Privatization
AND
Liberalization
IN THE
Middle East

Indiana Series in Arab and Islamic Studies

Salih J. Altoma, Iliya Harik,
and Mark Tessler,
GENERAL EDITORS

Privatization

AND

Liberalization

IN THE

Middle East

EDITED BY

Iliya Harik AND
Denis J. Sullivan

INDIANA UNIVERSITY PRESS
Bloomington and Indianapolis

The paper used in this publication meets the
minimum requirements of American
National Standard for Information Sciences—
Permanence of Paper for Printed
Library Materials, ANSI Z39.48-1984.

Manufactured in the United States of America

Library of Congress Cataloging-in-Publication Data

Privatization and liberalization in the Middle East / edited by Iliya
    Harik and Denis J. Sullivan.
        p.   cm. — (Indiana series in Arab and Islamic studies)
    Revised papers of a conference held at Northeastern University in
Boston in April 1990 and of the 1989 Middle East Studies Association
convention held in Toronto.
    Includes bibliographical references and index.
    ISBN 0-253-32697-4 (alk. paper). — ISBN 0-253-20748-7 (pbk. :
alk. paper)
        1. Privatization—Middle East—Congresses.   2. Free enterprise—
Middle East—Congresses.   I. Harik, Iliya F.   II. Sullivan, Denis
Joseph.   III. Series.
HD4276.5.P75   1992
338.956—dc20   92-5174

1 2 3 4 5   96 95 94 93 92

CONTENTS

Preface

Economic reform, structural adjustment, and privatization were global watchwords of the 1980s. Concerted efforts at promoting and implementing privatization are bound to continue to occupy center stage in the economies of the developing countries. Increasing international and domestic pressures are driving governments to address pressing economic questions, with special attention to changing outdated and inefficient policies.

This volume takes stock of the progress of economic liberalization and privatization in the Middle East and North Africa in the 1980s and highlights the problems and prospects of the economic-reform process. Some of the chapters were originally presented at a conference on "Privatization in Egypt and the Middle East" held at Northeastern University in Boston in April 1990. Others were presented at the 1989 Middle East Studies Association convention in Toronto. All have since been significantly revised and updated. As this book was being finalized, in summer 1991, the traumatic events of the war in the Gulf were still felt throughout the world. The editors, however, decided not to ask the authors to make revisions in light of those developments. For one thing, it was still too soon to tell how the Gulf episode would end and what the full effects on the region would be. We thought it best to leave the subject to future scholarly endeavors.

An examination of all the countries of the region is beyond the limits of this volume. We have chosen countries that have made reasonable progress in the liberalization drive and that have been the subject of scholarly research. The countries under review exhibit a variety of economic and political similarities and differences and therefore aptly serve the purpose of comparative analysis. All those included have taken some steps toward privatization, with varying degrees of enthusiasm on the part of political leadership. For example, Turkey responded early to the call by domestic elites for phasing out state control and ownership of economic activity. Egypt was slow in responding to pressure, which has largely come from outside donors.

Debates continue in most of the countries over the need, modalities, and pace of the reform. Privatization is a long-term process. The state will continue to play an important role in economic activity, if only by way of regulating, overseeing, and participating in the process of privatization. Important questions remain to be answered by proponents of privatization regarding the appropriate role of the state after privatization has been implemented, if it is not implemented, or especially if it should fail.

The present book constitutes a first step toward clarifying the issues involved in privatization. It is too early to predict how long the process will continue and how successful the countries of the region will be in meeting the stiff competition of the new world environment.

THE EDITORS

Privatization
AND
Liberalization
IN THE
Middle East

CHAPTER

1

PRIVATIZATION: THE ISSUE, THE PROSPECTS, AND THE FEARS

Iliya Harik

Privatization is a policy process whereby a government reduces its role as an owner and manager of business enterprises in the interest of other actors such as individuals or corporations. We have witnessed this process unfold recently in free-market economies such as Britain and Western Europe, in the centrally controlled markets of China and Eastern Europe, and in the interventionist regimes of many of the Less Developed Countries (LDCs). Privatization has occurred in conjunction with liberalization measures aimed at opening the economy for foreign investments, partially lifting controls, and encouraging private entrepreneurs. Typically, many state monopolies are terminated, controls of foreign exchange are relaxed, and tax benefits are extended to investors.

In this volume, we are concerned with privatization in one region of the LDCs, the Middle East and North Africa. First, it would be useful to indicate how the term *privatization* is used here. Most immediately, privatization signifies the transfer by the state of public-sector enterprises to the private sector and/or the liquidation of enterprises. Privatization, however, has been used in the literature, in a broader sense, to mean the *liberalization* of the economy in such a way as to expand the economic freedom of the private sector. Another aspect of the process involves partnership with the private sector through joint ventures or partial sale of public-sector shares.

In this volume, individual authors may differ in their use of the terms privatization and liberalization, but in general most have used the term privatization in the narrow sense of the denationalization of State-Owned Enterprises (SOEs) while employing the term liberalization in its broader meaning, which includes relaxation of economic controls and encouragement of the private sector. Liberalization reflects the partial withdrawal of the state from its hegemonic role as an entrepreneur and as a provider of welfare and other services. In short, liberalization signals the retreat of the patron state.

The Patron State. The role of the state in the LDCs in the postindependence period expanded considerably within a short time. Political-science literature refers to that development as authoritarianism, bureaucratic or otherwise. In this volume, our concern is with a specialized aspect of state expansion, its economic role, rather than with the whole phenomenon.

A patron state is a business entrepreneur and provider at one and the same time, and in the Middle East the development in that direction occurred shortly after independence. The rise by the state to the position of major businessman was achieved by assuming greater economic initiative and by acts of compulsion, and it was maintained by mass mobilization and bureaucratic regulation.

The emergence of the patron state gave rise to the intensification of economic dependency on the advanced industrialized nations. Both aspects of its developmental policies, business expansion and welfare, contributed to this situation. A number of calculations, some political and others economic, have led to increasing dependency. Nationalistic reasons as well as fear from competition in the world market drove policy makers to follow import-substitution policies, which created pressure on the productive units to meet domestic consumption needs. It also resulted in a shortfall in hard-currency revenue to meet the increasing expenditure on imports of capital goods, raw materials, and intermediate goods, whose volume had grown out of proportion because of the business expansion by the patron state and inadequate export performance. Intensifying this tendency has been the expansion in the welfare and free services extended by the state to the public to meet ideological commitments and to keep the masses from resorting to political agitation. The failure of the state to generate the financial resources to meet all these commitments led to the deterioration in the quality and quantity of the services offered and to a reduction in productivity, a kind of vicious circle in which lack of funds leads to low productivity and low productivity to lack of funds.

Economic policies of the patron state increased its dependency on the advanced industrial world. Originally founded on the premise of delinking and self-sufficiency, the patron state found itself achieving neither objective. On the contrary, it became increasingly in need of aid from external sources. This took the form of borrowing from foreign governments and international financial markets to feed the populace and maintain the welfare system as much as for productive purposes. The more it borrowed for nonproductive purposes, the deeper it sank into the financial hole and the less able it became to solve its economic problems. Extractive policies, which increased in direct relation to the extent of the shortfall in governmental revenue, proved to be counterproductive. Borrowing and deficit financing led the patron state to increasing dependency on the advanced industrial countries rather than self-sufficiency and delinking.

Caught in a financial bind, the custodians of the patron state eventually took the inevitable course of economic disengagement, first by encouraging the private sector and gradually relaxing controls, then by ultimately accepting, with reservation, the denationalization option. Trapped in the legacy of its own network controls and of enterprises which are in need of massive injection of funds and restructuring, the patron state was constrained to proceed with reforms at a slow pace, a course made even more imperative by fear of the political unrest likely to be generated by the disengagement process. The liberalization and privatization process thus was homespun in accordance with the internal logic of the system, a tendency reinforced by international forces. The influence of international actors has proved to be proportionate to the degree of deterioration in the domestic economy.

With liberalization, the state has enlisted the international community as a partner in resolving its economic problems as well as placing part of the responsibility on it. A successful outcome of this new development would be the integration of the less developed countries of the region in a positive fashion in the international economic system. At the same time, by opting for this course of action, the patron state has implicitly or explicitly agreed to change its character from a patron to a competitive system. Economic disengagement by the state has been associated with relaxation of political controls in most countries of the region.

EXCESSES OF STATE INVOLVEMENT IN THE ECONOMY

Unlike Eastern Europe, state hegemony in the national economies of the Middle East is rooted not in ideology alone but also in the nature of the economies of the region. The state stepped in to fill a gap in the industrial sector, which was extremely small, undercapitalized and oriented toward production of consumer goods. Hence, the familiar thesis that the state has, inevitably, a dominant role to play in the economies of underdeveloped countries.

The state, it is argued, has greater capacity to raise capital, is willing to enter more sophisticated activities such as heavy industry, and enjoys the advantage of central planning, which was considered an impetus for growth. The argument, however, has been overextended and certainly used by authoritarian regimes to justify their interventionist nature. In countries such as Turkey, Syria, and Egypt, where an experienced nucleus of an entrepreneurial class and a relatively significant middle class existed, the justification of the state primacy in the economy could not be accepted at its face value. Moreover, the manner in which the state thrust itself into the economy leaves little doubt that one of the main motivating forces behind state intervention has been political. Witness, for instance, the nationalization of the press in Egypt, an act that is totally political and has nothing to do with the development of the economy. Similarly, the state owned and controlled the press in Algeria, Tunisia, Libya, Syria, and Iraq. In Egypt, Syria, and Iraq, the state did not step in only where the private sector did not dare to tread, but it nationalized most existing businesses, including some very small ones. Such a step has no economic justification and can be understood only in ideological and political terms.

In contrast, state intervention in the economy by the monarchical governments of Saudi Arabia and Jordan (see Chaudhry, Brand) has been limited in comparison with those of the single-party states. Nevertheless, conservative regimes, too, found it necessary to play a prominent role in business, and this tendency is consistent with the thesis that intervention in LDCs is partly prompted by underdevelopment and weaknesses of the market.

The economic-primacy thesis, however, was never clear when it came to determining the extent of economic hegemony necessary by the state, and it was interpreted freely by different regimes. Most regimes assumed extensive powers and far-reaching direct involvement. The adverse economic effect is, of course, better understood at the present time in LDCs, and the main concern is how to execute the transition to a less controlled economy with the least pain possible and in the most productive manner. For as Dr. Said El-Naggar has put it, "To nationalize is easy, but to privatize is fraught with difficulties."[1]

Perhaps one of the most economically damaging acts of intervention by the strident ideological and/or military regimes has been the crushing of the small entrepreneurial class (a scarce developmental resource) in Iraq, Syria, and Egypt. In Tunisia and Algeria, the damage resulted from discouraging and hamstringing private entrepreneurs while in the other countries under consideration, the state sequestrated business and excluded most private entrepreneurs. Development economics calls for support and encouragement of entrepreneurs, whose scarcity in LDCs is one of the sources of weak economies and slow growth. Yet, suppression was exactly the sentence imposed on the agents of change in many Middle Eastern and other Less Developed Countries.

In the second place, as the main national entrepreneur, the patron state committed costly mistakes in poor investment decisions, in futile strategies such as import substitution, in monopoly environment, and in political interference with the management of state-owned enterprises. State hegemony in the patron state took not only the form of ownership of enterprises but also the form of management control of product mix, crops, prices, wages, and employment practices. Moreover, political interventions in state economic industrial firms had an antigrowth effect, resulting to a large extent from forcing industrial enterprises to provide social functions of welfare nature, which deprived them of whatever surplus available for reinvestment. Where there was a surplus, extractive measures and reallocation in favor of failing enterprises served the same antigrowth function. State enterprises, in short, have been riddled with waste and misallocation of resources and have proved to be ineffective in terms of cost.

A comparative study of private- and public-sector firms by Robert Millward concludes that technical efficiency is not necessarily greater in private firms than it is in public-sector enterprises.[2] Other comparative studies show the opposite to be true.[3] The comparative shortcomings of Millward's study aside,[4] the argument distracts from incontrovertible evidence of low returns on investments in the public sector, parasitic tendencies generated by the inacceptability of exit for hopeless enterprises, and the tendency toward decreasing levels of investments (see Sherif and Soos, Harik, Vandewalle, Chaudhry). The small cases of denationalized firms in Tunisia, such as Sitex, and privatization of hotels in Egypt and Tunisia show a definite improvement in performance.

The point, however, is not to compare public with private enterprises but, rather, to consider the conditions under which both sectors function. Official restrictions and interventions affect all businesses, though more in the case of the public than in the private one. It may well be that two identical firms, with ownership as the only difference between them, operating under the same rules will show comparable cost-effectiveness and performance. What should be noted, however, is that the public sector cannot operate, especially in LDCs, under market-economy rules because it would lose its raison d'être. On the other side of the coin, students of privatization ought not to lose sight of the fact that the patron state is capable of treating private enterprise in much the same restrictive way as public-sector firms. Hence, it is not structural change that is the primary issue in privatization but change in the rules under which an economy operates.

The argument against the economic primacy of the state should not, however, lead us to gloss over the strong thesis regarding the weakness and deficiencies of the market economy in LDCs. The state stepped in presumably to correct or make up for market failures: scarcity of capital, monopolies, sectoral imbalances, lack of economies of scale, small and timid entrepreneurial class, low investments, and distributional imbalances.

The irony of modern times in postcolonial countries is that liberalization and privatization policies are now being advanced in order to correct the failures of the centrally controlled economy: inefficiency, huge financial deficits, low productivity, parasitic tendencies, waste, shortages, noncompetitive products, low investments, low growth rates, and poverty (see Sherif and Soos, Chaudhry, Vandewalle, Harik). In effect, private and public enterprises alike are characterized by serious shortcomings. Here, we run the risk of shifting the arguments into an inquiry of underdeveloped economies, which in this context would constitute a diversion.

After more than three decades of state hegemony, it is clear that the state had extended itself and stretched the limits of its economic activities to the breaking point. The takeover approach had not been the only reform option open to the state as a remedy to the deficiencies of the market; indeed, the more productive course would have been for the state to get itself involved in providing infrastructure support, business promotion measures, worker training, finances, and expert know-how in the free market. With careful planning, the state could also have stepped into vital areas where the private sector feared to tread, particularly in the production of intermediate and capital goods. In return, the state could have exacted a price from the business community for its positive role in terms of distributional measures.

The tragic part of the developmental experiences of LDCs is that the takeover of the entrepreneurial role by the state has made only minor corrections of the market deficiencies it had set out to eradicate, and it compounded the picture by adding new problems to the old ones. Are LDCs then victims of their own economic designs or of their backward economies in the international system? The truth may be found in both, an observation which suggests the need for a balanced outlook at the reform process free from ideological biases and commitments.

BEYOND PRIVATIZATION: THE STATE'S ECONOMIC ROLE REDEFINED

Weaknesses in the economies of LDCs at the time of independence were not re-dressed by eliminating or strictly controlling market transactions. In the same or-der, shortcomings of the state as an entrepreneur will not be corrected by total privatization or total state withdrawal, assuming that is possible. The state which has created an enormous economic crisis bears the responsibility for the rehabili-tation of the public sector before it exits. This is the more so when it is realized that a return to normalcy cannot be achieved without sound economic policies which only the state can undertake.

Property. One way to get around this bifurcated vision of public versus private sector is to focus briefly on the question of property in the context of state-society boundaries. There simply is no such thing as a "green line" separating state and society as the argument over public versus private ownership suggests. The link-ages are rather too strong even in the most liberal economic systems. As it is commonly used, the term *ownership* is extremely vague. The bottom line is that ownership endows the holder with the right to transfer title, through sale or other means, as well as the right to consume the object or what it generates in the way of revenue. Yet, even in those basic senses, the right of ownership is not absolute but limited by other claims often of state and society. An owner of a lot of land in an area designated as a residential zone is not free to sell his property for use as a commercial enterprise. A farmer in the United States is not free to sell corn to Cuba nor is an exporter free to sell computers to the Soviet Union.

When property rights are viewed as claims to usage rather than title deeds, then it becomes clear that no single actor possesses all the property rights to an object or a service. Claims by others, especially those of the public, affect private ownership in a variety of ways. A farmer in Egypt cannot sell wheat or sugarcane for export nor is a manufacturer free to export undyed leather material. Similarly, consumption of returns from property are restricted by the state's claim for a share (taxes). Again, a farmer who owns an agricultural plot of land in Egypt or Tunisia does not have the right to build a house for his own use on the property. On the other hand, the same farmer can use free of charge the water from the canal, which is the property of the state. Here is a case where a person's private property rights are severely restricted while he is free to use public property. Similarly, that same farmer is not free to plant the crop of his choice and has to sell to one marketing agency. What meaning is left in ownership of a farmland if the owner cannot build on it, cannot grow what he wants, and cannot sell except at a fixed price and a designated marketing agent? Similarly, an owner of a rented apartment who cannot determine the rent rate nor dismiss the tenant finds little meaning left in the property title he holds.

Ownership for the Egyptian farmer or landlord is a limited-usage right to an asset restricted by the rights which others claim (in this case the state) to the use of that same property. Under those circumstances, ownership loses its importance to the titleholder and also its significance as a concept in development economics.

The ownership concept may well be archaic to do us much good; yet, if it is viewed in a different perspective, it may yield a theoretical dimension to the issue of privatization with which we are concerned. The first step is to disaggregate the concept into its component parts. Once that is done, property ceases to be a concrete object and becomes a "bundle of rights" that can be separated and aggregated in different combinations under different circumstances. In the examples given above, it is clear that the two main agents with combined claims to certain rights are the state and the private individual or the corporate economic agent. We should also add subnational communities as actors who share claims to usage with individuals, corporations, and the state.

Privatization may then be redefined as the rearrangement of title claims to usage of property rights and the rights to offering services, whereby the state gives up some of those rights to other parties but never strips itself of all of them. Privatization thus is not equivalent to "a state exit" from economic enterprises because, as a representative of the public, it has rights in practically every economic activity under its jurisdiction whether undertaken by individuals or collectivities.

In its economic activities, the patron state stepped beyond the limits observed generally by the conventional state. Theoretically, the state is an agent representing the rights of the public; but in practice, it develops extra claims of its own, and it is in those areas that it has faltered and stepped on the rights of others.

The state is a partner in all business enterprises, public or private alike. The bottom line of the partnership of public and private ownership lies in the provision by the state of such services as infrastructure, security, and other external economies in return for which it charges taxes and imposes regulations in the name of the public. In other words, it claims a right to a portion of the returns from labor, to capital, and to a say in the management rules under which the enterprise is run.

The state has far greater presence as a partner in private businesses in market economies than has been suggested in the literature on privatization. Here are some of its major roles:

The state is a regulator; that is, it determines how claims to the rights of usage could be exercised: safety conditions in the work place, facilities for the handicapped, labor laws, nondiscrimination, antitrust and antifraud measures, quality controls, price controls (true of the United States as of the Middle Eastern countries alike, but to a different extent), and management of social security.

The state is a promoter: provides subsidies, export facilities, information, research and so forth. The state is a gate keeper providing the private agent with rights of entry and of exit. The state creates fortunes and bankruptcies by monetary policies, such as determining interest and foreign exchange rates. Finally, the state is an insurance agency of last resort (guarantees of bank deposits) and an employer of last resort as in most developing countries. Those diverse roles which the state performs obtain in capitalist and socialist systems alike, but to varying degrees; and they attest to the intricate web of relations between state and society.

Under such perspective, it becomes necessary to look at ownership claims as a continuum rather than as a bipolar phenomenon suggested in the classification of property into public and private sectors. Here, ownership ceases to be viewed in exclusive terms of the propertied and the propertyless but, rather, of the number of rights the propertied actors enjoy, the more the wealthier of course.

The inference that should be made from this perspective on ownership is that the debate regarding the public and the private sectors may be off the track. The issue goes beyond private or public property and concerns the rights to which each is entitled. There is no such thing as a purely private property or purely public property. The rights of enjoyment of the object, whether it is public or private, are shared to varying degrees by multiple actors. Public ownership is not absolute either. The state's usage rights in a publicly owned enterprise is restricted by the rights of workers, the degree of which varies from country to country but which is there in all of them. It is also limited by its needs of others for capital, to wit the heavy burden of the debt. It is also limited by the rights of the public to a reliable and fairly priced product. The state sector in some of the countries of the region under study cannot dispose of its products at will; for instance, it cannot export certain items strongly demanded domestically, as is the case in Egypt.

In turn, private agents do not enjoy all the usage rights to what they claim as private property. How private is a hotel sold by the state to a private actor when the state retains the right to control employment practices, wages, and prices? Under Nasser and well into the late 1980s, agricultural land was held as private property, yet the farmer enjoyed very few property rights while the state enjoyed the major ones, including the right to determine kinds of crops, prices, and marketing. In Egypt, in Iraq, and, to a lesser extent, in Tunisia, the state's claims remained strong even after privatization policies were set in place. Ownership title is thus less important than other rights of usage. In other words, it does not so much matter who holds title to a firm but what are the policies that govern its operations. That is why the state continues to loom large even in a market economy.[5]

A second important inference is that privatization alone in the LDCs does not constitute a major change or an economic impetus for growth and prosperity unless it occurs in conjunction with liberalization policies in which the state gives up some of its claims against business and pursues sound economic policies. Protectionism and monopolies, for instance, can hardly be more of an improvement when enjoyed by private business than they are under the public sector. In many of the patron states, even under *infitah* in Egypt (see Sherif and Soos, Posusney, Said Aly, Sullivan), the state continued to hold to its role as partner: controller, gatekeeper, protector, regulator, and fiscal decision maker. In other countries, such as Iraq, Syria, Jordan, Algeria, and Tunisia (see Lawson, Chaudhry, Brand, Vandewalle, Patton, Harik), the same thing prevailed. Consequently, we notice that in two of the Arab countries with the oldest track record in privatization and liberalization, Tunisia and Egypt, the balance sheet continues to show very limited progress toward privatization (see Sherif and Soos, Posusney, Sullivan, and Harik).

Does it really matter then whether the public sector is privatized or not? In principle, of course not; the public-sector managers should be able to change the performance equation markedly if given more rights to run the enterprises upon which they preside in a free, professional way. Public-sector managers have been much maligned in the literature for their incompetence,[6] a thesis not yet demonstrated to be true. Public-sector failures have been due to political leaders who actually make the vital business decisions and basic policies. Managers of state economic firms who see that the competitiveness of their enterprise is negative do not even have the right to close up shop. The state will not even allow a public-sector firm to be declared bankrupt (see Sherif and Soos) and in some cases not even private firms.

Is Decentralization Possible? If public-sector firms could, like their private counterparts, improve their performance under a system with freer access and more rights' claims, then the argument for decentralization of the state economic firms should prove to be a promising reform measure. Under conditions of decentralization, it is argued, managers would be in a position to make strictly professional business decisions regarding investments, employment, product mix, pricing, marketing, or liquidation. However, we do not yet have empirical grounds for testing this hypothesis. In some countries where decentralization has been a much discussed issue, such as Egypt, Turkey, Tunisia, and Algeria (see Sherif and Soos, Sullivan, Posusney, Patton, Harik, Vandewalle), presumably the state has already decentralized public-sector firms although, in practice, most are still under the direct control of the line ministry, with the minister in charge serving as the director general and the cabinet continuing to reserve to itself all the important decisions pertaining to the fortunes of the enterprise. In Algeria, breaking up the large state conglomerates took precedence over enterprise autonomy (see Vandewalle).

Why do we not have genuine cases of decentralization of the State Economic Enterprises (SEEs)? The answer is instructive: decentralization of SEEs is extremely difficult politically. The state which has used the public sector for its own political purposes (such as patronage, power base, income redistribution, social benefits to the largest number of people, etc.) has not lost those political interests nor has it found a substitute for them—hence, the resistance of regimes to undercut themselves and jeopardize their survival. Is it then surprising to see that the most radical changes made in the economies of the LDCs have occurred in countries which have had a change of regime, such as Turkey (see Patton), Senegal, Poland, Brazil, Argentina, Chile, and now Peru, or in countries under irresistible pressures from international agencies (see Sullivan, Said Aly)?

Still the question remains: Is the private sector immune from the political vicissitudes which afflict the public sector? To a certain extent, yes, but not fully; for here, government functions and prerogatives are one step more removed from those of the managers of public enterprises. Private businesses in all the liberalizing regimes examined in this volume have enjoyed greater freedom of action than SEEs. Still, in a politically dominant regime such as we witness in the patron state, private-ownership rights are attenuated by those of the state in the form of claimed rights to partial control of entry, exit, prices, wages, employment, marketing, and other rights (see Sherif and Soos, Posusney, Patton, Harik, Chaudhry, Lawson). This is true also of monarchies such as Jordan and, to a lesser extent, Saudi Arabia (see Brand, Chaudhry). Among the countries under study in this volume, the greatest progress in attenuating state rights have occurred in Turkey, Tunisia, Jordan, and Egypt.

As is evident from the preceding, the role of the state in a free-market economy is quite vast and, in many cases, legitimate. This may be a point which is lost on many leftist opponents of privatization. Privatization does not eliminate the state functions in the economy; rather, it reaffirms the partnership. With property defined as a set of usage rights which combines and disaggregates in various proportions, it follows that freed private entrepreneurs will not enjoy the opportunity of laissez-faire nineteenth-century practices. The state continues to play most of the roles outlined above, which in effect means the enjoyment of a share of the returns of capital and labor. It is supposed to continue to protect the public against abuse of monopoly prices and unfair business practices. Should we consider Western democracies as our measuring rod, the likelihood that the state would abdicate its protective measures of citizens' rights in a market economy is quite slim.

The Redistribution Argument. Scholars sometimes recognize that the state used the public-sector firms for political purposes. In some cases,[7] this argument is turned in support of the public sector. It is argued that the record of the state economic firms should not be measured solely in terms of market valuation but also in terms of the social functions they perform. State economic enterprises provide commodities and services to the public at affordable and artificial prices and also extend employment, often redundant.

It is surprising that some economists find strength in the state economic firms where they are at their weakest.[8] Subjecting public-sector managers to the onus of making socially rather than economically based decisions has been the most deleterious practice on the performance of state economic enterprises and eventually for those who socially benefited from them. Financing social-welfare measures by extra-taxation of productive units is an efficient recipe for low growth and economic decline.

The discouraging aspect of the public-sector case does not lie in its inherent inefficiency but, rather, in its definition and structure. It is of no comfort to maintain that if we take into account social services made by SEEs, their performance record would appear positive. The problem is that the social function assigned to the SEEs has drained their resources and taken away their capacity to generate and use the surplus for reinvestment, renovation, innovation, and research. The public sector cannot be defined (and actually has not, in fact, been so defined) as a purely economic enterprise. Being political is an essential aspect of the definition of the public sector. To recommend freeing the public sector from political interference is equivalent to suggesting change in political regimes. No sooner is the public sector deprived of its political functions than it will cease to be of interest to the policy makers. They will not have it unless it delivers those political goods expected of it.

The political aspect of the public sector cannot be separated from the economic one, and that is why we hardly have any cases of genuinely decentralized public-sector firms in the LDCs. To make state economic firms autonomous is to alter the very definition and raison d'être of the public sector. This is where the argument for privatization is at its strongest, not necessarily because of the inherent superiority of the private sector but, rather, because of the unlikely prospect that dominant regimes would tolerate public-sector autonomy or willingly accept self-imposed limitations on their powers of interference. To the extent political considerations are given as much weight and even precedence over economic ones, growth will not meet expectations.

The concept of autonomy for the public-sector firms enjoys widespread support among international agencies and even national governments. The argument is a variant of the thesis that, in advanced industrialized societies, management has been separated from ownership. True as a sociological observation, the disaggregation thesis has not been shown to be an unqualified success. The conduct of managers in large, private corporations tends to be self-serving and is often characterized by complacency and inertia in a manner reminiscent of public-sector managers. In countries such as Yugoslavia, Mexico, and the Philippines, SEE autonomy has produced signs of lack of fiscal discipline.

One form of autonomy, developed in Egypt and in Tunisia in a very small number of cases, holds some promise. It creates firms as subsidiaries of more than one SEE subject to free management according to market consideration. The Export Development Bank and Misr-Iran Bank in Egypt are cases in point, and they have proven quite successful although there is no evidence that the government is in a rush to replicate this pattern in other cases. In Tunisia, state banks played a central role in the transition to privatization. State banks, sometimes as a group, act as the purchasers of public-sector firms to run or to resell them (see Harik).

Assuming autonomy is possible in the context of dominant political regimes; the task of demonstrating its success has not yet been made. We do not have many such cases from which to gather data, let alone studied ones, to suggest that SEE autonomy improves the economic performance of firms.

The most damaging argument against autonomy of SEEs remains political. In dominant regimes of the LDCs, respect for legal and constitutional arrangements is not compelling and may or may not exclude political interference. Perhaps even more serious is the fact that political instability and violent regime changes portend poorly for the autonomy argument. A new regime is not necessarily bound by the rules and actions of its predecessors in cases where personal rule is a more dominant form than statehood.

It may be added, too, that economic-reform periods in LDCs occur as a response to urgency and come in spurts and starts. The attention span of top leaders and regimes, moreover, is not impressive. No sooner does the head of the system divert his interests to other matters, or find pressure for some reason receding, than interest among subleaders wanes. Such shifts in interests and fortunes could affect the private sector, too, but not to the same extent unless a regime is bent on extractive and destructive measures.

Why does the reform-oriented state such as we see in many countries of our region not reduce its claims to ownership rights in relation to private-sector firms in a more definitive way? Why not allow the private sector more freedom of action? In part, because the state's own public sector would be thrust into full competition with the private sector, a course it is not structurally endowed to perform. Given full competition without shedding its social role or bureaucratic shackles, the public sector would not stand a chance (see Sherif and Soos). An inferior competitive role would result in a mounting financial drain on the treasury and, eventually, would lead to liquidation of SEEs, too radical an option for officials to be entertained. The state would rather seek divestiture than take that option.

It seems from the preceding that the crowding-out hypothesis takes the form of a two-edged sword; it cuts both ways. The hypothesis has originally been advanced as the limitation of available space for the private sector due to the growth of the public sector. Now, with the transition to liberalization, some public-sector firms, especially those which produce consumer goods, seem unable to compete with the private sector even under conditions of protection extended to them by the state. They may be crowded out by private competition were they free to exit. Instead, they continue to operate at a loss. Large public-sector firms, however, continue to block the entry of new actors by virtue of their massive capitalization and market-network advantage.

However, the crowding-out thesis, as it has been advanced in purely economic terms, is limited since the major reason for the exit of major private firms has been nationalization and/or official restrictions on the scope of action rather than financial and economic deprivation. Official measures that benefit the SEEs reflect political interests and unfair advantage secured by force.

According to yet another argument, the crowding-out thesis becomes irrelevant altogether. Some have maintained that the small remaining private sector in a state-run economy has the versatility and clout to turn the state sector to serve its economic interests. The point is made in class-analysis terms to the effect that the public sector has been serving the private interests of the bourgeoisie.[9] The basis of this bold assertion is the clientele relationship which private entrepreneurs carve out for themselves in the public sector. Being the largest business "corporation," the state has found that small, private entrepreneurs could provide its enterprises with inputs and services. This was particularly significant in the construction business in Iraq, Syria, Egypt, Tunisia, and Algeria.

Yet, on balance, the argument of the subservience of the SEEs holds no water whatsoever. The private sector under the etatist systems of the Middle East and North Africa remained minuscule, and, in some cases (such as Syria, Iraq, and Egypt), it was extensively reduced from what it had been before the state took over. Moreover, even what was left of private enterprise was subjected to severe restrictions and crippling bureaucratic impediments, many of which continued to exist under liberalization. After nearly twenty years of *infitah* in Egypt and Tunisia, the public sector still generates 65 percent and 60 percent respectively of manufacturing-value added (see Harik).[10]

Though it has registered growth, the private sector itself has not been free of problems (see Patton). It has not shown remarkable vigor in any of the countries under consideration (see Lawson, Chaudhry, Harik, Vandewalle), with the qualified exception perhaps of Turkey. The transition to a market system meant that an entrepreneurial class had to be rehabilitated and rejuvenated, the financial markets redeveloped, and capital and know-how provided. Inexperience and adventurism characterizes many private enterprises, especially among new entrants, with the result that failures are quite frequent (see Brand, Chaudhry, Patton, Harik).

PRIVATIZATION AND FOREIGN INFLUENCE

The strongest charge against privatization, however, has been political in nature. First, it is argued that, because it has been sponsored by foreign actors, privatization reflects the interests of advanced industrial states which occupy a prominent place in the world economy, such as those of Western Europe and the United States. The foreign agencies urging privatization are mainly the IMF, the World Bank, and the USAID (see Said Aly, Sullivan). Second, it is considered to be a response to the political interests of the business classes, foreign and native, who put claims on the state and seek relief from obligations to the public. Businessmen understand both that achieving their economic interests requires political action and that, by their location and wealth, they enjoy considerable leverage. Finally, business classes seek to dominate the state with a view to affect the distribution of national income in their own favor at the expense of the mass population. A variant of this last point is that the poor are bound to become poorer in a free-market economy because the increasing wealth of the few and the linkages of the economy to advanced industrial nations contribute to inflation and lower purchasing capacity of the poor. Cognizant of this argument, political leaders fear that privatization and rapid liberalization of the economy may lead to political turmoil, a turmoil which could undermine their regimes (see Posusney, Lawson, Brand, Sullivan, Patton, Said Aly, Vandewalle).

There can be no doubt that privatization has a significant political dimension.

Foreign states, international agencies, and national entrepreneurs are involved in its support. Moreover, its immediate beneficiaries are business entrepreneurs, and the immediate losers are workers and state functionaries (see Lawson, Posusney, Chaudhry, Said Aly, Sullivan). However, the risks from those tendencies are overdrawn. Detractors tend to portray privatization as a politically insidious intrusion by foreign agents.[11] As far as the Middle East and North Africa are concerned, it should be understood that privatization and liberalization have been homespun while foreign actors have lent a much delayed supporting hand. How could one attribute liberalization and privatization to foreign actors in such radical states as Iraq and Algeria? The IMF has not been allowed into state councils of Algeria, Iraq (see Vandewalle, Chaudhry), or Syria. Egypt and Tunisia, which have been the most implicated by this charge, started on the liberalization track on their own at the beginning of the 1970s. Sadat had moved in that direction before he mended his fences with the United States, a measure which did not come about until after the 1973 war. Jordan's first liberalization reforms in the early 1980s ignored the IMF recipes (see Brand). Moreover, it is instructive to note that AID did not become involved in the privatization question until 1986 (see Sullivan) and only with a very small proportion of the aid package. For the previous decade of assistance to Egypt, AID devoted far more (indeed, a major portion of its assistance) to the public sector.

No less significant in support of the public sector has been the role of the World Bank, whose financial support and technical assistance has gone mainly to public projects. In the majority of its recent structural-adjustment loans, reform, rather than dismantling of the public sector, is stipulated.[12] Moreover, structural-adjustment lending by the World Bank, though growing, is still small, accounting for over 6 percent of total lending in the period 1979–86 but rising to 17.5 percent in the 1986 fiscal year.[13]

The IMF, which is much maligned by critics of privatization, in turn has devoted considerable attention to the reform of the public sector, not its elimination. "Of the ninety-four IMF-supported adjustment programs in LDCs during the 1980–84 period, the majority contained policy recommendations relating to non-financial state enterprises,"[14] most of which pertained to subsidies, prices and investments in the public sector. Those suggested reforms are also disliked because of their immediate effects on the middle- and low-income population, but they are basically in the interest of public firms.

After twenty years of liberalization, the privatization record of Egypt and Tunisia has been meager and can hardly demonstrate a national response to pressure from the outside. Turkey, which is officially part of the Western World, has made slightly more progress on that path.

It is the market economy of the international economic system, not the actors listed above, which has the real influence on the economies of the Third World countries. The integration of the world economy into a single international market has created facts that the LDCs started to understand in the early 1970s, as witnessed by their binding together in the United Nations to change the international economic order in such a way as to give them more elbow room. Though viewed negatively and as interventionist by the advanced industrial societies, the Declaration of a New International Economic Order in 1974 marked the beginning of the bend in the river. The Declaration reflects the keen awareness shown by leaders of LDCs that they are bound inextricably with the world economic system and that adjustments had to be made on both sides. Western observers saw in the Declaration only the demands made by the LDCs for adjustment on the part of the advanced industrial countries, but they overlooked the signal by the LDCs that they, too, were adjusting to the changing world environment. Most liberalization policies in Latin America, Africa, and the Middle East started at that same time as the Sixth Special Session of the General Assembly of the United Nations. LDC leaders were not responding only to the international system, but they had their own domestic reasons for the change in policy.

The growing economic interdependence of the world economy offers opportunities and serious problems to developing countries. International interdependence has meant, among other things, lowering trade barriers and free market competition. Competition, internationally or domestically, should not be understood to mean absence of state supervision and regulation. Similarly, international competition is regulated by international organizations such as the General Agreement on Tariffs and Trade (GATT) and the Organization for Economic Cooperation and Development (OECD), by North-South dialogues, by summits of the major industrial powers, and by lateral state negotiations.

Regardless of supervision and regulation, free-market competition poses serious problems to LDCs. First, there is the imbalance in the economic powers of the competitors: huge disparities in technology, capital, and enterprise size. The LDCs are a small league competing with a major one, and the outcome is a foregone conclusion. Insistence on unqualified free trade as if the parties are competitive is totally unrealistic. That is why private businessmen themselves pose as the major opposition to structural adjustment (see Brand, Patton, Harik). There is considerable concern among indigenous manufacturers and industrialists that free imports could put them out of the market. On the other hand, prolonged import-substitution stands, such as we have witnessed in so many countries of the region, is an invitation to inefficiency, waste, and continued economic dependency. A balance between protection and free competition in the world market should be a major concern of the state.

A second problem of a free, competitive market on the domestic level is that totally free entry of investors is an invitation to rapid exit as well. Since crowding the market removes the advantage of the economies of scale and pushes down profits, it leads to considerable waste of resources. In league with businessmen, the state limited the entry into the market in some countries of the region (see Brand, Harik). Controlling business access is disturbing to many observers: on the left, because limited entry to the market works to the advantage of large businessmen; on the right, because it limits free competition. The state, nevertheless, has to play that role to prevent the dissipation of capital and the loss of competitiveness in world markets. This function, however, has to be exercised selectively with caution and fairness; but, just as there are domestic considerations for limiting liberalization, so are there domestic factors pushing in that direction.

The Domestic Factors. If foreign actors were not the major cause for the change in policy toward economic liberalization, then what was? A multiplicity of domestic factors contributed to the turn toward liberalization: increasing production costs of SEEs, financial drain on state treasuries, increasing deficits, the failure of import substitution strategy, and shortages of foreign exchange investment capital, and modern technology (see Sherif and Soos, Patton, Harik, Vandewalle, Chaudhry, Brand). The declining revenue and diversion of funds from national budgets to support state enterprises was particularly alarming because it started to affect the state's welfare programs, both in quantitative terms as well as in quality. This plus the slowing down of the economy smelled of political trouble for the various regimes.

At any rate, the moves made in the direction of liberalization in the states of our region have not occurred under pressure of political groups or ideological conversion. Indeed, to this day, business groups have not shown strong political tendencies or involvement that could swing the boat in one direction or the other (see Harik, Chaudhry, Lawson, Posusney, Vandewalle). The main drive for change came from the fact that regimes were losing credibility and legitimacy among the general public in proportion to their inability to deliver. Having total control over the national economy deprived political leaders of sharing the burden and the responsibility for failure with others. State treasuries were, moreover, drying up.

The takeover of responsibility for the economy in the 1960s was partly viewed as a power buildup for political leaders, but it ended up as a liability. Being the major-domo, the state posed as the mainly responsible agent for the declining fortunes of the public. Thus, the state moved toward economic liberalization both in order to partition the blame and responsibility and in the hope that an injection of fresh economic actors and capital would help a declining economy to regain its fortunes.

As for the fear that a free business class could hijack the state apparatus and subject it to its own interests,[15] the chances are not yet very high. For one thing, none of the liberalizing regimes has shown any interest in relinquishing much power. Political democratization, which has the potential of giving businessmen greater influence over the economy, has made very modest progress in a small number of these countries (see Brand, Vandewalle, Lawson, Harik). Under a democratic regime, businessmen enjoy a natural advantage, but that does not mean they can do away with the interests of other groups. Under a reasonably working pluralist system, a balance of interests develops. Organized labor, moreover, may have greater leverage in a pluralistic system than in single- or dominant-party states (see Posusney).

The concern many people express regarding the distributional effects of privatization and liberalization is of course justified. Experience has shown that structural-adjustment programs, during the initial stages, cause considerable unemployment and displacements, affecting entrepreneurs, professionals, and workers alike. What remains to be demonstrated is whether the purchasing capacity per capita declines in the process of transition to liberalization. Transition is quite a new phenomenon, and we do not have sufficient data to reach even tentative conclusions regarding this question. In none of the cases studied in this volume is there an inkling as to where things stand with respect to distribution. For one thing, the number of cases is small, the period of transition short, and the economic data not adequate. There is evidence of conspicuous consumption (mostly in Egypt, and to a lesser extent in Tunisia) caused more by external factors than by the domestic economy.

The object of concern with respect to distribution is whether the economic standing of the lower-income groups is advancing or declining rather than whether the income gap has widened. What is quite established, however, is that income distribution tends toward greater egalitarianism in direct relation to the advanced level of the economy. Income distribution in the advanced industrial societies is more equitable than in the LDCs, regardless of the nature of their political systems. This is, of course, a long-term trend and should not be confused with the trickle-down-effect thesis. One lesson may have been learned from the experience of LDCs in the politics of independence: a person will not have either freedom or a full stomach without actively working for them. The assumption that *étatisme* would guarantee the basic needs of the poor has had only very limited applicability, while freedom and human rights were hardly respected.

The studies in this volume confirm findings from other LDCs regarding privatization. Insofar as divestiture is concerned, the record is quite modest—several firms in Turkey and Iraq; a few service and industrial firms in Tunisia and Egypt; none in Algeria, Syria, or Jordan. Moreover, most of the privatized units are small, with the exception of Teletas in Turkey. More progress has been made in the sale of state-owned hotels, where the majority in Tunisia and an impressive number in Egypt have been privatized. The prospects for the future, however, are not yet clear. Tunisian authorities do not seem to have more than a fraction (less than 10 percent) of the industrial firms in mind for divestiture (see Harik), and Egyptians have focused mainly on small firms under local and provincial governments.

Again, in line with findings in other LDCs, considerably more has been achieved in the direction of economic liberalization and deregulation in most countries under examination. Restrictions on entry and exits have been relaxed considerably; many state monopolies have been terminated; foreign firms have been invited to invest in almost all the countries of the region, including Algeria and Iraq; and national entrepreneurs have been encouraged and supported through relaxation of rules regarding foreign exchange, investment, imports, exports, and employment practices. Tax holidays were granted to investors and free zones established.

In Turkey, Tunisia, and Egypt (the countries with the longest track record of liberalization), the private sector has made reasonable progress, but it is still hampered by the state's resistance to relinquish more of its controls and bureaucratic procedures (see Patton, Sherif and Soos, Harik). Despite the liberalization drive, the state continues to control the prices of a large number of commodities, especially pertaining to food. In Egypt, external trade has not been fully opened up for the private sector, especially exports, and the state continues to maintain some areas closed to private investment. In Algeria, Syria, and Iraq, the private sector enjoys a very limited scope of freedom.

Under the hampering effects of restrictive policies, it is not time yet to assess whether liberalization has succeeded to produce economic recovery or not; and until full liberalization is achieved, all we can do is just monitor the growth in private economic activities and note its impact on the economy.

OBSTACLES TO DIVESTITURE

The slow pace of denationalization is not accidental. It is the hardest part of the transitional period. Not only is there a significant ideological residue of resistance and vested interest by labor and civil servants, but there is reluctance ·and fear on the part of policy makers of what they see as major economic dislocations and political turmoil. Political concerns aside, there are a number of major hurdles in the way of divestiture even where governments are favorably disposed:

First, private savings are much too small to serve as funds for purchasing SEEs (see Harik, Chaudhry). The small financial market in the LDCs are unsuited and unprepared for the conversion of state economic enterprises to private hands. Decimated during the socialist takeover period or originally negligible in size, the entrepreneurial class itself is not ready, nor will it be in the near future, to replace the state. Moreover, there is a tendency for entrepreneurs to prefer starting their own enterprises rather than buying out ailing public-sector firms. SEEs are either not attractive because of a history of losses and labor privileges, and/or they are too large to handle. Most sales so far have been made direct to a single buyer or a few buyers in all the countries of the region except Turkey, where some equity has been put up for public subscription. Failure to involve a large number of citizens in the sale of SEEs gives rise to concerns that divestiture will substitute a small-business oligarchy for what was state monopoly.

A second major hurdle in the way of denationalization is the financial disadvantage the government will undergo by selling unattractive firms to reluctant buyers. The tendency is for businessmen to take advantage of the urgency with which the government is faced and to push the price down, sometimes by ganging up against the government. There have already been a few cases in which offers for sale have been withdrawn because of this condition. Governments are faced with two difficult options: sell a financially ailing firm as is, or tidy it up before putting it on the market. In the first case, a government will be obliged to sell at a depressed price, and even then it may not find a buyer. In the second case, it will have to muster huge resources and skill, both of which it lacks. That is why many states are reluctant to fully give up public-sector firms and to prefer to encourage businessmen to start new enterprises.

Finally, foreign buyers, the most capable and available, are not the most acceptable to nationalist regimes—and for legitimate reasons (see Patton, Posusney).

It is obvious that the divestiture course is very hard to implement in the LDCs and may take decades to achieve. The inescapable fact, nevertheless, is that a beginning has to be made, and it would require all the skill and ingenuity of governments. In certain cases, liquidation may be a better solution; it will cause a short-term loss but stop a long-term drain on the national treasury. In other cases, tidying up public firms, even with outside help, may be the best solution, as is the case in Sitex in Tunisia. Again, foreign buyers cannot be barred in contemporary economies even though they may be subjected to limits in numbers and privileges.

While most states in our region have shown willingness to entertain sales to foreign firms, allowing foreigners a major share in the national economy is not likely to occur in any of the countries of the Middle East and North Africa. In Egypt and Algeria, the memories of foreign control of business is still vivid, and the determination to defend the national economy against any form of foreign control is strong. It is one thing to entertain limited transactions with foreign firms in the interest of the national economy and another to see national control over the lifeline of the country pass to foreign hands. The dilemma is quite serious. Given the opportunity, foreign capital could become the dominant force in many of the countries under consideration, especially with the trend toward swapping debt for equity in so many LDCs. On the other hand, not accepting this option means that the divestiture process will not make significant progress in the foreseeable future. Some experts, such as Dr. Said El-Naggar of the IMF, envisage a twenty-year period for divestiture to be completed, which, barring foreign sales, is quite unlikely. With the integration into the world economy becoming a crucial matter in the LDCs, foreign buyers cannot be ruled out; but alternatives to transnational corporations deserve serious attention by nationalist regimes if they desire national control and integration into the world economy at one and the same time.

Since the state is likely to continue to hold on to a large part of public-sector enterprises, it is important to find ways to stop the financial drain on the treasury. Here is where the call for reforming the public sector takes its urgency. Even if they do not make a profit, SEEs should be made to break even. It is obvious, though, that their numbers must be reduced, particularly by eliminating those that have had a long track record of losses, and their future prospects are dim. Joint ventures, which were ill-conceived and mostly unsuccessful in Egypt (see Sherif and Soos), could be reconsidered rather than ruled out for the future. In some experiences, as in Tunisia, foreign involvement and partnership in ailing SEEs has proven quite constructive (see Harik).

Given the limited scope possible for divestiture, are there any courses of action helpful for the LDCs? By searching through the accounts in this volume, at least six ideas and courses of action are suggested or could be inferred:

First, governments should show more readiness to put an end to the parasitic tendencies in the public sector. Firms that are running chronic deficits and show little sign of competing must be liquidated.

Second, the state should free state economic enterprises from the responsibility of financing the welfare system and restore equilibrium between wages and the cost of living. The practice of overtaxing productive units to meet the basic needs of the masses of the population is most harmful to growth and the national economy. Of all the income distribution schemes, this is the most economically damaging. Social welfare should be treated as a separate item in the budget. Programs need to be devised to reduce the pain of those most vulnerable to privatization. Retooling of workers should enjoy a priority consideration.

Third, considerably more can be done with regard to removing obstacles to entry of private businessmen and to reducing state interference in pricing, product mix, and marketing, especially in exports and crop controls. A more active state role in promoting exports is called for in the manner in which it has been done in Turkey (see Patton).

Fourth, it should be realized that new business ventures by the state will not turn better results than the previous experience, a lesson that does not seem to have been learned by many governments. The state is not meant to be an entrepreneur but, rather, to be a promoter of business growth. The partnership between business and the state would achieve the best results if it were based on the principle of assigning to each side its proper role.

Fifth, incentives should be provided for national businessmen to buy all the small- and medium-sized firms after they had been tidied up by the government in the manner in which it had been done in Tunisia. SEEs will not receive a very fair price; the question is to minimize the losses rather than to refuse to sell at an unattractive rate. Autonomy of SEEs will remain a wish formally subscribed to by governments but not respected in practice. There is, however, a variant of autonomy in "warehousing" and in subsidiaries of SEEs. These methods have been successfully tried in Tunisia and Egypt. Two or more state-owned banks, often the most successful public enterprises, buy a firm and run it while they bring in other buyers as partners. A subsidiary is a business firm formed by a consortium of public-sector banks and/or corporations (such as the Export Development Bank and the Misr-Iran Bank in Egypt), which seem to have enjoyed considerable autonomy because they are one step removed from the reach of policy makers. Additional reform measures could be introduced to allow wider public participation in SEEs. To encourage private participation and strengthen the money market, the state can open up public-sector firms, large and medium ones, for public subscription. To succeed, such a measure should start with successful firms and shares be made lucrative to potential buyers. This has only been done in Turkey (see Patton), but Tunisia is taking a reluctant step in that direction. Egypt has resisted this option steadfastly. Though an attractive idea, sale of firms to employees has not yet proven to be a viable option. It is being tried with one company now in Egypt (see Sullivan, Posusney, Sherif and Soos), while a variant of this in Tunisia did fail (see Harik).

Sixth, and most important, the state should upgrade its performance as a promoter through responsible financing, research, and new technologies. The partnership of business and the state should be geared toward joint benefit rather than extraction and obstruction.

PRIVATIZATION AND DEMOCRATIZATION

Finally, what do the studies of privatization in the Middle East and North Africa tell us, if anything, about transition to democracy? It is clear from practically all the cases at hand that the state is not withdrawing but, rather, redefining its role in the economy. When the state sells a public firm, it does not cease to draw revenue from it; it does not end all service activities affecting the particular firm; it does not end its regulatory role nor its mediation between labor and management. In the same vein, both businessmen and labor have gained more freedom to make choices: labor regains the power to bargain and to strike; businessmen, the power to make investment, marketing, and management decisions. As both sides gain more freedom, the change will be reflected politically. Authoritarian governments would find it increasingly difficult to exclude the various groups from the councils of state. This is true of authoritarian monarchies (Jordan and Saudi Arabia) as of the single- and dominant-party regimes. The growing stature of private groups will undoubtedly have a progression effect, which could be stopped only by an act of force.

Although it is not possible to find a direct causal linkage between privatization and democracy in either direction, it seems nevertheless clear that the two reinforce one another. Some states in our region introduced economic liberalization and democratization measures on their own before any public pressure forced them in that direction. In those cases where mass action occurred, such as Algeria and Jordan, democratization measures were speeded up (see Vandewalle, Brand). However, the thesis that political liberalization may be associated with a transition from a *rentier* economy to one in which the state may have to be domestically extractive (see Brand) is suggestive, but it is not possible to substantiate from the limited experiences of our region. A state that reduces its economic burdens might cease to be in need of extractive measures. Moreover, economically extractive regimes are not associated with liberalization but, rather, with political repression. In general, however, democratic regimes tend to show strong tendencies to placate public pressure by granting concessions (see Patton).

Economic liberalization in varying degrees has been introduced in almost all states of the region as a result of the failure of state economic enterprises and the futility of state intervention. Economic failure had undermined regime legitimacy and spurred leaders to cut their losses by cutting back on their economic involvements. Some regimes proceeded with liberalization on both fronts (Algeria, Tunisia, Egypt, Turkey, and Jordan), but others held basically to economic reforms (Syria, Iraq, and Saudi Arabia). It thus appears that where the economic damage has been severe, the state has tended to adopt a dual approach of economic and political liberalization. Where the state economic resources for reform were strong and the political damage caused by economic failure manageable, the state shunned political liberalization and dealt with the crisis through economic measures.

The transition to democracy in our region undoubtedly will continue to be just as slow as the transition to economic liberalization, because the social forces which could bring about a turn around have not yet demonstrated a pressure-power equal to the task. It is clear that both economic and political liberalization have moved at a controlled and relatively equal pace. The balancing of interests of social, political, and economic groups is going to be rough and uncertain in the promised competitive future of these countries.

Given the limited weight of trade-union organizations and of businessmen associations, it is not likely that either labor or capital will take over the state. Businessmen are politically handicapped by the disrespect shown them by intellectuals who propagate the image of the businessman as avaricious, exploitative, and not quite patriotic. At any rate, neither businessmen nor labor groups are likely to become distinguished leaders in the struggle for democracy. The interests businessmen share with the state are too strong to allow them to pose as an independent political adversary, and labor will continue to need state support in securing favorable legislation and mediation with business.

We will continue to see conglomerate interests coexist and compete in what may look like a populist coalition of diverse and vaguely defined groups. This would be quite similar to what has prevailed during the authoritarian patron state to this day, with the exception that the voice of the people will have more weight than it had in the past. Democratization may or may not take the form of parliamentary democracy of the Westminster pattern. What is certain, though, is that the councils of state will be broadened and that individuals and groups will have more freedom to express themselves and to act upon their beliefs.

Radical groups nourished by the turbulent transition in the economy will pose constant challenges to the democratic fulfillment in these societies. Authoritarian regimes may continue, therefore, to perpetuate themselves by posing as barriers to radical movements. While democracy will be nourished and gain strength by privatization, the latter is not a precondition for the former. Privatization and economic liberalization have occurred at the hands of authoritarian regimes in all the cases studied here, except Turkey. Democracy, on the other hand, holds the promise of economic improvement and growth, but there is no necessary connection or evidence to the claim. Forces opposed to sound economic measures could be just as strong if not stronger under a democratic system (see Patton). Democracy has to be valued and sought for itself, not for its economic rewards.

In short, the question of economic reforms goes beyond the issue of public versus private sector. It belongs in the policy-making sphere—how it is made, and for what objectives. For just as the state can hurt the private sector, it can do the same to its own public sector by ill-advised policies, as we have seen happen in many cases discussed above. The art of making sound economic policy thus comes before the issue of structural changes in the direction of privatization.

Notes

1. Said El-Naggar, ed., *Privatization and Structural Adjustment in the Arab Countries,* International Monetary Fund (1989), p. 14.

2. R. Millward, "Measured Sources of Inefficiency in the Performance of Private and Public Enterprises," in Paul Cook and Colin Kirkpatrick, *Privatization in Less Developed Countries* (New York: St. Martin's Press, 1988); see also R. Millward and D. M. Parker, "Public and Private Enterprise: Comparative Behavior and Relative Efficiency," in R. Millward et al., *Public Sector Economics* (London: Longman, 1983).

3. See Alan Walters, "Liberalization and Privatization: An Overview," in El-Naggar, *Privatization and Structural Adjustment,* pp. 24–26; see also Richard Pryke, "The Comparative Performance of Public and Private Enterprise," in John Kay, Colin Mayer, and David Thompson, eds., *Privatization and Regulation: The UK Experience* (Oxford: Clarendon Press, 1986); and Kwan Kim, "Enterprise Performance in the Public and Private Sectors: Tanzania's Experience," *Journal of Developing Areas* 15, no. 3 (April 1981).

4. See, for instance, the criticism in Cook and Kirkpatrick, *Privatization in Less Developed Countries,* p. 12.

5. For more on this point, see Harik, "The Patron State and the Future of Arab Development" (written in Arabic), *al Mustaqbal al ʿArabi* (March 1989).

6. This is particularly true among leftist apologists in Egypt, both scholars and intellectuals. See Killick and Commander, "State Divestiture," *World Development* 16, no. 12 (1988); and John Waterbury, *The Egypt of Nasser and Sadat,* (Princeton: Princeton University Press, 1983).

7. See, for instance, Cook and Kirkpatrick, *Privatization in Less Developed Countries;* and Killick and Commander, "State Divestiture," p. 1471.

8. In addition to Killick and Commander, "State Divestitute," see statements made by a number of Egyptian economists in a round-table discussion published by the Beirut monthly journal *al Mustaqbal al ʿArabi,* August 1989.

9. See Waterbury, *The Egypt of Nasser and Sadat.* A variant of this argument can be found in Joel Migdal, *Strong Societies and Weak States* (Princeton: Princeton University Press, 1988).

10. Cook and Kirkpatrick, *Privatization in Less Developed Countries,* p. 6.

11. The round-table discussion in *al Mustaqbal al ʿArabi.*

12. See Mosely, in Cook and Kirkpatrick, *Privatization in Less Developed Countries,* pp. 125–40.

13. Killick and Commander, "State Divestiture," p. 1466.

14. Cook and Kirkpatrick, *Privatization in Less Developed Countries,* p. 28.

15. More than an intimation of this possibility can be seen in Waterbury, who maintains in *The Egypt of Nasser and Sadat* that the public sector in Egypt was run in the class interests of private businessmen.

CHAPTER

2

EXTRA-STATE ACTORS
AND PRIVATIZATION IN EGYPT

Denis J. Sullivan

The government of Egypt has committed itself to a "radical" reform of the economy, which it has controlled and poorly managed for the past several decades. President Mubarak's May Day 1990 speech calling for privatization and liberalization, his "1,000 Day Reform Program" announced in December of that year, and his government's 1991 signing of a standby credit agreement with the International Monetary Fund were all intended to mark a new direction for economic policy making in Egypt. Whether they have, in fact, done so is doubtful because, although these steps are important, they have not ended the long-standing and continuing debate over whether and how to privatize. That this debate still lingers attests to the reality of a fundamental disagreement over economic decision making within Egyptian state agencies.

On one hand, this debate centers on the question of which takes precedence—economics or politics. For the past many years, those calling for political stability have won out in this internal governmental struggle. Maintaining stability and the status quo has taken precedence over economic development objectives, the goal of so-called reformists within the economic and political elite. On the other hand, the debate is a more fundamental one, centering on the question of what kind of economic system should Egypt follow—socialist, capitalist, Islamic, or other.

This debate is not merely an internal Egyptian governmental one. Various voices are heard from within and outside the government, from within and outside Egypt. It has only been since 1987 that the concept of privatization entered into this debate, and now that issue is at the top of the list of those discussing economic reform.

Privatization is a political process[1] wherein the state initiates and directs its own economic restructuring. Selling State-Owned Enterprises (SOEs), whether through divestiture, joint ventures, liquidations, or asset transfers, is the primary method of achieving privatization. Privatization also involves the state's establishing a policy climate more conducive to the private sector. In virtually all of these cases, reform is a top-down process.

As it is not only the state that debates or lobbies to promote economic reform, so, too, is it not only the state that has influence over the restructuring *process*. Various institutions, both inside and outside a given country, also affect this process. Labor unions, business associations, local communities, charitable associations, and Private Voluntary Organizations (PVOs) can and do influence the governmental decision-making process. International donors, multinational corporations, and world powers also exercise influence in this realm.

This chapter focuses on *extra-state actors* involved in the process of privatization in Egypt. Extra-state actors refers to institutions other than the Egyptian state that are involved in this process: Egyptian societal groups as well as institutions from outside Egypt. The latter include foreign donors attempting to persuade the government of Egypt to promote privatization. The emphasis from "below" the state level is primarily on grass-roots organizations that have been formed in recent years as a direct response to the failure of the state to provide basic services for specific communities. These organizations are pressuring the state either *to* provide such services or *not to* interfere with their efforts to fill in where the state has failed to fulfill its social-welfare role.

Whether the effort at reform comes from outside Egypt or from societal groups inside Egypt, the fact is that the state continues to have as much influence over the process as any other group. The ultimate responsibility for reform, at present, therefore belongs to President Husni Mubarak. To whom, among his advisers, the President listens is a crucial question that cannot be disregarded by outside groups trying to influence the pace of reform inside Egypt. The President's advisers include a bevy of *reformists* in the Egyptian government and an equally powerful group of *gradualists,* who recognize the need to improve economic efficiency but caution against any drastic moves toward immediate reform. The reformists are represented by Yusef Wali, Minister of Agriculture, who is also a Deputy Prime Minister and Secretary-General of the ruling National Democratic Party; by Atef Abeid, Minister of Cabinet Affairs; and by Fouad Sultan, Minister of Tourism. The gradualists are represented by Kamal Ganzouri, Minister of Planning, who is also a Deputy Prime Minister and the leading figure in this group; and by another like-minded person, Muhammad Abdel-Wahhab, Minister of Industry.

Even though these bureaucratic rivalries for power, position, and prestige are not my immediate concern, they cannot be ignored.[2] Egyptian officials do acknowledge the need to reform the public sector; to cut price subsidies on energy, food, and transportation; to end government control of certain economic sectors; and to promote the private sector. A new public-sector law is being debated in Parliament at present. Two committees have been set up to study—and promote?—the issue of privatization. One, under Yusef Wali, is a Steering Committee, the responsibility of which is to implement the "Partnership in Development" project of the United States Agency for International Development (USAID or AID).

Former Defense Minister Abu Ghazala is the chairman of a committee to study privatization priorities in industry.[3]

With all this apparent activity at reform, the real question of the government's commitment to economic adjustment and reform concerns the pace at which reform will be implemented. To date, the arguments of the gradualists seem to have won out over those of the reformists: "the social disruption will be too great so we must guide any reform, over a long period of time, to prevent the truly needy from losing the protection of the state."[4] Such internal Egyptian differences may be the guarantee of continued political inertia and economic stagnation.

With this internal division in mind, this chapter shifts the focus to those efforts aimed at promoting reform and privatization from outside the Egyptian state, or extra-state actors.[5]

MULTILATERAL AND BILATERAL SUPPORT FOR PRIVATIZATION

The International Monetary Fund (IMF)

The IMF and World Bank—and in many cases, USAID—work closely together in developing countries. The IMF often behaves as the "advance team," imposing conditionality on a government in the form of a standby credit agreement.[6] Once this agreement is reached, the World Bank (and/or USAID) is prepared to provide Structural Adjustment Loans (SAL) or other forms of project assistance for long-term development.

In Egypt, economic reform has been the primary goal of the IMF since the mid-1970s. In May 1987, a standby agreement was reached between the IMF and the Government of Egypt. The IMF provided $342 million and paved the way for Egypt to reschedule its debt payments through the Paris Club, a group of eighteen member states, formed in 1977, who are Egypt's largest creditors.[7] This standby agreement collapsed by November 1988 after the IMF had disbursed the first payment of $160 million. The IMF accused Egypt of reneging on its promise of economic reform while Egypt claimed it was merely slowing down the pace of reform for fear of widespread social unrest.

Periodic talks between the IMF and Egyptian officials continued since 1988 and were aimed at reaching yet another standby agreement. Tentative agreement between the IMF and Egypt was made in September 1990, and the IMF team continued discussions with Egyptian officials on the steps necessary to finalize the agreement. Talks in early February between top-level Egyptian ministers—then Foreign Minister Esmat Abdel-Meguid (now Secretary-General of the Arab League) and Cabinet Affairs Minister Atef Abeid—and the Managing Director of the IMF, Michel Camdessus, resulted in Camdessus's recommendation for board approval of a standby credit arrangement "provided the government carries out elements of the economic reform programme announced by Prime Minister Atef Sedki in his

28 January People's Assembly speech."[8] The Letter of Intent, stipulating Egypt's commitment to a specific reform and liberalization package, was finally signed by Egypt and the IMF in Cairo on 9 April 1991. Final approval was given in May at the Fund's board of directors meeting. With this approval, the IMF was expected to extend $400 million in credits to Egypt.[9]

Moreover, with the IMF's "seal of approval" for the government's economic-reform program, Egypt received a 50 percent reduction in its debt to the Paris Club. Creditors agreed to cancel 30 percent of the debt in two phases beginning July 1, 1991. Another 20 percent would be cancelled on 1 July 1994, at which time the remaining debt would be rescheduled, perhaps with a twenty-five-year repayment schedule.[10] The United States cancelled $7 billion in Egyptian military debt because of Egypt's stance in the Gulf War against Iraq and had been actively pressing other creditors to follow suit.

Elements of Reform

One of the primary elements of the IMF-supported reform program proceeded despite the difficulties facing the Egyptian economy as a result of the Gulf crisis. The government announced at the end of February 1991 that banks were allowed to exchange foreign currency at free-market rates, essentially ending the multi-tiered exchange-rate system and establishing a single unified rate.

In addition to foreign exchange-rate reform, the IMF has been pushing for other policy reforms, which include: reducing the budget deficit (which reached LE 7.2 billion in 1989 and LE 14 billion in 1990, the latter approximately $4 billion) to 6 percent of total national output and causing it to disappear over the next five years; gradually cutting subsidies for some food (though the government insists it will not touch subsidies on staples) and other commodities and eliminating them entirely over the next seven years; raising energy prices, over the next five years, to the international market level; raising bank interest rates (which the government also has allowed); and reducing the number of civil-service posts and military spending.[11] Indeed, the government of Egypt has come to terms with the IMF on virtually every issue. It has raised prices for gasoline, cigarettes, and bu-tagas; raised bank interest rates; and accepted the IMF's budget deficit targets.

The last two items that had been preventing a standby agreement were the implementation of a sales tax and bringing domestic energy prices into line with world levels. The IMF apparently pushed hard for the introduction of this very controversial sales tax, which was introduced on 1 May 1991. It is a 10 percent tax on luxury goods and imports. The latter will be taxed in order to gain more revenue and to protect "infant [local] industries" from foreign competition. By replacing the consumption tax, the government hopes the new tax will raise $300 million in the first year.[12] The government has also, apparently, agreed to raise domestic energy prices to their international level. These reforms will hit everyone hard, but primarily the lower and middle classes, who have survived the economic crisis afflicting Egypt since the mid-1980s largely by government subsidies on food, housing, transportation, telephone service, fuels, and electricity.

Egypt's Strategic Position

The IMF and similarly motivated agencies such as the World Bank, USAID, and even Arab donors only recently are beginning to see their objective of economic reform in Egypt come into fruition. In the past, Egypt has been able to fend off such "leveraged persuasion" from foreign donors because of its strategic importance to foreign interests (e.g., American, French, Saudi, Kuwaiti) in the Middle East. Pointing to the events of January 1977, Egyptian officials have been able to convince foreign donors that drastic reforms would lead to political instability in Egypt. In 1977, under pressure from the IMF, the United States and several Arab states, President Sadat announced the reduction of various food and other subsidies. This led to "food riots" throughout Egypt and, as a result of these riots, to several days of uncertainty regarding the stability of the Sadat regime; the subsidies were quickly reinstated.

Sadat's reversal, reinstating subsidies, was not questioned by American officials. The priority of political stability over economic reform has been the hallmark of U.S. foreign policy in Egypt. At the same time, other officials of the American foreign policy establishment harbor a concern for economic reform and argue that stability can be achieved by focusing on economic issues. Egyptian officials who observe this internal American difference of opinion are able to exploit it. They are most successful in addressing American fears that yet another U.S. ally (after Iran) could topple in the Middle East. For example, when rioters took to the streets of Caracas, Venezuela, in early 1989, after the government accepted an IMF package, Egyptian officials used this event to reiterate their call for understanding and leniency by the IMF and Washington. When riots erupted in Jordan later that year, IMF conditions were even further resisted. More strikingly, when Egypt joined the U.S.-led defense of Saudi Arabia against Iraq, Egypt was able to utilize its military and political assets to soften the demands of the IMF for strict economic reform. Egypt, therefore, has consistently exhibited an ability to fend off those who press too hard for economic reform.

The IMF attempt to get Egypt to sign a standby agreement in order to then restructure its international debt became less critical, although still necessary, from the standpoint of the Government of Egypt (GOE) with the announcement of debt relief by the United States and by Saudi Arabia and other Gulf Arab states in late 1990.[13] Prime Minister Sedki's assurance of economic liberalization and reform is all the more significant because in the past, when international pressure on Egypt was lessened, the government of Egypt was less willing (or able) to pursue reform.

It was this posture of delaying reform that resulted in IMF officials' losing patience with the GOE. Much of this impatience has been due to the difference in perspective between the IMF and Egyptian officials over what constitutes structural reform. Much is also due to the IMF's recognition of Egypt's political leverage and the allies it has in its camp against moving too far, too fast in reforming its system. These allies include some White House officials, members of Congress, and State Department officials. Perhaps their impatience is also due to changes in Eastern Europe, where formerly socialist governments are much more forthcoming in their desire to restructure and reform their economies than is the GOE. Indeed, Paris Club members were arguing in early 1991 that Poland was a "much more deserving case"[14] for debt relief and other international assistance than was Egypt. The United States did forgive 70 percent of Poland's debt in March 1991 as a reward for Poland's push for market reforms.

Whether or not the government is itself enthusiastically or otherwise committed to these reforms is an important question. Many analysts feel that the GOE is agreeing to IMF conditions simply to get short-term benefits of standby credits and debt relief.[15] If this view is correct, the GOE could renege on its pledge once the sacrifices become too difficult for Egyptian society to handle. Others say that even though the same government (i.e., same group of cabinet members), which in 1987 agreed and later reneged on its pledge of reform, has agreed to the 1991 program, this time it is committed.[16] Indeed, given Egypt's previous record of reneging on its commitment to reform, the IMF is not taking Egypt at its word alone. IMF support for Egypt's reform will be under constant review with an IMF delegation visiting Egypt every three months to assess progress of the reforms. "Aid given by the IMF and debt rescheduling agreements will be suspended if the delegation is not satisfied with the pace or degree of achievement in implementing the reforms."[17]

The success of the IMF in assuring Egyptian commitment also affects the prospects for other international donors and creditors who are poised and ready to work with a cooperative, reform-minded government in Egypt.

The World Bank

The International Bank for Reconstruction and Development (IBRD or World Bank) provides support worldwide for policy reform in general and industrial restructuring in particular. Recently, the Bank's International Finance Corporation (IFC) established a Corporate Finance Services Department to assist member governments with privatization. Also, in 1988, the Multilateral Investment Guarantee Agency and the Foreign Investment Advisory Service were established "to help increase the flows of direct foreign private investment to our member countries through policy advice and active promotion of the investment opportunities in our member countries."[18]

In Egypt, the Bank had allocated, as of 1990, $300 million in lines of credit for private investments in three areas: small and medium scale industries, export promotion, and construction. Bank officials say that the demand for these credits is "very weak." They attribute this weak demand to the government's support for the failing public sector and to a policy climate that inhibits private initiative.[19] Bank officials emphasize that Egypt's industrial economic activity since the nationalizations of the 1960s has been based on the Soviet model of development. While they recognize the attempt by Sadat to modify this model, they bemoan the fact that the government tries to retain fundamental control over the economy by way of central planning; investment licenses; controls over import, export, credit, and, until February 1991, foreign exchange decision making; and a dual set of rules and regulations for public and private enterprises.

World Bank activity in Egypt consists of industrial and other specialists seeking to prepare the groundwork for a major investment on the part of the IBRD in the form of a Structural Adjustment Loan (SAL) and other projects. (This will occur with Egypt's signing a standby agreement with the IMF.) A memo of understanding on the SAL, linking Bank loans to progress on Egypt's economic reform process, was signed 19 March 1991.[20]

The World Bank seeks to promote private sector industrial investment but will not do so until the IMF secures a commitment from the government of Egypt to provide an "appropriate" policy environment—that is, a more liberal policy climate, one which encourages private sector investment and which diminishes the capacity of the state to control (read, to inhibit) economic activity. At the same time, the Bank does not shy away from funding public sector activities. In Egypt as in most developing countries, this sector still comprises a large percentage of economic activity in various fields, particularly industry. The Bank is involved in trying to make this sector run more efficiently.

The World Bank can point to no specific instance in which their financial or technical assistance has led to the privatizing of a state-owned enterprise in Egypt. Yet, in the spring of 1991, World Bank officials were in Cairo attempting to draw a list of twenty companies to be privatized as part of the SAL agreement.[21] Until this point, the Bank has been in a "waiting game." It has been waiting for the government and the IMF to agree to a stabilization program. It further waits for private-sector investors to apply for the $300 million the Bank has made available for private investments.

In the meantime, the World Bank continues to pursue its traditional projects as well as some unique ones. For Egypt, these include promoting public-sector reform, investigating methods to facilitate deregulation and to promote private investment, a first-ever (in Egypt) project to work with the government to promote the tourism sector (essentially, a series of loans for infrastructure development, e.g., in Sinai and Fayoum), and a first-ever "social equity fund" to help people displaced by privatization and other liberalization schemes. The tourism project was proceeding even before the government reached agreement with the IMF. This is primarily because the World Bank has deep trust in Tourism Minister Fouad Sultan, a noted supporter of privatization and economic reform. The social equity fund has had difficulties in its early stages and has become highly politicized with President Mubarak's cousin being named the director of this important project.[22] Still, the fund project is expected to proceed apace as the government and other foreign donors, who will transfer some of their aid into the fund, are exhibiting keen interest in it.

An important question is raised when one considers the extent of IMF and World Bank pressure on the GOE to commit to a thorough remaking of the Egyptian economy. That question is: to what extent are the reform efforts dictated from outside Egypt and to what extent are they a product of Egyptian decision making? If one believes officials of the GOE and the IMF, the recent reform package is a GOE product that is simply "supported" by the IMF. The opposite view is suggested by an official of the World Bank who works on Egypt. He said that the package is entirely created by the IMF and World Bank and that both organizations had worked hard to get the GOE to agree to their conditions. While the question may not be answerable, I will try to suggest below that the answer lies somewhere in between these two extremes as the so-called reformists from within the government try to promote liberalization in Egypt and find encouragement and allies in extra-state actors.

The United States Agency for International Development

While there has not been much movement in the direction of privatization in Egypt—with the exception of the sale of three tourist hotels and several hundred governorate-owned small-scale enterprises (e.g., beehives, minibus services, and poultry farms)—there has been considerable interest in the concept. One AID official suggested in March 1989 that "18 months ago, privatization was a dirty word, and was not even mentioned in GOE circles."[23] By March 1990, AID had issued its Request for Proposals, seeking bids from contractors who can assist in achieving "substantial privatization activity in Egypt. The purpose is to assist in the development of procedures and implementation of divestitures of governorate and national state owned enterprises."[24] In February 1991, USAID had shortlisted two groups for the estimated $3 million to $4 million "Partnership in Development" project (a euphemism for privatization). Final decisions had been hampered by the Gulf crisis but were expected within the year.[25]

Prior to this point, AID officials had seen considerable progress toward their goal of promoting reform in Egypt's agricultural sector. Whether this was due to AID's efforts or to an internal GOE decision makes little difference to many at AID. The fact is that Dr. Yusef Wali, Minister of Agriculture, spearheaded the removal of delivery quotas of certain crops and the raising of the procurement prices offered by the government. AID is using this example of reform to encourage similar reform measures in other sectors. A top economist at AID-Egypt is convinced that Egypt will continue in the direction of economic reform if it can overcome the remaining political obstacles, most notably a lack of consensus within the government over the appropriate path toward reform. He is convinced of Egypt's commitment "not because the Egyptians have suddenly been enlightened to the wonders of market liberalization," but because Egypt "ran out of money to service its debt and couldn't borrow more to continue to support its economic policies."[26]

AID's ability to promote economic reform in other sectors faces various obstacles. The politics of the aid program in Egypt put AID officials in a position in which they have ironically low political leverage over the GOE. This is a result of AID's subservience to the wishes of the White House and Congress over the form of aid to Egypt (i.e., cash versus project aid), and its competition with the U.S. Embassy in Egypt, the Departments of Agriculture (USDA) and Commerce, and other bureaucracies which stake a claim in the aid program.[27] Given this competition between various American bureaucratic institutions, the United States hardly speaks with one voice regarding economic aid to Egypt. Perceptive Egyptians have taken advantage of this disunity to prevent the United States or AID or the IMF from pushing a reform package on Egypt before Egypt is ready to accept one.

Movement toward meaningful reform is, therefore, slow; but some AID officials would say that there is movement nonetheless. These officials point to the creation of an Employee Stock Ownership Program (ESOP) of an Alexandria-based tire company as the most significant effort toward privatization to date. AID initiated this program but, because they could not attract an American tire manufacturer, turned to Pirelli of Italy. Yet, AID was not allowed to join in privatizing an existing public-sector tire company; it had to help create an entirely new company, find a foreign investor, and find two thousand employees to work in the company *and* to invest in the ESOP. This is an effort aimed at encouraging the private sector, not at selling off part of the public sector; yet, it is touted by AID as a successful effort toward their goal of privatization in Egypt. More than two years after the initiation of this project, the Alexandria Tire Company/ESOP had yet to be conducting business. The employees/partial-owners had not even been hired.

This model of privatization fits into the Egyptian debate over privatization on the side of those who take a conservative view of the issue (i.e., those calling for "encouragement" of the private sector, *tashjiic qitaac al-khaas*). It also is a strange position for USAID officials to be in since they are the ones calling for a more liberal view of privatization (i.e., "selling off" of the public sector, *biic qitaac al-caam*).[28]

To date, the government has not privatized, in whole or in part, the assets of any industrial state owned enterprise. Three hotels (the Sheraton Hurghada, the San Stefano in Alexandria, and the Cairo Meridien) were sold off to the private sector. These sales were executed not by any external pressure but as a result of a commitment by Fouad Sultan, Minister of Tourism.[29] Other than these sales, "privatization" in Egypt has been limited to joint ventures, an ESOP in a *new* company, price reform in agriculture (again, the result of a commitment to reform by Minister of Agriculture Yusef Wali), the sale of hundreds of Small and Micro-Enterprises (SMEs), and private management of publicly owned hotels and restaurants.

In addition to its grand strategies to promote privatization, AID has various other projects to promote the private sector. One of the most important is the Commodity Import Program (CIP) for the private sector (there is also a CIP for the public sector). Together, the public and private sector CIP totaled $200 million in 1990, $150 million of which is for the private sector. Interestingly enough, many private-sector businesspeople have begun to criticize USAID for decreasing the public-sector CIP to only $50 million in 1990 from a high of $313 million in 1981. They say that the private sector's declining viability is related to the declining availability of resources, which can be traced in part to a declining commitment of funds by USAID to the public sector. The feeling among many Egyptian private businesspeople is, as one businessman put it, that the "public sector is still an important part of the economy. If it goes without American aid, the private sector loses out as well."[30] This businessman is pointing to the strong ties between the public and private sectors in Egypt, and he is certain that the strength of one is closely linked with that of the other.

USAID is also involved in trying to promote the business fortunes of small- and medium-scale businesses through projects such as the Banking Credit Guarantee Corporation, the Egyptian Small Enterprise Development Foundation in Cairo and a similar agency in Alexandria, and the International Executive Service Corps' projects to give Egyptian companies the services and expertise of retired executives from the United States. All but the latter of these were started only recently, and so it is premature to pass judgment on their effectiveness in achieving their objectives.

While American officials in the United States and in Cairo are in general agreement on the need to promote the private sector and to institute widespread economic reform, they reflect the divisions within the Egyptian community as to the wisdom of the speed and details of such reform. The main division is over what is economically rational (essentially the position of AID) versus what is politically feasible (the main concern of the U.S. State Department and the White House, and perhaps Congress as well, especially the Subcommittee on Europe and the Middle East in the House Foreign Affairs Committee). The *gradualists* within the Egyptian government are thus supported in their caution by those Americans concerned primarily with political issues while the *reformists* are looking to those with the least political clout—USAID officials—in their quest to reform Egypt's economic system. The gradualists, both Egyptian and American, seem to have had the upper hand in this complex struggle since the late 1970s. The question is: will the global move toward restructuring and privatization improve the prospects for Egyptian and American reformists in the 1990s?

This question is certainly on the minds of those officials in the multilateral and bilateral agencies involved in pushing Egypt along the path of economic restructuring, including privatization. The concern for restructuring and reform is also a major issue for millions of Egyptians who have suffered from the state's inability to provide them with adequate housing, healthcare, education, municipal services, and other basic needs. Rather than wait for the government to reform itself, thousands of communities throughout Egypt have begun to "take matters into their own hands."

PRIVATE, RELIGIOUS, AND COMMUNITY ASSOCIATIONS

Traditional (governmental) bureaucracies, to a large extent, have failed in their responsibilities of formulating, planning, executing, and monitoring Egypt's development objectives. Instead of working to promote development, the government is involved in crisis management and must work to avert financial collapse. It continues to be unable to solve or even deal effectively with a host of basic problems: unemployment, inflation, housing shortages, deteriorating municipal services, and poor quality healthcare and education, to name but a few. "The main effort at development is from locals, through PVOs, not from the government."[31] Community-based, grass-roots development initiatives have increased significantly in recent years in rural and urban areas. Two of the more interesting aspects of these initiatives are that they have emerged largely without coordination and that a main impetus behind them comes from local mosques and churches.

Out of frustration over the government's inability to recognize the needs of specific communities and to target these communities with development projects in response to those needs, religious groups have developed efficient social services, most notably schools, trade-skill centers (carpentry, sewing), day-care centers and healthcare clinics (some to the extent of being hospitals). In some cases, filling this gap in services has been extremely profitable.

Thus, the entrepreneurial role so necessary to promote growth and development is not being taken up by the GOE exclusively. Egypt's bureaucracy has become defensive and nonactivist as the government struggles with economic crisis.

Islamic, Christian, and secular associations are stepping in to help. An official of Catholic Relief Services, an international PVO working in Egypt, reports that "mosques are providing alternative support services as foreign donors push the government of Egypt *out* of such services in their efforts to reform governmental policies such as subsidization of food, medicine, etc.; privatization; and budget cutting."[32] As a result, individuals are looking to these associations instead of to governmental agents for assistance, support, and healing.

Voluntarism (including that of a religious nature) has a long history and solid reputation in Egypt. Islamic associations, originating in the nineteenth century, rapidly increased in number after World War II and in the late 1950s. The need for such groups diminished somewhat during the 1960s as government sought an increasing role in the daily private lives of its subjects.[33] Yet with the failure of government to effectively displace private initiative, there has been a gradual reassertion of voluntarism in Egypt.

Private religious (Islamic, Coptic Christian, and other Christian) associations are evident up and down the Nile and in villages and large cities. They range from small organizations of only five people operating out of satellite villages to large "societies" (even corporations) employing scores of healthcare professionals, educators, and clerical staff in middle-class suburbs of Cairo. In general, these PVOs are part and parcel of the *jam'iyyaat khayriyya* or charitable associations which are registered by the Ministry of Social Affairs. Their services are largely determined by their own members though the government can demonstrate considerable oversight functions.

Village Associations

On the village level, the focus of many of these PVOs is on education and job training as well as on providing healthcare to mothers and infants, day care, and municipal services (e.g., sewage facilities and potable water projects). In a satellite village of Taha, near al-Minia, job training consists of a small room with half a dozen Singer sewing machines run by mothers whose children attend school in the room next door. Other such training, geared mostly toward males, includes carpentry centers where instruction on the use of certain machines can be had. The major contribution of these programs is the mere fact of providing access to equipment otherwise unavailable to individuals for use in building and repairing household necessities. This allows persons to maintain their own clothing or household items and to contract their services to others in the village in need of such assistance.

Community Development Associations and PVOs

Urban areas also house these associations. The short history of Ezbet Zein, on the southern edge of Cairo, provides an important case study in their development.[34] Originally a squatter community developed in the early 1960s around a factory, Ezbet Zein still has neither public sewerage nor public schools. In the late 1970s, leaders of the community approached the Ministry of Social Affairs (MOSA) for financial support to make their mosque a more permanent structure. MOSA officials responded that it could not use public money to rebuild mosques. Instead, MOSA suggested the residents form a Community Development Association (CDA), the headquarters of which could be in a mosque, to which MOSA would contribute some human and financial resources.

After 1979, the CDA of Ezbet Zein began a nursery school and a vocational training program. The mosque was rebuilt as a two-story building, the upper level to be used for community services. The association is run by a fifteen-member board, which is responsible for collecting *zakat* (donations given by Muslims for charity) and supervising the various programs and community services they have developed over the past decade. These services are teaching the Koran (no charge), running a sewing center, and providing day care. (The MOSA provides the teacher, and the CDA pays one-third of her salary.) The CDA receives some foreign assistance, as do many PVOs in Egypt. This CDA also provides medical services to the community. It rents a room to a doctor who in turn charges low fees to his patients. Through its remedial tutoring program, the CDA retains one-half of the charges. It has also organized a food cooperative and septic-tank cleaning services.

Louise White reports the 1983 budget for this CDA at just over LE 7,000. About four-fifths of this income comes from *zakat* and other donations from the community. The day-care and sewing centers recover about 70 percent of their costs from fees and the sale of garments. MOSA's contribution is not included in these budget figures because the staff support they provide comes out of the national government's budget.

Thus, the community is meeting the challenge to provide educational, health, social, municipal, and family services. It is building organizations to provide for community members in the absence of government provisions; it is developing community participation in decision making; and it is learning the basics of self-reliance, if not self-governance.

Mustashfa Sayida Zeinab

Connected to the Mosque of Sayida Zeinab in Cairo is a hospital (*mustashfa*). Founded in the late 1970s, this hospital has four beds and treats anywhere between 100 and 200 patients per day. Patients are seen by medical staff between the hours of 5 p.m. and 8 p.m., though there is a doctor on duty twenty-four hours per day. In 1989, a patient paid LE 2 for a physical exam (the cost used to be 25 piasters and increased gradually to this level). The Mosque of Sayida Zeinab pays the doctors for operations, costly medicines, and other treatments beyond the means of the patients. The doctors work for government hospitals in the mornings and come, in the evenings, to Sayida Zeinab or one of the other mosque/hospitals around Cairo that are affiliated (loosely) with Sayida Zeinab (e.g., Rod al-Farag, Shubra, Qalya, etc.). These eighteen mosque/hospitals are developing an informal network of sharing doctors, referring patients elsewhere for more appropriate treatment, and so forth.

An office assistant at Sayida Zeinab hospital says the medical staff includes "good doctors who know the patients and their problems. People have such faith in them that some people come from the Sudan for our services!"[35] He stresses that this hospital, and the many others like it, is not affiliated with the government and receives no money from official sources. The mosque raises money through the *zakat* and other donations.

This Islamic association is responding to and meeting specific community needs, namely affordable and quality healthcare. In turn, it is establishing links with similar organizations throughout Cairo, especially in poorer areas of the city, and it is building a system of cooperative (intercommunal as well as intracommunal) and autonomous (from the government) institutions. It even uses the same doctors the government uses, but it pays them more; and it decentralizes the provision of services by community, enabling these city doctors to become much more known and approachable.

Mustafa Mahmud Society

Perhaps the most widely noted of the urban PVOs is the Mustafa Mahmud Society in Muhandiseen, a middle- to upper-class section of greater Cairo. Mustafa Mahmud is a well-known and generally respected physician. He is an ex-Marxist, "born again" Muslim, scientist, television personality, founder of this society, and otherwise an entrepreneur. Turning to Islam after years of adhering to Marxism as a solution to Egypt's ills, he initiated a television program (*al-'ilm wal-'imaan,* "Science and Belief") dedicated to the precept that Islam and science are completely compatible and self-supportive. He founded his society in accord with this theory: in the name of Islam, to promote the general welfare and to provide top salaries to the medical staff at his health center.

This Islamic society is part aquarium, part library (for the study of Islam), part observatory (to mark the precise dates for beginning and ending of holy days), and very much a health center and hospital. Similar to the Sayida Zeinab operation, the Mustafa Mahmud Society links a mosque with a hospital—the former raising the funds, the latter providing health services. Such services run the gamut from physical exams, blood testing, urinalysis, and diagnoses to kidney dialysis, appendectomies, and heart treatment. Dental and psychological services are also provided. In August 1987, the Society did not have facilities for patients to stay overnight; thus, it technically was not a "hospital." By 1989, a high-rise apartment building in Mohandiseen was renovated and donated to the Society as a hospital. The benefactor is a Kuwaiti with strong ties to Dr. Mustafa Mahmud.[36]

This capitalist enterprise founded in the name of Islam is hardly representative of the vast number of Islamic PVOs in urban settings, but it is a model of achievement with financial benefits accruing to the staff and quality healthcare for thousands of patients.

While urban and rural CDAs and PVOs operate to serve their communities first and foremost, they are also sending a message to the government and society in general. The message is that if the state will not improve the quality of services promised to the people of Egypt, then the people of Egypt will provide their own services as best they can. Of course, they are unable to provide all such services. Moreover, it is inherently uneconomical to do so. But in the face of poor or non-existent services, the alternative of costly, quality services is the clear choice for those who are able to take advantage of them.[37]

The International Connection

While these religious associations and PVOs are homegrown, local, Egyptian institutions, they often have an international connection. The relationship between Egyptian organizations and international actors is mutual, with each side seeking out the other. For instance, Egyptian PVOs often find that their own government is unable or unwilling to offer them financial support, and so they turn to foreign-aid agencies. The Dutch Embassy in Cairo is heavily involved in funding local development initiatives as are the USAID and the Canadian International Development Agency (CIDA).

There is a conscious effort on the part of many development specialists (in USAID, CIDA, and other development agencies) to seek out PVOs because they are viewed as the organizations best placed to promote these donors' objectives, which include providing projects directly in local communities. This gives PVOs the financial, political, and bureaucratic support needed to pursue their own development projects, whether it be potable water, a day-care center in a village, a greenhouse on the edge of the desert, a healthcare center for mothers and infants, or a job-training program. For instance, USAID provided the funding for a kidney dialysis unit for the Mustafa Mahmud clinic. CIDA provided a $20,000 grant for a small operating room at the Zakr el-Rahman Islamic healthcare center in Zeitoun, a working-class area outside Cairo. The Dutch Embassy provided funding for the Center for Development Studies, founded in 1990, whose mission is to train people who run PVOs and CDAs to build the capacity of these local organizations.

Other countries and governments continue to take an interest in Egyptian developmental affairs and even back up that interest with financial support. For instance, the Mustafa Mahmud Society receives considerable funding from Kuwait (i.e., essentially private individuals who support the goals and practices of the Society). This funding helps explain how the Society can operate in such an effective way in which patients pay only LE 2 for an initial consultation while doctors make up to LE 600 per week.[38] This Kuwait connection is hardly a unique situation. Saudi Arabia and other Gulf states support Islamic movements and personalities in Egypt. Saudi Arabia funds a Muslim charitable association, *jamʿiyyat ansar as-sunna,* that teaches its members the Koran and gives them a social education with a strong Wahhabi bent.[39]

Religious, community-based PVOs are not only Islamic in orientation or design. There are scores of Coptic and other Christian PVOs throughout Egypt which also provide basic educational, health, municipal, and other services to their own communities. In practice, this includes providing such services to Muslim members of their communities as well as to their own religious communities. One of the most successful of Egypt's PVOs is a Coptic organization near al-Minia. The Coptic-Evangelical Organization of Social Services (CEOSS) has its own international connection, a Dutch church that has supported the work CEOSS has done throughout the years. CEOSS runs a hostel, trains peasants in certain skills (sewing, carpentry, and farm-related), and operates a school. It is a favorite of USAID officials, who view it as a model of local development and small-scale enterprise.

Economic and Political Associations

The focus on religious charitable organizations is not intended to ignore the existence of militant, politically inspired, or corrupt Islamic organizations in Egypt. It is intended to counter the argument that depicts Islam, or religion in general, solely as a reactionary, militant phenomenon incapable of promoting the general welfare.

Egypt does face a direct challenge from militant organizations, all of which pursue distinct agendas in the name of Islam. The following discussion focuses on student and economic organizations in Egypt and suggests some reasons behind their onetime (and future?) significance. Much like charitable organizations and CDAs, these groups respond to a failure of the state to satisfy basic economic, social, or political demands. They take advantage of the failure of the state to enhance their own legitimacy and their own agenda.

Jama'aat Islamiyya, or Islamic (student) associations, "became the dominant force on Egyptian university campuses during Sadat's presidency."[40] One month before his death, Sadat ordered these groups disbanded, their infrastructure destroyed, and their leaders arrested. While these and other groups remain active, militant groups seem to have lost their appeal, or at least have lost their "ability to constitute a movement that might serve as the mouthpiece of civil society in its confrontation with the state."[41] The personification of that confrontation is, after all, gone now and President Mubarak is adeptly confronting, and perhaps manipulating, the various subgroups of the Islamic "force," thus defusing their organizational power.

Much is being asserted about the continuing influence of Islamic groups on Egyptian university campuses, with analysts pointing to the increasing number of women donning traditional Islamic dress. To be sure, this is readily apparent. But whether this superficial variable suggests that there is something "revolutionary" going on within students (as individuals or as a community) has yet to be determined. Gilles Kepel suggests one reason for this "phenomenon of the 'return to the veil' on the part of female students, encouraged by the *jama'aat.*"[42] Given the problems of campus life (overcrowded classrooms, housing, and buses being primary among them), the *jama'aat* worked to solve many of these and women responded accordingly. *Jama'aat* demanded and achieved segregation of the sexes in different rows in the classrooms to alleviate the problem of having two or even three persons for each seat, a situation that often results in

> promiscuity that threatens the female students' modesty. Similar embarrassment is suffered during the daily journey to the campus in an equally jam-packed bus. In a prudish society in which relations between the sexes occur late and are strictly circumscribed by marriage, the jostling bus in which bodies are pressed one against the other becomes a site . . . of which the female students feel themselves the victims.[43]

The *jama'aat* responded to the latter problem by organizing a minibus service for the female students

> to preserve their dignity from the assaults to which they are subjected on public transport. . . . Its success was immediate. But since demand exceeded supply, it was first preferable, and later compulsory, for the women to dress in 'Islamic style'—veil, long robe, gloves—if they wanted to use this means of transport.[44]

Thus, to many women, adhering to an Islamic dress code (which is easily justifiable in terms of local norms, practicality, and even emerging fashion) is a small price to pay in order to enjoy the special privileges fought for by the *jama'aat*.

This is not to suggest that there are no women making such a political or religious statement by their style of dress. Indeed, many such individuals found on Egyptian university campuses and especially found in poorer neighborhoods do represent more of this consistent, determined, respectful adherence to traditional norms and outward symbols of internal feelings. Guenena, in her research on *al-jihad,* found the "phenomenon of the veil" to be one that is very much class-based.[45]

Islamic student organizations have demonstrated an ability to achieve results for their communities. The problems of overcrowded classrooms, buses, and housing cannot be attributed directly to the government. Yet, solutions to these societal problems have not come from government but from Islamic student groups who have a distinct political (i.e., Islamic) agenda. Again, as was seen with Islamic *charitable* organizations, local groups are fending for themselves since government cannot or will not help them.

Another arena in which a group working in the name of Islam took advantage of government inefficiency or neglect was over the issue of investment. Islamic Investment Companies (IICs) operated for years beyond the control of the government. IICs were initially successful in attracting investors due to the failure of the official, regulated banking industry to provide sufficient rate of return. With interest rates of between 5 and 10 percent, and with inflation averaging 20 to 25 percent, government banks provided a guaranteed negative rate of Return on Investment (ROI). IICs took advantage of this government failure to provide positive ROI with their unregulated activities and claims of upwards of 20 percent "participation in profit."[46]

Of the over 100 Islamic investment companies in 1988, roughly fifty were considered large or medium sized. Total funds of the latter were estimated at nearly $3 billion.[47] Depositors numbered in the hundreds of thousands and included Muslims and Christians alike. Economic ventures were largely in commodity speculation, hence the concern by the traditional banking system and the government. Other ventures were in tourism, industry, agriculture, trade, and real estate.

With several of the large Islamic investment companies unwilling to cooperate with the government's call for public disclosure of investment activities, the government cracked down. In June 1988, a new law called upon the companies to issue investment and financing notes, instead of deposits, and to open their books to official inspection. Total amounts of investment notes were to be limited to ten times the capital available to the company from its shareholders.

The failure of some IICs to comply with government requests prompted the government, in November 1988, to seize the assets of al-Rayan, one of the largest IICs, and to attempt to retrieve overseas funds estimated at over $400 million. Economists in Egypt were predicting that depositors' claims of up to $3 billion would be unmet due to the illegal practices of investment-company owners. Al-Rayan's (and other companies') illicit practices—pyramid system of paying dividends from incoming deposits, embezzlement, and smuggling money abroad—has left tens of thousands of Egyptian investors bereft of their money. Based on the corrupt practices of a small, but powerful, minority of the owners or managers of IICs, the Islamic solution to banking and investment has been dealt a terrible blow, and the confidence of hundreds of thousands of investors has been lost.

CONCLUSION

Private initiative, international pressure, internal bureaucratic and political struggles—all are being brought to bear on the government of Egypt to move the state away from its oligopolistic control over economic affairs. Foreign donors offer incentives of increased aid (World Bank), threats of lack of progress in debt rescheduling (IMF and Paris Club), and promises of shift in aid from project funding to cash transfers (USAID).

Private groups, such as Islamic and other community-based associations, respond to the government's failure to reform itself by doing what is needed for themselves. The state may have the leisure of time and may be able to constantly fend off pressure to reform itself, but individual members of society face immediate threats to their survival if healthcare is inadequate or nonexistent, if potable water is unavailable, if education facilities are lacking, if day care is not provided to allow parents to work. Individuals cannot wait for the state to reform itself. They are thus turning inward instead of looking outward for solutions. They respond with their own private initiatives in their own communities. It is only then that the government and international donors take notice of these groups and seek to support their activities financially in order to better monitor them, if not control them.

We see the Egyptian state responding to different pressures from *extra-state actors* in different ways. With the IMF, even while accepting many of its demands, the GOE asserts its political and military significance to the United States in order to avoid making the most difficult decisions demanded by the IMF. For example, it rejects the IMF's usual demand for a quick end to subsidies and other reforms, and it has the political leverage to succeed. President Mubarak, on many occasions in 1991, has boasted of the "unprecedented, lenient terms" he has won to get IMF backing. With the World Bank, the GOE seeks help in the form of reforming its public-sector institutions. With USAID and other bilateral donors, it again uses its political leverage to avoid making massive reforms.

When reforms are undertaken, they are often the type that are suggested by internal elites (Yusef Wali, Fouad Sultan, Atef Abeid). Even if they seem to fit with the demands of external powers, the impetus is still from within. Much of this impetus is a result of independent decision making on the part of a reformist, as in the case of Fouad Sultan. Some of the impetus is a result of internal pressure on a bureaucracy or government official to reform pricing structures and other governmental controls which act against the interests of a certain economic sector, as in the case of Yusef Wali in agriculture.

The need for economic reform in Egypt is clear. Privatization is one of several mechanisms that can be used to attain that reform. Alas, privatization is, for the most part, still a top-down process. But if that process is dormant, then actors other than the state have no choice but to encourage reform while at the same time proceeding with their own agendas in case it never occurs.

The state remains the key to long-term prospects for further economic growth and development. International actors might be catalysts or supporters of reform. Communities will provide the basis for development. But the state must make the difficult decisions to restructure itself. The state must continue to take an active role in mobilizing the national resources found in each of the country's communities, and the state must sustain a national commitment to economic progress.

The issues, then, for the government of Egypt, are: whether it will decide to reform Egypt's economic system; whether privatization can serve as one way to achieve some of this restructuring; whether to commit the political capital (and thus the prestige of President Mubarak himself) toward this process; and, finally, whether to accept some of the assistance that is being offered from outside Egypt in order to benefit private individuals and companies inside Egypt.

Privatization should not be conceived of as an attempt to sell off the Egyptian state to *foreign* capitalistic interests—and it must not be implemented in this way, either. It should be seen as one way of unburdening the state and the people of Egypt who suffer accordingly. Privatization includes both selling off state-owned enterprises as well as establishing a policy climate more conducive to *Egyptian* private-sector investment. Once the government decides to pursue this course of action, it will be placing some trust in the private sector. Such a demonstration of trust demands a reciprocal demonstration of responsibility on the part of private-sector interests.

Privatization, if it is pursued in Egypt, does not end when the sale is made. It is an ongoing process in which the state will retain some form of oversight and regulation to ensure that the ideals of the Egyptian "Revolution" are not abandoned, even if the failed tactics to achieve these ideals must be.

Notes

1. This assertion holds true for both developed and developing countries. See Yair Aharoni, "The United Kingdom: Transforming Attitudes," and Stephen Haggard, "The Philippines: Picking Up After Marcos," in Raymond Vernon, ed., *The Promise of Privatization: A Challenge for American Foreign Policy* (New York: Council on Foreign Relations, 1988). This issue was further extended to Egypt and numerous Middle Eastern states by Said El-Naggar in remarks made before the Conference on Privatization in Egypt and the Middle East, Boston, 3 April 1990.

2. For details on the bureaucratic and political rivalries over the development process in Egypt, see my "Political Economy of Reform in Egypt," *International Journal of Middle East Studies* (August 1990).

3. This latter committee, however, has not been publicly active, and it is likely that this

position was simply created for Abu Ghazala, Mubarak's way of retiring the powerful Field Marshall in a less humiliating fashion.

4. Interview with undersecretary at the Ministry of Planning and International Cooperation, 25 February 1987.

5. From late 1990 through much of 1991, the government of Egypt was under less pressure to pursue reform. Egypt's important position in the multinational coalition against Saddam Hussein has removed most of the pressure from Egypt to pursue a coherent and difficult economic adjustment and reform program. When the war is over, however, attention will necessarily return to these crucial issues.

6. A standby agreement is the most common form used by the IMF to apply conditionality on a recipient nation. It commits the recipient to carrying out a package of policies decided upon in prior negotiations. Robert Wood, *From Marshall Plan to Debt Crisis: Foreign Aid and Development Choices in the World Economy* (Berkeley: University of California Press, 1986), p. 126.

7. See Robert Springborg, "Economic Assistance and the Limits of Policy Leverage," chap. 7 in *Mubarak's Egypt* (Boulder, Colo.: Westview Press, 1989), for a detailed outline of the Paris Club, IMF, and USAID efforts to impose austerity measures and other economic reforms on the government of Egypt.

8. Michel Camdessus, "Egypt: IMF Talks Make Progress," *Middle East Economic Digest,* 15 February 1991.

9. Speech by Michel Camdessus before a joint session of the American Chamber of Commerce in Egypt and the Egyptian Businessmen's Association, May 13, 1991.

10. *Middle East News Agency* report, quoted in *Egyptian Gazette,* 26 May 1991, p. 1.

11. See Regina Soos, "A Glimpse at the Egyptian Economy," *Business Monthly* (American Chamber of Commerce in Egypt, July 1989): 10–11.

12. Sherine Salama, "New Sales Tax: A Bit Confusing, Much Criticized," *Middle East Times,* 21–27 May 1991, p. 1.

13. The total amount of debt relief comes to approximately $15 billion, lowering Egypt's foreign debt from roughly $50 billion in mid-1990 to approximately $36 billion in early 1991. See Alan Richards, "Egypt's Problems of the 1990s: Foreign Debt," *Middle East Times,* 1–7 January 1991, p. 6. $36 billion is a sizeable figure and Egypt is still seeking further debt relief. Secretary of State James Baker pledged to President Mubarak in March 1991 in Cairo that the United States would back a further debt-forgiveness program as a reward for Egypt's role in the anti–Saddam Hussein coalition as well as for its adoption of difficult economic demands of the IMF.

14. Camdessus, "Egypt." And "the Club" made good on this argument by relieving, in March 1991, one-half of the $33 billion owed to them by Poland.

15. This view is best represented by the economist Alan Richards.

16. This view is best represented by Heba Hendoussa, an economist who also serves as consultant to the Ministry of Industry.

17. Azza Ali, "Economists Assess Impact of IMF Agreement," *Al-Ahram Weekly,* 9 May 1991, p. 4.

18. Linda Likar, "Multilateral and Bilateral Support for Privatization in the Middle East" (Washington, D.C., 1990, Mimeographed), p. 7.

19. Interview with World Bank official, Middle East Department, 4 June 1990.

20. *Al-Ahram,* 20 March 1991, p. 1.

21. Interview with World Bank official, Cairo, 26 May 1991.

22. Interview with World Bank official, Cairo, January 1991.

23. Interview with AID official, Office of Investment and Finance, Cairo, 26 March 1989.

24. USAID Request for Proposal, no. Egypt 90–011, 25 March 1990, p. 7.

25. Camdessus, in "Egypt," reports that the two groups are Ernst & Young of the UK and a joint venture of the U.K.'s Coopers & Lybrand and Bechtel of the U.S.

26. Interview with AID economist in program office, Cairo, 11 March 1987.

27. For an analysis of the interbureaucratic struggles facing USAID officials, see my "Bureaucratic Politics in Development Assistance: The Failure of American Aid in Egypt" in *Administration & Society* (February 1991).

28. For an overview of where USAID stands on privatization, see "Privatization" (Concept paper, USAID-Cairo, Office of Finance & Investment, June 1987). Of course, not all USAID employees are in favor of privatization. As one official in charge of several aspects of the privatization program put it: "[P]ushing for privatization is an uphill battle. Even within AID there is opposition to it. We have many supporters of the public sector within the mission and detractors of the private sector, the latter being still referred to as exploitative and insensitive leaches" (Cairo, 26 February 1991).

29. When Sultan announced plans to sell the San Stefano in February 1988, a firestorm of protest erupted in Parliament (led by NDP members) and President Mubarak had to halt the sale. Sultan waited until the matter was off the minds of most legislators, and then he proceeded with the sale as originally planned.

30. Comments by an official of a large trading company at a business symposium held at the Marriott Hotel, Cairo, 10 December 1990.

31. Interview with official in Ministry of Social Affairs, Cairo, 3 August 1987.

32. Interview with Catholic Relief Services official, Cairo, 2 August 1987.

33. Morroe Berger, *Islam in Egypt Today: Social and Political Aspects of Popular Religion* (Cambridge: Cambridge University Press, 1970); see, especially, chap. 4, "Voluntary Benevolent Societies."

34. Most of the information on Ezbet Zein is taken from Louise G. White, "Urban Community Organizations and Local Government: Exploring Relationships and Roles," *Public Administration and Political Development* 6, no. 3 (1986).

35. Interview with assistant, Sayida Zeinab, 27 March 1989.

36. Interview with Director of the Society, Cairo, 2 August 1987. The new Mustafa Mahmud Hospital greatly expands the healthcare center, which, until 1988, had no facilities for overnight patients. This building is prime property in a major urban area and doubtless is valued at upwards of $1 million.

37. In addition to the economic issue, there is a potentially very significant political question surrounding these Islamic organizations: are they also promoting a larger cause, the Islamic alternative, which may serve as a direct challenge to the predominantly secular system? This question is equally significant for state and society alike in Egypt.

38. These figures are based on discussions with patients and doctors at the Society, August 1987.

39. Gilles Kepel, *Muslim Extremism in Egypt: The Prophet and the Pharaoh,* trans. Jon Rothschild, (Berkeley and Los Angeles: University of California Press, 1985), p. 184.

40. Ibid., p. 129.

41. Ibid., p. 241.

42. Ibid., p. 142.

43. Ibid., pp. 136–37.

44. Ibid., p. 143.

45. In attending various meetings of "young women involved to various degrees in the trend," she found a distinct difference between middle to upper-class women who were committed to Islam but not comfortable with wearing the veil nor with accepting simplistic answers to complicated issues and those less educated, lower-class groups of women in which the *niqab,* or full veil, was quite prevalent. These groups of women exhibited a strong degree of consensus on accepted principles of Islam, community, social norms, and so forth. Nemat Guenena, "The Jihad: An 'Islamic Alternative' in Egypt," *Cairo Papers in Social Science* 9, no. 2 (Summer 1986): 87.

46. The latter term is used, rather than a specified "interest rate," since "those who practice usury are sternly rebuked and warned that they face 'war from God and His prophet'

(Quran 2:279)." John Esposito, *Islam: The Straight Path* (New York: Oxford University Press, 1988), p. 34.

47. *Middle East Economic Digest,* Special Report on Egypt, 14 October 1988, p. 44. See Said Aly in this volume for further details on the IICs.

CHAPTER

3

PRIVATIZATION IN EGYPT: THE REGIONAL DIMENSIONS

Abdel Monem Said Aly

Because of its strategic geographic location, its international political significance, and a history of foreign intervention and domination, Egypt's economic development has been influenced as much by external factors as by internal ones. The Egyptian economy has been guided by diverse foreign economic principles ranging from free-market economy to Keynesian economics as well as from state capitalism and import substitution to export oriented growth, deregulation, and privatization.

Under Nasser Egypt had highly centralized political and economic systems. During the 1950s and 1960s,[1] the government imposed controls on virtually all private economic, political, and social activities—banking, the majority of industry and other commercial activity, cooperatives, local councils, education, information agencies (press, broadcasting, and television), professional and labor unions, and even the religious institutions. In addition, it undertook a series of broad obligations to the Egyptian people: provision of basic human needs such as subsidized food, healthcare, and housing; free education through the university level; and guaranteed employment. By the end of the 1960s, one-fourth of working Egyptians were paid directly or indirectly by the government.[2] Egyptians were living within the larger context of the state.[3]

After the October 1973 War, Egyptian civil society gained ground. The centralized and socialist legacy of the 1960s lost its logic. The firm grip of the state loosened in politics as well as economics. Different indicators show the erosion of state dominance over the economy and the reemergence of private-sector initiative. New liberal legislation was enacted in the spirit of *infitah,* including Law No. 43/1974 (later amended by Law No. 32/1977), on the investment of Arab and foreign capital and free zones, and Law No. 159/1981, on joint stock (Egyptian ownership) companies.[4] Another liberal law for investment was passed in 1989.[5]

The result of this shift in policy has been the consolidation of the private sector. From 1974 to 1986, the private sector's share of industrial output rose from 23 percent to 33 percent.[6] Joint-venture banks and private Egyptian banks for investment, savings, and foreign exchange were established. The economic situation in Egypt, though not ideal, has nonetheless attracted business initiatives. As of June 30, 1987, the Investment Authority had approved 1630 projects with a total capital investment of LE 7.3 billion and LE 14.3 billion investment cost.[7] The private sector has extended its activities into new areas such as insurance and international trade, and it has intensified its share in industry, air transportation, agriculture, land reclamation, education and housing.[8]

Not only are private-sector initiatives on the rise, the government has also taken steps to deregulate private-sector activities and stimulate domestic-capital formation as well as in-flow of foreign capital. Actual percentages of gross fixed investment in the public sector have been reduced from 79 percent in FY 1983 to 70 percent in FY 1986. While the Nasserist concept of economic planning in the form of five-year plans has been resurrected, the substance and direction of these plans in no way seeks to exclusively reestablish a state-run public sector as the major socioeconomic force in Egypt. Between the 1982-83 to 1986-87 five-year plan and the 1986-87 to 1991-92 plan, the percentage of GDP investment in the public sector has been scaled down from 77 percent in the former plan, with 23 percent going into the private sector, to approximately 50 percent investment in both private and public sectors.[9] The state share of GDP investment percentage remains high due to government involvement in oil production and the Suez Canal enterprises.

The state, however, did not concede its economic powers easily. While it was generally willing to give room to the private sector, the state has been less willing to sell public-sector firms. Nor has it been willing to allow the private sector to control or dominate the more sensitive and strategic sectors of the economy. Up to 1989, there had been only two public firms sold, namely the Sheraton Hotel in Hurghada and the San Stefano Hotel in Alexandria. When one of the Islamic investment companies asked the government to establish a transportation-network company for Cairo and Giza, the president himself declared that he could not agree to the establishment of a private company "that dominates the transportation movement" in the capital.[10]

The state has always emphasized its ability to stay in charge of economic activities. When the Islamic investment companies seemed able to rely on their own transnational resources to control the money markets in Egypt, the government decided to interfere and regulate their activities. In June 1988, the government promulgated Law 146 requiring, *inter alia*: that the companies prepare audited financial statements of their activities; that they seek (by November 8, 1988) and obtain government approval to restructure their operations and remain in business (or else they would be required to liquidate operations and refund deposits); and that in the future, the government would oversee the most important aspects of their activities.[11]

The lesson that can be drawn from this confrontation is that the state remains in charge of national economic activities; on the other hand, the private sector is in Egypt to stay. Law 146 sought regulation of Islamic companies but nonetheless legalized their activities in Egypt.

This discrepancy between the rise of the private sector in Egypt and the state's persistent efforts to control economic activities can be explained by the interplay between various domestic, regional, and global factors. This chapter will focus on the regional dimensions of privatization in Egypt. Regional factors have had positive as well as negative effects on privatization in the country. The issues that affect the course of privatization in Egypt emanate from (1) the oil revolution in the region and the resulting politico-socioeconomic consequences and (2) the Arab-Israeli conflict. Both factors have contradictory effects on the Egyptian position in the centralization-privatization continuum. The following two sections will elaborate these points.

REGIONAL INCENTIVES FOR PRIVATIZATION

The Oil Revolution

The October 1973 war changed qualitatively the oil policies of the Arab producing states. Of particular importance was the policy of restricting production and increasing prices by Arab oil-producing countries. These nations were able to double their revenues to unprecedented levels. The oil returns of Arab OPEC members in 1965 were a mere $2.169 billion. By 1970, returns reached $51.5 billion, and in 1980, they skyrocketed to $204.244 billion. Since then, revenues have declined annually to $182.9 billion in 1981, $134.7 billion in 1982, $101.7 billion in 1983, and $102.4 billion in 1984.[12] The 1989 returns were not expected to be more than $68.7 billion.[13]

In spite of this precipitous decline in oil prices, two decades of accumulated revenues have motivated the colossal developmental plans of the Arab oil-producing countries. The oil era, in its rise and fall, has led to an extensive change in the Arab world. Egypt has been markedly affected by this tidal wave of change, which gave rise, among other things, to privatization.

The oil revolution has contributed vast resources to the Egyptians as a result of the growing Egyptian-Arab interdependence.[14] The well-known phenomenon of labor migration to the Arab oil-producing countries has provided extensive employment opportunities as well as capital to Egyptian individuals. According to conservative estimates for 1974 to 1984, 3.3 million Egyptians migrated to work in the Arab oil-producing countries. They transferred to Egypt $33 billion in cash transfers, bank deposits, goods and commodities—almost three times the American economic aid available to the Egyptian government over the same period.[15] The following years show that remittances seem to continue at the same average level: they were $3.063 billion for 1985-86, $3.012 billion for 1986-87, and $3.387 billion for 1987-88. The total 1974–88 reached $44 billion.[16] Less conservative estimates state these transfers at much higher levels. Nazli Chucri has put the figure for 1983–84 alone at $18 billion.[17]

Remittances are not the only source of income transferred to Egyptian society from its Arab connection. In 1982, 613,000 Arab tourists visited Egypt, or about 43.41 percent of the total number of tourists. By 1987, Arab tourists approached 657,000, representing 36.6 percent of total tourists. The Arab share in Egyptian tourism is so large because Arab tourists tend to stay longer and, thus, to spend more than European and American tourists. In 1985, the Arab share of tourist nights was 43 percent. By 1987, their share reached 48 percent.[18] The number of Arab tourists increased only slightly in 1988 (2.4 percent). In 1989, however, the number grew by 44.3 percent, and their tourist nights grew by 26.2 percent.[19] Arab journalism, broadcasting, and television are dependent on Egyptians working in Egypt. Egyptian private-sector hospitals are preferred by the middle-income groups in the Arab oil-producing states. Consequently, it is not surprising that many Egyptians, even if they stay at home, have a source of income related to the Arab countries.

The result of this flow of capital to Egypt has been the consolidation of the Egyptian private sector. Foreign investment capital in Egypt as of June 1987 stood at LE 7.3 billion: 65 percent of which was Egyptian (most of it generated from Arab countries), 18 percent Arab, and 17 percent foreign.[20] Furthermore, a recent study of small-scale manufacturing in Egypt found that remittances have a significant effect. Gunter Meyer surveyed two popular quarters (Bab al-Shariya and El-Gamaliya) in Cairo, between September 1985 and April 1986, interviewing 2,343 owners and employees of 531 manufacturing enterprises. He found that 12 percent of the employees had worked abroad at least once. One out of four owners in the enterprises studied had worked abroad, with a record 37 percent in shoe-producing firms.

The results of the survey show that 35 percent of the proprietors of manufacturing enterprises who were former labor emigrants had used their remittances as a principal source of capital to establish new workshops of their own. A large number of the workshops, which were equipped with the most advanced machinery, belonged to returning migrants.[21]

The Egyptian-Israeli Peace

The October 1973 war was the prelude for changing Egypt's regional environment by paving the way for the Egyptian-Israeli peace treaty of March 26, 1979. Egyptian economic development could now evolve for the first time under the shadow of peace.

Throughout most of its modern history, Egypt's development has occurred under the shadow of conflict with external powers. First, there was the Egyptian confrontation with revolutionary France when Napoleon's army invaded the country in 1798. Then, Muhammad Ali struggled to gain independence from the Ottoman Empire. This was followed by the protracted conflict for independence from Great Britain, which continued from 1881 to 1956.

The conflict with Great Britain overlapped with the Arab-Israeli conflict which started in 1948, accelerated in the mid-1950s, and became particularly significant for Egypt in 1967 when Egyptian territories came under direct Israeli occupation. The "national question" has thus dominated the evolution of Egyptian society and politics. The need to mobilize for war against Israel was one of the reasons behind the state's domination of political and economic life.

The Camp David Accords and the subsequent Egyptian-Israeli peace treaty have allowed Egypt to live under a new promise of peace. Political and socioeconomic restructuring of the country, long suppressed in order to unite the country to combat the external threat, was given a chance to evolve. The legacy of the 1960s has lost some of its luster and logic. The firm grip of the state has loosened in politics as well as economics. Peace with Israel has become but one pillar of Egyptian politics, which also includes an alliance with the West, particularly the United States. The open-door policy, or *infitah,* and a degree of democratization[22] occurred in conjunction with the peace initiatives.

This "package" of policies put Egypt closer to the Western practice of a free-market economy. By the end of the 1970s, socialist ideas and Nasserist policies lost their charm. The power of ideas was not, however, the sole factor that inspired Egypt to give more room to the private sector. The Egyptian-Israeli peace treaty was linked to a very generous American and Western aid program. After the reestablishment of diplomatic relations between Egypt and the United States in 1974, the United States rewarded Egypt with $250 million. In 1975, Egypt was included on the regular roster of American aid appropriations, receiving both loans and grants. The ratio of loans to grants was tied to Egypt's movement toward peace with Israel. In 1975, loans represented 78.6 percent of all aid compared to 21.4 percent in grants. In 1983, loans were 21.2 percent of aid and grants were 78.8 percent. As of 1985, all American aid (economic and military) was in the form of grants. In the period from 1975 to 1989, Egypt received over $25 billion in U.S. assistance. Direct investment from the United States at the end of 1987 was $1.7 billion, of which $1.4 billion was in the petroleum sector.[23]

The United States is not the only supplier of aid to Egypt. Europe and Japan contribute aid, both in loans and grants. Table 1 shows the increases of development assistance given to Egypt by the members of the Development Assistance Committee of the OECD (excluding the United States).[24] The Japanese grant-aid program alone through 1989 cumulatively amounted to $340.7 million.[25]

Western aid in general and American aid in particular has targeted the Egyptian economy for transformation to a private-centric one. A key element of the USAID mission-growth strategy for Egypt has been to provide incentives for production increases and an expanded role for the private sector.[26] Although direct American aid to the Egyptian private sector did not exceed 5 percent of the total economic aid to Egypt (1975–89), it was intended that the investment in infrastructure and other projects (about 42 percent) would facilitate the work of this

TABLE 1
**Development Assistance to Egypt
(in millions of dollars)**

	1970–71	1980–81	1986–87
Australia	—	8.606	7.950
Austria	—	4.209	18.001
Belgium	.134	2.950	—
Canada	—	20.034	14.076
Denmark	2.814	8.190	20.194
Finland	—	2.583	7.087
France	9.080	52.884	103.322
Germany	9.192	92.972	144.960
Ireland	—	—	—
Italy	22.080	4.278	30.480
Japan	—	96.984	133.480
Netherlands	—	19.572	28.084
New Zealand	—	—	—
Norway	.080	—	—
Sweden	—	—	—
Switzerland	—	2.223	5.368
United Kingdom	—	22.320	17.451
E.E.C.	3.744	44.275	46.845
Total	47.124	382.08	577.298

Source: *Development Cooperation* (OECD, December 1988): 211–20.

sector.[27] The improvements during the 1980s in energy supplies, roads, and tele-communication have given the Egyptian private sector the opportunity to work in a more healthy, productive environment than was the situation in the 1970s when infrastructure development was virtually at a standstill. Foreign aid has been in-strumental in achieving this result.

REGIONAL DISINCENTIVES FOR PRIVATIZATION

The Oil Revolution

As mentioned above, the oil revolution has provided capital to the Egyptian private sector, allowing it to participate in the national economy. This revolution, how-ever, in addition to other factors, has fostered the transnationalization of the Egyp-tian economy. The revolution in the world capitalist market and communications technology has provided Egyptian society with transnational instruments to bypass the national government. The world's stock, money, and commodity markets have given Egyptians the opportunity to invest, to speculate, and to transact with the world economy without being forced either to deposit in public-sector banks or to abide by the government's exchange rates. Faisal Islamic Bank (FIB) has invested $500 million (about one third of total deposits) outside Egypt.[28] More important, the FIB practice is not an exception. As Mohammad Said demonstrated: "The most staggering feature in the operation of the banking system in Egypt is the contrast between its high reliance on mobilization of Egyptian savings, on the one hand, and its tendency to 'invest' outside Egypt altogether on the other."[29] This feature is shared by commercial banks (Law 43 "banks"), which are majority-controlled by Egyptians, and investment and business banks established according to Law 43 (of these thirty-three banks, twenty-two are branches of foreign banks and eleven are joint ventures and private banks).

In 1984 and 1985, the net-credit position of commercial and business banks in relation to banks abroad was slightly less than 1.5 billion Egyptian pounds worth of foreign exchange. Since then, it rose to LE 2.0 billion for 1986, LE 2.678 billion in 1987 and LE 7.287 billion in 1988.[30] Even the public-sector commercial banks have deposited an average of 13.25 percent of their total assets in foreign banks between 1981 and 1986. All of this leads to the conclusion that "the banking system is a major channel for reverse transfer of money capital from Egypt to the developed world."[31]

Although this capital transfer is due largely to the domestic constraints on investment, the linkages with transnational capitalism have drained substantial capital from the Egyptian market. More important, however, is that the capital transferred to Egypt has been concentrated in a small number of Egyptians. One concern that the Egyptian government has with the privatization of public enterprises is the small number of private investors to whom the government could sell these enterprises. The government fears that selling national assets to a limited number of individuals would concentrate economic power in the hands of a few, which the government wants to avoid.[32]

The Egyptian government's fears were compounded by the rise of the Islamic Investment Companies (IICs). These companies were but one of the major outcomes of the oil revolution.[33] They have utilized both the resources of the oil revolution and the deficiencies of the Egyptian economic system to acquire political as well as economic powers. Although details of the IICs are sketchy, we do have the following information about their activities in Egypt:

First, most analysts in Egypt now agree, and official records confirm, that the number of important IICs before the promulgation of Law 146/1988 was 104.[34]

Second, the number of depositors in these companies is half a million, which means that an estimated two million Egyptians (at least) have been directly affected by this phenomenon (each one representing a member of a family of four). Only ten of the IICs account for 90 percent of the depositors (about 452,200 individuals). The top four (Al-Rayan, Al-Sherif, Al-Hoda Misr, and Al-Saᶜad) account for 375,000, or 75 percent, of the total.[35]

Third, the amount of deposits in these companies is estimated between LE 5-8 billion (or US $2-3 billion).[36] The top four companies account for LE 4.3 billion of this total.

Although these estimates are much less than previously estimated, they remain quite substantial. By comparison, deposits held with the Egyptian commercial banks amounted to some LE 30.8 billion as of June 30, 1987. This means that the top four companies hold funds amounting to the equivalent of 14 percent of total commercial bank deposits and some 21.1 percent of the deposits held by public-sector commercial banks (LE 20.3 billion as of June 30, 1987).[37] If the rest of the IICs were included, the percentages would be much higher.

These companies have alarmed the Egyptian government for different reasons:

First, the IICs became the economic symbol of the rising Islamic tendencies in Egypt. These tendencies were partially a product of labor migration. After being exposed to the more conservative cultures of the Gulf area, many migrant workers returned to enhance and consolidate the Islamization of Egypt. As the Islamization of Egypt accelerated and as the "Islamic economy" gained momentum, the IICs' phenomenon could be understood as a result of this context. The shift in ideological makeup of Egyptians toward Islam has made them ready to deposit their money in the IICs. These companies became very attractive because they offered salvation for a populace that was increasingly religious. IICs not only used nonusurous concepts of economics, they also used Islamic symbols. Their names (Al-Sherif, Al-Rayan, Al-Saʿad, Al-Hoda, Al-Hillal, Badr, etc.) are all drawn from the Islamic lexicon in theology, history, and morality. The founders of the IICs grew their beards and wore the *galabeya* as a non-Western or Islamic dress. They opened their speeches and their advertisements with Quranic verses. They contributed to charities and Islamic philanthropic activities. In short, IICs carried many of the signs of the Islamic revival in Egypt.

Second, only two of the IICs' founders are known to be associated with the Islamic political movement. Abdel Latif Al-Sherif, the founder and chairman of the board of Al-Sherif Investment Company, is a Muslim Brother. Ahmad Al-Rayan, the last chairman of the board of Al-Rayan Company, was the amir (prince) of an Islamic fundamentalist society during his university years.[38] All of the IICs, however, recruited leading religious personalities either from the traditional Al-Azhar institutions or from the ranks of the Muslim Brothers in order to ensure that investments were made according to Islamic principles. Abdel Sabour Shahin, an ex-Muslim Brother, a member of the Consultative (Shura) Assembly and a professor of Quranic studies at Cairo University, was a consultant and, for a short time, a board member of the Al-Rayan company. Ahmad Al-Mahalawi, a religious orator in one of Alexandria's famous mosques, was the leading religious personality in Al-Saʿad company. Mitwali Al-Shaʿrawi, the ex-minister of al-Azhar, was a confidant of and consultant to Al-Hoda Misr company. The list of religious consultants to the IICs included prominent personalities such as Salah Abu Ismaʿil, a member of the People's Assembly; Hafiz Salama, a religious orator; and Abdel Monʿim Al-Nimr, an ex-minister of endowment.[39]

Third, political Islam found in the IICs an economic model for activities. As these companies distributed high returns for their depositors, it was considered by Islamic political activists as a vindication of the economic efficiency of Islam. The staunchest support came from the ranks of the Muslim Brotherhood, who considered the banking interest rates as a form of *riba* (usury).

The Brothers have propagated the idea of an independent Islamic economy for quite a while. They have sponsored the creation of the Islamic banks. Their prominent members in Egypt sponsored the establishment of Al-Taqwa (piety) Bank in the Bahama Islands to work according to the Shariʿa.[40] The Muslim Brothers defended the IICs in newspapers and in the People's Assembly. Ahmad Sayf-Al-Islam, son of Hasan Al-Banna, the founder of the Muslim Brotherhood movement, and a member of the People's Assembly has declared his support and admiration of the IICs.[41] Sheikh Mohammad Al-Ghazali, a prominent Islamic personality and an ex-member of the Brotherhood, declared that IICs represent the true economic manifestation of Islam. Al-Ghazali accused the IMF of being the source behind the government regulations and curtailment of the IICs.[42] Hasan Al-Gamal, a Brotherhood member and a member of the People's Assembly, described Law 146/1988 as being "a conspiracy against the Islamic solution and the Islamic movement. This conspiracy was made by Israel, America, Zionism,and international communism. IICs were fought, it was claimed, because they worked in the name of Islam."[43]

Whether the IICs are truly Islamic or not is not the issue here.[44] What is at issue, however, is that the IICs became a part of the Islamic phenomenon in Egypt. The IICs corresponded to a rising trend in Egyptian attitudes and politics. Accordingly, the supporters of the IICs were supporting "the Islamic Solution" for Egypt's problems. Their enemies, inside and outside Egypt, were considered enemies of Islam. This was not exactly what the Egyptian government was hoping to "open" the door for. The confrontation that ensued between the government and the IICs—private sector, Islamic companies—has contributed to slowing down the privatization of the Egyptian economy.

The Arab-Israeli Conflict

As mentioned above, the Egyptian-Israeli peace treaty has loosened the grip of the state over Egyptian politics and economics. Further, the treaty has allowed for foreign aid to come to Egypt from the West in general and from the United States in particular. This economic assistance has improved the Egyptian infrastructure and made it more hospitable for private investment.

These outcomes of peace, however, have negative side effects on the privatization of the Egyptian economy:

First, the large sums of foreign assistance (in addition to the revenues from the Suez Canal, high oil prices, and substantial worker remittances) have made it possible for the Egyptian government to ignore making fundamental economic reforms. The so-called open-door policies, promulgated with the hope of invigorating the economy through economic liberalization measures, have not altered the basic controls on resource allocation and production. Price distortions and administrative regulations continue to discourage growth, efficiency, and privatization. The state might have lost some of its powers in proportional terms due to the growth of new centers of powers in the country. In absolute terms, however, state powers have continued to grow. Employment figures show the predominance of the state. In 1951–52, Egypt had 350,000 public employees, or about 2.2 percent of the Egyptian population. At the end of the Nasserist era, in 1969–70, the figure grew to 1.2 million, or 3.8 percent of the population. In 1986, 4.8 million Egyptians were on the public payrolls, or almost 10 percent of the entire population and some 35 percent of the labor force of 13 million.[45] External aid has provided the government with resources to penetrate, to mobilize, and to control the society. Even American aid to Egypt has been directed to the government. Out of $14.98 billion of economic assistance, only $751 million, or about 5 percent, went to the private sector from 1975 to 1989. In the same period, $1.2 billion, or about 7.6 percent, went directly to the industrial public sector alone.[46]

Second, the availability of externally generated resources, including foreign assistance, has made importing technology much cheaper than creating it. The weakness of the Egyptian base of research and development is one of the most significant structural problems of the Egyptian public and private economies. By the late 1980s, Egyptian private-sector industries had started to suffer, or completely close down, because of their high reliance on foreign technology. As the country started to suffer from the lack of foreign resources, its ability to import became more limited. Ironically, out of the $14.98 billion of American economic assistance to Egypt, only $289 million, or 1.9 percent, was spent on science and technology.[47] It would have been much more beneficial to Egypt if foreign aid were helpful in teaching Egyptians how to catch the fish!

Third, Egyptian-Israeli peace has opened Western gates for Egypt to borrow and accumulate debts on a large scale. By 1987-88, Egypt owed $43.1 billion to Western states and institutions.[48] By 1990, Egypt was classified by the World Bank as one of the severely indebted states.[49] As the Egyptian government became increasingly constrained by its debt problem, and as foreign resources became less able to fill the empty state coffers, government worries about the political as well as the social consequences of its economic weakness became acute. The fear was that bold moves toward privatization would not only undermine the state's political stand in favor of the new Islamic Capitalists of Egypt but that it also would exacerbate the plight of the poor, thus contributing to social instability.

Fourth, in spite of the Egyptian-Israeli peace treaty, the absence of a comprehensive solution to the Arab-Israeli conflict has allowed both the government to justify substantial defense spending and the military to legitimize its continued dominance over the country. Israel's qualitative military advantage, not to mention a quantitative advantage in certain areas, makes Egyptian perceptions of a continuing Israeli threat understandable.[50] Consequently, the Egyptian army expanded not only in numbers but also in roles.[51] In 1987, Egypt's direct military expenditure was 8.2 percent of GNP.[52] This does not include investments in military industry which seems to monopolize Egypt's best resources in research and development.[53] This high profile of the military institution in the national economy has become a strong disincentive for privatization in Egypt.

As a comprehensive Arab-Israeli peace remains elusive, and as the Iran-Iraq conflict lingers, regional stability may not be attainable. The regional arms race is but one of the major results which tends to strengthen the hands of the military. Currently, Egypt is participating in this arms race.[54] Under the banner of national security, the Egyptian military establishment is less inclined to accept liberalization in politics as well as economics.

PRIVATIZATION: PROSPECTS FOR THE 1990S

The preceding sections show that the regional environment has generated incentives and disincentives for privatization. The oil revolution created resources for the Egyptian private sector and increased its linkages with transnational capitalism. In the meantime, it has intensified the Islamization of the private sector. The Egyptian-Israeli peace has loosened the grip of the state, but the Palestinian *intifada* and the continuing tensions between Israel on the one hand and Syria and Iraq on the other are enough to keep Egyptians insecure in their peace arrangement with Israel. Peace also provided Egypt with substantial Western aid, the donors of which are pressuring the government of Egypt for more privatization. At the same time, however, this aid has directed resources to the government that allow it to avoid basic economic reforms.

The end result of these competing forces may explain, to some extent, the contradictory attitudes of the Egyptian government toward liberalization in politics as well as economics. In the latter area, although the private sector had made progress throughout the 1970s and the early 1980s, such progress was halted by the mid-1980s. The second half of the decade witnessed the decline in the economic fortunes of the country as well as a struggle between the government and the Islamic Investment Companies, which ended with the former regulating the latter.

In spite of the ability of the government to curtail the economic base of the private-sector Islamic movement, there seems to be some prospects for privatization in Egypt. Domestic factors, such as widespread unemployment and the inability of the government to contribute to national investment, will constitute the basic pressures for more reliance on the private sector. Regional factors will contribute further to this tendency. If oil prices increase during the coming decade, the government may be more willing to attract Egyptian and Arab capital for investment. Western donors and institutions will continue to exert pressure for economic reforms in which privatization is an essential part.

However, one should not expect a radical transformation of the Egyptian economic system, as such a transformation would be linked to changes in the nature of the political regime. And such a transformation will certainly be a gradual process.

Notes

1. See Joel S. Migdal, *Strong Societies and Weak States: State-Society Relations and State Capabilities in the Third World* (Princeton, N.J.: Princeton University Press, 1988), pp. 181–92. For the control of religious institutions, see D. Crecelius, "Al-Azhar in the Revolution," *Middle East Journal* 20 (Winter 1966); and B. Borthwick, "Religion and Politics in Israel and Egypt," *Middle East Journal* 33 (Spring 1979).

2. Ghassan Salame, "Introduction," in Ghassan Salame, ed., *The Foundation of the Arab State* (London: Croom Helm, 1987), p. 2.

3. Iliya Harik, "Continuity and Change in Local Development Policies in Egypt: From Nasser to Sadat," in L. J. Cantori and I. Harik, eds., *Local Politics and Development in the Middle East* (Boulder, Colo.: Westview Press, 1984), p. 85.

4. Egyptian National Bank, *Economic Bulletin*, no. 4, 1987, pp. 229–31.

5. Said Al-Naggar, "On the New Investment Law," *Al-Ahram*, 31 May 1989.

6. U.S. Embassy, Cairo, *Economic Trends Report: Egypt*, December 1986, p. 8.

7. Egyptian National Bank, *Economic Bulletin*, no. 3, 1987, p. 211, Arabic version.

8. See Amani Kandil, ed., *The Transfer towards the Private Sector* (Cairo: Center for Political Research and Studies, 1989).

9. "Foreign Investment: Making Participation Pay," *Business Monthly* 3 (October 1987): 6.

10. *Al-Ahram*, May 12, 1989.

11. U.S. Embassy, Cairo, *Egyptian Economic Trends*, March 1989, p. 18.

12. Bahgat Korany, "The Crisis of the Arab Society: A Research on the Premises and Consequences of the Contemporary Arab Political Economy," *Al Mustaqbal Al Arabi*, no. 60 (February 1984): 45.

13. Kiyotake Tsuji, *Forecast: OPEC's 1989 Oil Revenues and Current Account* (Tokyo: The Japanese Institute of Middle East Economies, 1989), p. 8.

14. See Abdel Monem Said Aly, "Back to the Fold: Egypt and the Arab World," *Occasional Papers Series*, CCAS, Georgetown University, Washington, D.C., September 1988.

15. Nadir Firgani, *Going After Salary: A Field Research on Egyptian Migration to Work in Arab Countries* (Beirut: Center for Arab Unity Studies, 1988), pp. 80 and 220.

16. Ahmad Al-Naggar, "Temporary Migration from Egypt" (research paper prepared for the Arab Research Center, Cairo, 1990), pp. 16–20.

17. Nazli Chucri, "Dimensions of National Security: The Case of Egypt" (research paper prepared for the World Resource Institute, March 1987), p. 7.

18. Central Agency for Public Mobilization and Statistics, Cairo, *Statistical Yearbook*, 1988, pp. 213–16.

19. *Al-Ahram*, 22 Feb. 1990.

20. General Authority for Investment and Free Zones. The figure reflects approved projects as of March 31, 1987, as found in "Foreign Investment" (see n. 9).

21. Gunter Meyer, "Employment in Small-scale Manufacturing in Cairo: A Socioeconomic Survey," *British Society for Middle Eastern Studies Bulletin* 14, no. 2 (1988): 6.

58 / **Privatization and Liberalization in the Middle East**

22. See Abdel Monem Said Aly, "Egypt: A Decade After Camp David," in William B. Quandt, ed., *The Middle East: Ten Years After Camp David* (Washington, D.C.: The Brookings Institution, 1988).

23. U.S. Embassy, Cairo, *Egyptian Economic Trends,* March 1989, p. 19.

24. Calculated from *OECD 1988 Report, Development Cooperation,* December 1988, pp. 211–20.

25. Embassy of Japan in Cairo, *Japan Information Bulletin,* no. 42, 15 April 1989, p. 4.

26. U.S. AID, Cairo, *Status Report: United States Economic Assistance to Egypt,* November 1989. Also see the chapter by Sullivan in this volume.

27. U.S. AID, Cairo, *Status Report* (see n. 26).

28. Interview with Mahmoud El Helw, Chairman of the Board, FIB, *Al-Ahram al-Iqtisadi,* 5 May 1986, p. 34.

29. Mohamed E. Sayed Said, "The Political Economy of Migration in Egypt 1974–1989" (paper presented at the seminar on "International Worker Migration: Political, Economic and Social Change in Turkey and Egypt," Istanbul, Turkey, 28–30 June 1989), p. 55.

30. Ibid., p. 61.

31. Ibid.; and *Arab Strategic Report 1986* (Cairo: Center for Political and Strategic Studies, 1987), p. 434.

32. World Bank, *Egypt Industrial Sector,* vol. 1, memorandum, 13 June 1989, p. 37.

33. "Islamic Investment Companies" has been the most commonly known name in English-language literature on the subject. "Islamic Finance Houses" is also used in the literature. The translation from Arabic of *Sharikat Tawzif Al-Amwal* is "Capital Employment Companies." All, however, refer to closed companies, which attracted savers either to deposit their savings in exchange for returns (without participation in the decision making in any form) or to own shares or stocks in the company. Further, these companies utilized "Islamic" forms of investment such as *mudarabah* (capital-labor participation), *musharaka* (venture-capital participation), and *murabaha* (cost-plus operations), which attract depositors who view interest as a form of usury (prohibited by Islam). See Abdel Monem Said Aly, "The Myth and the Reality: The Four Faces of the Islamic Investment Companies," in Louis J. Cantori, *Democratization in Egypt* (forthcoming).

34. *Al-Ahram al-Iqtisadi,* 21 November 1989.

35. Egyptian National Bank, "Capital Employment Companies," *Economic Bulletin,* no. 4, 1987, pp. 232–33.

36. Abdel Kader Shuheib, *The Penetration: The Story of the Capital Employment Companies* (Cairo: Sinai for Publishing, 1989), p. 84.

37. Egyptian National Bank (see n. 35), p. 233.

38. Gehad Auda, "The Islamic Movement and Resource Mobilization in Egypt: A Political Culture Perspective" (paper presented to a conference on political culture and democracy in developing countries, Hoover Institution, 14–17 September 1988), p. 65.

39. Ibid., p. 70.

40. Prominent Muslim Brothers in Egypt participated in the establishment of this bank: Ahmed Al-Naggar, Ahmad al-Salt, Gaber Rizk, Ahmad Seif Al-Islam Hassan Al-Banna, Saleh Abu Raqiq, Abdel Azim Lukma, Youssef Al-Qaradawi, and others. *Al-Ahram,* 21 September 1987.

41. *Rose Al Youssef,* 7 July 1987; and *Al Ahali,* 29 June 1988.

42. *Al-Shaab,* 10 October 1989.

43. Shuheib, *The Penetration,* p. 144.

44. Reports in the Egyptian press about immoral and unethical practices by the IICs particularly in Al-Rayan group are many. For a summary see Shuheib, *The Penetration,* chap. 9, "The Scandal."

45. Robert Springborg, *Mubarak's Egypt: Fragmentation of the Political Order* (Boulder, Colo.: Westview Press, 1989), pp. 137–38.

46. U.S. AID, Cairo, *Status Report* (see n. 26).

47. Ibid.

48. U.S. Embassy, Cairo, *Egyptian Economic Trends,* p. 21.

49. *World Debt Tables 1989–90: External Debt of Developing Countries* (Washington, D.C.: World Bank, 1989), p. 51.

50. See Abdel Monem Said Aly, "Quality vs. Quantity: The Arab Perspective of the Arms Race in the Middle East" (paper presented at the Canogic Conference on Arms Control and the Proliferation of High Technology Weapons in the Near East and South Asia, Bellagio, Italy, 23–27 October 1989).

51. This expansion excludes the high mobilization period of 1967–74. See Springborg, *Mubarak's Egypt,* pp. 95–134.

52. *World Almanac 1990,* p. 706.

53. Said Aly, "Quality vs. Quantity."

54. Ibid.

CHAPTER

4

EGYPT'S LIBERALIZATION EXPERIENCE AND ITS IMPACT ON STATE-OWNED ENTERPRISES

Khaled Fouad Sherif and Regina M. Soos

State-Owned Enterprises (SOEs) have recently come to the fore of industrial reform efforts in Egypt as policy makers face increasing pressure to reduce the state's
fiscal burden and to satisfy international donors. A product of the legacy of nationalization and the large public-investment program of the 1960s and early 1970s,
the SOEs have become a major contributor to the annual budget deficit in Egypt.[1]
The poor performance of most Egyptian SOEs is attributable in part to restrictive
management and financial regulations governing the operations of SOEs. However,
it is also directly tied to the type of economic liberalization policies implemented
by the Egyptian government during the past fifteen years. In contrast to public
enterprises in heavy industries, or state monopolies of key services, many of the
sectors in which SOEs operate have been opened up to private-sector investment.
In the face of renewed private-sector competition, and in the absence of reform
of the management and financial regulations governing the SOE sector, the financial performance of most SOEs declined markedly. As many critics of the Open-
Door Policy feared, this part of the state sector has indeed become the victim
of economic liberalization. The fact that the government continues to operate
these firms, which are losing money and producing nonessential products,
has become the focus of the ongoing debate over privatization in the Egyptian
context.

In this chapter, we first describe the current regulatory and management environment in which SOEs in Egypt operate and the consequences for SOE financial
performance. Then we discuss the policy stances of the Egyptian government toward
various alternatives for reform of the SOE sector, with an emphasis on the policy
options of liquidation and privatization. Finally, we provide two examples of how
the implementation of economic liberalization has increased the financial liability
of two SOEs and how it has affected the state budget, threatening to obstruct the
possibility for further reform.

REGULATIONS AFFECTING SOE PERFORMANCE

In the early 1960s, during the era of "Arab Socialism," the Egyptian government initiated a lengthy nationalization program which transferred a variety of assets from the private to the public sector. Direct state involvement in the economy expanded into industry, agriculture, key services, and much of the wholesale and retail trade. Today, the Egyptian government manages 120 SOEs, some forty of which fall under the Ministry of Industry. These firms found their way into the public sector either as a result of nationalization or through the extensive public investment program of the mid-1960s and early 1970s.

SOEs are defined here as those commercial industrial establishments producing a wide range of nonessential consumer goods who have profit maximization as their sole objective and are a part of the Ministry of Industry's portfolio. The largest groups of SOEs are found in the engineering (electronics) and food-processing industrial sectors. Many SOEs in Egypt are chronic money losers with extremely low rates of return.

Financial Performance

Over the last two decades, Egyptian SOEs have provided the treasury with very limited returns. For example, the net rate of return on revalued public assets for Ministry of Industry supervised SOEs was only 2.1 percent during the periods 1980-81 through 1987-88 versus an annual inflation rate of 18 percent during the same period.[2] The weak financial returns from SOEs have had serious negative impacts on the treasury, and it is estimated that the financial deficit from these enterprises now accounts for roughly 6 percent of the national fiscal deficit.[3] Weak returns from Egyptian SOEs have not only had negative impacts on the budget deficit, but the debt-equity ratios of a number of firms have now spiraled due to their inability to adequately balance their cash inflows with their current liabilities position.

SOEs under the Ministry of Industry employ approximately 310,000 workers, or almost 2 percent of the civilian labor force. The share of SOE exports to total exports is also very small, amounting to less than 2 percent of total production.[4] Given their minimal returns and limited exports, SOEs have contributed little to GDP growth. Between the years 1965 and 1987, SOEs accounted for less than 2 percent of the increment in real GDP.[5] The backward and forward linkages between Egyptian SOEs and other economic sectors are not strong. SOEs in the food-processing sector, for example, purchase agricultural products but do not seem to generate significant growth in the agricultural sector by demands for greater output and/or product diversification. Additionally, most Egyptian SOEs (which were created during the import-substitution drive of the 1960s) do not operate in compar-

TABLE 1
**Financial Performance for Six State-Owned
Enterprises in Egypt**

SOE	% Return on Assets	% Profit Margin	Current Ratio*	% Debt Ratio
El Nasr Bottling Co.	1.6	1.2	.93	51
Misr Dairy	0.3	.93	.67	84
Edfina	1.8	1.9	1.15	61
Kaha	2.3	2.1	1.21	54
Al Ahram Beer	3.1	2.2	1.34	59
Biscomisr	2.1	2.1	1.26	57

*Estimates in Egyptian pounds ($1 = 2.51 Egyptian pounds) based on revalued capital.
Source: Estimates derived from balance sheets and income statements of the above-mentioned firms (1984 through 1987) are by consent of the Ministry of Industry. The calculations for the return on assets, profit margin, current ratio, and debt ratio do not include adjustments for implicit subsidies on electricity, energy, and water granted to these six firms by the state.

ative advantage areas and are dependent upon imports for a significant portion of their inputs from abroad.[6] Thus, the development of backward linkages has not been significant.

Industrialization in Egypt has, since the early 1960s, tended to stress import-substitution practices even when the chance of developing backward linkages was small. This strategy has survived the various changes in Egypt's economic system that have taken place over the last five decades: a free-enterprise system during the periods 1930 through the late 1950s; a mixed economic system which existed for a small period during the late 1950s and early 1960s; the planned economic system of the 1960s and early 1970s; and Egypt's well-known Open-Door Policy, which began in 1973 and initiated liberalization in a number of key sectors where investment was once completely reserved for the public sector.

The import-substitution policies pursued since the 1930s until today led Egypt to stress the production of basic consumer goods such as manufactured food, soft drinks and other beverages, and some manufactured textiles. For various reasons, a large number of these SOEs are now financially unviable.[7]

A detailed ratio-analysis exercise was undertaken to assess the financial performance of six Egyptian SOEs. The companies examined were the El Nasr Bottling Company, Misr Dairy, Edfina, Kaha, Biscomisr, and Al Ahram Beer. All of the aforementioned companies fall under the Ministry of Industry's Food-Processing Holding Company. The findings of the ratio analysis undertaken are found in table 1.

During the period between 1984 and 1987, return on assets for the aforementioned six firms did not exceed 3.1 percent (i.e., implying that for every pound invested in assets the most successful of these companies is earning a meager 3 piasters in income). The profit margin for these firms during the same period did not exceed 2.2 percent (i.e., the most successful of the six companies studied made a profit of only 2.2 piasters on every pound in sales, suggesting negative economic returns).

With regard to liquidity and solvency, the most viable firm of those examined is Al Ahram Beer while the financially weakest is Misr Dairy. Misr Dairy's current ratio is .67, which would make the company insolvent by financial standards (bankruptcy does not take place because the government absorbs all outstanding liabilities at the end of the fiscal year). With regard to debt, the debt ratio for Misr Dairy (84 percent) is the highest in comparison to the other five firms (i.e., roughly 84 percent of the assets of this firm are financed by government debt with minimal self-financing coming from the company itself).[8]

While the debt-equity ratio is an important determinant of creditworthiness for private enterprises, it is often considered irrelevant for SOEs because the government is most often the major source of finance. However, the distinction between debt and equity is related to the financial autonomy and accountability of SOEs. An SOE is likely to be more autonomous in financial matters and, accordingly, to plan its operations better, if it finances the major portion of its needs through retained earnings. While the distribution of financing between equity and debt does not affect the rate of return on capital (both dividends and interest are payments to capital), a large equity participation by the government could weaken the financial discipline of SOEs, permit low or negative profits to be continued, and constrain the reuse of generally limited government funds.[9] In all of the aforementioned six SOEs examined, none are generating the liquidity required to be able to play an active role in supporting their own depreciation allowances, or to add to their equity. These six firms are supported by tremendously high transfers from the government; and at least two firms, Misr Dairy and the El Nasr Bottling Company, would automatically become insolvent if state transfers were to stop.

The Egyptian government is concerned over the low rates of return made by Egyptian SOEs who, as commercial enterprises, were never envisioned to have serious negative implications on the state's finances. Large SOE deficits, low levels of export, and high foreign-exchange expenditures are all symptoms of one major weakness in a majority of Egyptian SOEs: a low financial rate of return. Estimates of rates of return from SOEs from the periods 1980-81 to 1986-87 show that the average gross rate of return on assets for firms under this category (estimated at their book values) was only 6.2 percent.[10] In addition, the net rate of return on revalued assets was only 2.1 percent.[11] The government is also alarmed by the decline in rates of returns by SOEs. During the periods 1980 through 1986-87, the net rate of return (on book-value assets) declined from 11 percent to only 6 percent. During the same seven years, the net rate of return on revalued assets declined from approximately 8 percent to only 2.1 percent.[12]

Payment arrears in SOEs have also become a major problem. Between 1980 and 1987-88, arrears in SOEs increased at an average rate of approximately 11 percent per annum.[13] The existing system for handling arrears also creates system-wide distortions. A typical example may look like the following: An engineering (electronics) SOE does not pay the steel industry because their cash flow position is weak. In turn, the steel industry does not pay the Egyptian Electricity Authority (EEA) for consumption of energy, and so forth. As a result, accounts-receivable collection periods become more lengthy in many enterprises dealing with SOEs, causing liquidity problems, and managers are forced to spend more of their time chasing after unpaid bills. In fact, EEA has an accounts-receivable collection period from SOEs which exceeds eleven months on average.

By financial standards alone (if it were not for government liquidity support), the leverage, profitability, and liquidity ratios for a large number of SOEs would have led them straight toward insolvency. Yet, the government has been acting as the major barrier preventing insolvency and any possible liquidation of SOE industrial assets. In fact, no Egyptian industrial SOE has been liquidated since nationalization took place in the early 1960s.

Pricing Industrial Products

Many state officials are claiming that the weak financial returns from SOEs can be attributed to their inability to price output above cost for social considerations. In fact, over the last decade the growth of the price index of SOEs has never exceeded the growth of annual inflation. Even though prices are kept down to protect living standards in companies producing essential commodities, experts are now questioning the logic of why the government still insists on keeping price controls on Egyptian SOEs producing a wide range of nonessential products.

For pricing purposes, the output of SOEs and Public Enterprises (PEs) in industrial establishments, falling under the auspices of the Ministry of Industry, is divided into two groups. The first group is made up of goods which are defined as essential products (these commodities can be either final products or intermediates).[14] But the Government of Egypt (GOE) has tended to regard an array of commodities from state-owned food-processing firms, for example, as being essentials (e.g., soft drinks, soap, and industrial detergents). The prices of products in this group are set by a committee made up of the Prime Minister, the Minister of Industry, and other key ministers. This committee is known as the Higher Policies Committee. Price setting for commodities in the second category does not require Higher Policies Committee approval (e.g., nonessentials like bubble gum, chocolate, corn flakes, etc.). The authority to set the prices of commodities falling under this category lies in theory with the holding company and the board of the firm producing that commodity, but it is the holding company which has the strongest say in price-setting decisions.

The GOE has used state holding companies that control SOEs as a mechanism to fight off inflation over the last several years. The government is usually slow when it comes to adjusting SOE prices, regardless of the fact that their product mix is made up of nonessentials. For example, the Ministry of Industry used to provide companies like El Nasr Bottling (Coca-Cola) with sugar at one-third of its price. When the Ministry decided to remove this subsidy, it took the Higher Policies Committee more than a year to allow for the required price adjustments to offset the increased price of sugar. One reason for slow price adjustments can be attributed directly to the overriding belief by many government officials that the state industrial sector exists to combat economic ills like inflation.

The slow pace of price adjustments due to centralized decision making has had three main implications for SOE industrial performance: (1) it hinders the ability of firms to achieve profit maximization objectives, (2) it creates distortions in incentives, and (3) it limits accountability in SOEs. In addition, the slow pace of price adjustments, which in many cases applies to both SOEs and the private sector (e.g., soft drinks), has directly affected their profitability. It has also constrained supply and discouraged investment.

The lack of accountability caused by centralized pricing decisions is one of the major distortions facing the entire system of state-owned enterprise. In a system where SOE prices are subject to outside interference, there is a tendency for SOEs to blame their minimal returns on the lack of adequately timed price adjustments instead of on inefficiency.[15] To differentiate between SOEs that are efficient and making limited financial returns because of the lack of adequately timed price changes and SOEs that are both inefficient and making limited financial returns is a very complex task. Minimal price flexibility affecting SOE financial performance (along with various other controls) and the lack of a properly functioning evaluation system have made it very difficult to differentiate between firms that are efficient versus those that tend to be inefficient. Due to the lack of a performance-evaluation mechanism that gives the right signals on efficiency, inefficient enterprises are seldom held responsible for poor performance.[16]

Financial Management Policies

The system of financial-management policies under which SOEs in Egypt operate primarily affects the efficiency of enterprises by limiting the flexibility and accountability of management. There are three broad categories of financial policies relevant to SOEs: policies relating to the financial capital structure of SOEs, policies affecting the distribution of SOE surplus, and policies tied to foreign borrowing by SOEs.[17]

There are two main aspects of policies relating to the financial capital structure of SOEs: the issue of "debt versus equity" participation by the government, and the availability of bank credit for working capital. In 1973, in an effort to relieve the pressure on government funds and to encourage greater financial discipline in SOEs, it was decided that investment funds for SOEs would no longer be provided as equity participation by the state. Instead, investment funds would be made available to all public enterprises on a loan basis. Operationally, this policy change went into effect in 1980 with the creation of the National Investment Bank (NIB), which operates outside the jurisdiction of the state budget and which strictly enforces the servicing of funds loaned to state and public enterprises. However, the aggregate impact of this policy change has been diminished by conflicts with other policies and by the fact that a key element necessary to ensure financial autonomy and accountability—price flexibility—has not accompanied the change in policy.

The banking sector has provided the other main source of working capital for SOEs. Until 1982-83, credit policy for both public and private enterprises was fairly liberal. In August 1983, a more stringent credit policy went into effect. Since the new policy was aimed primarily at reducing the supply of credit to the private commercial sector to discourage foreign-exchange speculation, it did not create significant liquidity problems for SOEs. This, along with the fact that interest rates on bank credit have been largely negative (i.e., less than the inflation rate), encouraged many SOEs to borrow excessively, leading to a high ratio of debt to equity and a large debt-service burden in many SOEs.

The second category of policies, those governing the distribution of the surpluses of SOEs in Egypt, is quite rigid and, to a certain extent, is inconsistent with the financial policies discussed above. Approximately 80 percent of the surplus of an SOE must be transferred to the state, 10 percent is allocated for the workers' welfare, and the remaining 10 percent is retained as statutory reserves. Hence, on the one hand, the system requires that SOEs surrender their surplus to the state while, on the other hand, financial discipline is enforced by requiring them to pay interest and amortization on funds loaned to them from the NIB. In theory, it is possible for an enterprise to retain a larger share of its distributable surplus as provisions for depreciation, for inflation, or for bad debts, by entering into a lengthy bureaucratic process of approval. In practice, however, by understating their true distributable surplus, many SOEs succeed in retaining a large portion of their surplus without engaging in this time-consuming approval process.[18] Nevertheless, the overall effect of these rules concerning the allocation of SOE surpluses has been to constrain the flexibility of SOEs to plan their growth strategy: they do not have the control over financial resources necessary to respond quickly to developments in the market; nor do they have the requisite flexibility in selecting and approving investment projects, because the bulk of the investment financing is obtained from the state budget. Both factors also represent disincentives to management.

The policies regulating an SOE's access to foreign borrowing have been more flexible but with mixed results for financial discipline and accountability of SOEs. There are two ways that SOEs obtain funds through foreign borrowing. In the first, the central government provides domestic currency loans to SOEs from funds borrowed from foreign sources. In this case, the central government retains responsibility for servicing the debt in foreign currency. However, SOEs are also allowed to borrow directly. This usually takes place in the form of suppliers' or buyers' credits, which are guaranteed by the public-sector commercial banks and which are dependent on approval from the Loans and External Debt Department

(LEDD) of the Central Bank in the case of prospective loans with a maturity period of more than one year.[19] In this option, the enterprises concerned bear responsibility for servicing the debt. Prior to 1985, SOEs found little difficulty in contracting external loans directly. However, this flexibility was inconsistent with other micro-level controls on the operations of SOEs, and no effective penalty for wrong decisions in contracting loans was applied. As a result, in many instances the debt-service burden was shifted to the central government. In January 1985, the flexibility of SOEs to negotiate foreign borrowing directly was significantly curtailed.[20]

Exchange-Rate Policies

The exchange rate and trade regime are both key determinants of the overall incentive structure for SOEs. Two major effects of the policies pursued in these areas have been to discourage exports and to distort production incentives for both the public and private sectors.

Until February 1991, when the government of Egypt liberalized the exchange rate—essentially floating it against foreign currencies—this exchange rate in Egypt has generally tended to be overvalued and fragmented as a result of the complex exchange-rate policy pursued in the last two decades. During the 1960s, tight control over the exchange rate was maintained. In the two decades since then, partial liberalization of the exchange rate has occurred only intermittently. The fragmented and highly overvalued exchange rate which has prevailed in Egypt for the last decade and a half has substantially distorted incentives. According to IMF calculations, the weighted-average real-effective exchange rate for the economy as a whole appreciated by 54 percent between January 1979 and April 1985 and depreciated by about 18 percent between April 1985 and January 1988.[21] This result suggests that the exchange rate by itself caused a significant disincentive to export from the period between January 1979 and April 1985. Recent devaluations have also not helped SOEs to export because holding companies continuously place limitations on exports if the state feels that it must protect the domestic market from shortfalls in supply.

The trade regime in Egypt, too, has undergone frequent changes. Generally, though, trade policies have favored production for the domestic market over exports. Before the nationalizations of the 1960s, tariffs and import controls were the two major instruments of the import substitution strategy, while after the nationalizations, public investment and direct controls became the primary instruments. In both periods, the development strategy pursued remained biased against exports.[22]

By 1973, tariffs again became an important determinant of production. The broad pattern of the nominal tariff was similar to that of the 1950s and 1960s, with a high average tariff on consumer goods and low average rates for capital and intermediate goods not locally produced. One significant change, however, was the substantial increase in the level of exemptions granted, mainly as concessions to Law 43 companies.[23] The resource-pull effect of the tariff structure along with pricing and subsidy policies has led to a significant distortion of production incentives, in many cases discouraging those activities with high economic rates of return.

In addition to tariffs, another commercial policy instrument that has been used actively has been quantity restrictions on imports. Import controls have been used in response to balance of payments difficulties. The combined effect of an overvalued exchange rate, the tariff structure, and the use of trade controls has caused a substantial bias against SOE exports and a large distortion of production incentives.

SOE Operations and Management

The government has also done little to reform the organizational pattern of SOEs or to develop their management practices. SOEs in Egypt today virtually cannot fire employees (unless in serious cases of proven absenteeism or when bodily harm is inflicted upon a colleague or superior), and they are not free to set their own salary and incentive scales.[24]

Wage rates are uniform for all SOEs, meaning that an engineer at the El Nasr Bottling Company is likely to receive a wage comparable to that of an engineer at Misr Dairy if they have approximately the same level of seniority. Similarly, SOE managers in the aforementioned companies with comparable levels of experience would also receive identical wages. Additionally, both white-collar and blue-collar employees in Egyptian SOEs are paid considerably lower wages than the market wage for their skills. Much has been said in favor of moving toward a system in which SOEs determine their own wage policy in light of their financial situation, but no effective measures have yet been implemented in this regard.

Additionally, all SOEs are still constrained by the fact that they can only allocate a maximum of 10 percent of their residual to incentives. The board of directors of the given state firm in theory has the right to decide how to distribute the residual among employees, yet it is actually the holding company supervised by the Ministry of Industry which sets the guidelines for the pattern of how any residual will be distributed. Equity has been the overriding factor when it comes to formulating policy with regards to the disbursement of residual. Thus, incentives in the form of residual are virtually uniform among public employees across all SOEs regardless of the firm's financial position. In fact, incentive pay in the form of disbursement of residual, even when a residual is nonexistent, is virtually guaranteed to employees across the entire SOE network. As a result, companies like Misr Dairy and El Nasr Bottling, as well as a host of other SOEs, currently face serious morale problems because the wage and incentive payments of their employees are in essence guaranteed regardless of their firm's profit or loss position.

In addition, depressed salary scales in SOEs have attracted low-caliber management professionals who are working in a system where autonomy and accountability are seldom linked.[25]

SOE Input Distortions

SOEs continue to receive a whole range of explicit and implicit subsidies that the private sector must survive without. These subsidies are reflected in the disparities of prices of inputs like electricity, fuel, and other public utilities and services.

SOEs currently pay on average 2 piasters per kilowatt hour (KWH) for electricity while private industrial firms are charged between 4 and 11 piasters per KWH for power.[26] It is estimated that the long-run marginal cost (the general rule for calculating economic electricity tariffs) is roughly 13.2 piasters per KWH, which also implies that the private sector receives subsidized electricity but to a lower degree in comparison to SOEs. Since national electricity sales are currently running at about 33.3 billion KWH per year (roughly 35 percent of sales are directed toward industrial enterprises), the implicit subsidy for this service is estimated at approximately LE 2.8 billion annually. This figure represented roughly 5 percent of gross domestic product in 1988.[27]

In addition, SOEs are also given preferential fuel prices and preferential water tariffs, and they can acquire foreign exchange from the state at preferential prices in comparison to the private sector. Yet, regardless of these implicit subsidies, SOEs in the majority of cases are generating much lower financial returns compared to their private sector competitors.

Barriers to Entry Affecting Private Investment

There is no doubt that private-sector investors, both local and foreign, benefited from substantial improvements in the investment climate in Egypt during the 1970s and 1980s, changes which occurred mainly through legislative reforms. The most recent of these efforts is the new, "unified" investment Law 230, which was passed in July 1989. It brings together most of the established incentives which existed under Law 43 with those provided by Law 59 for the New Communities and, in fact, makes them more generous. Foreign investors may now establish companies with 100 percent foreign shareholding; they are allowed to own land and real estate related to their projects; and tax exemptions have been extended for longer time periods.

Unexpectedly, however, the new law also introduces two major drawbacks from the point of view of the business community: The first requires companies to allocate at least 10 percent of the profits to workers. The second allows for increased discretionary power on the part of the Prime Minister and Ministry of Industry, especially regarding pricing and profit levels but not necessarily limited to these concerns.

The prominence of the bureaucracy in the procedures for obtaining investment approvals is certainly not new. In the past, private investors found difficulty entering areas where SOEs were heavily involved because of the GOE's fear that additional competition would infringe on returns from SOEs. These barriers to investment were manifested by the existence of "prohibited products" lists used by the

General Organization for Industrialization (GOFI) to deny investments when existing production was judged to be sufficient, or by other bureaucratic mechanisms which made obtaining an investment license from state authorities difficult and time consuming. The Investment Authority has assured potential investors under Law 230/1989 that preliminary approvals will be issued within two weeks from the submission of the application, and that "one-stop" investment procedures will reduce bureaucratic red tape to a minimum.

Nevertheless, bureaucratic delays continue to plague the investment process in other areas where the procedures remain unaffected by the issuance of the new investment law. This bureaucratic tangle begins with two major steps that must be undertaken to establish a Law 159 private commercial enterprise in Egypt.[28] These are the most difficult steps to pass through. Both the Ministry of Economy and GOFI require that a private-sector investor submit investment applications and a detailed feasibility study to their institutions. Both institutions have committees in place to assess the feasibility studies presented. These committees include representatives from virtually every key government organization and holding company (e.g., Investment Authority, Central Bank, Ministries of Economy and Industry, Federation of Industries, Holding Companies for Food, Electronics, Textiles, Metals, Mining, etc.).

Take, for example, the GOFI committee reviewing Law 159 investment applications. The GOFI committee has fourteen members and each member has a separate set of guidelines upon which he or she approves or disapproves the establishment of a Law 159 company.

The Ministry of Industry (MOI) representatives are primarily interested in maintaining protectionist policies for a number of SOEs. Their presence on this committee is meant to guarantee the kind of import-tariff protection that the MOI feels is warranted for local SOEs and, in some cases, to secure protection for state enterprises from domestic private competitors. The Ministry of Planning, Finance, Economy, and Central Bank representatives are concerned with the conformance of a Law 159 proposal to the Five Year Plan, foreign-exchange budgets for new and existing private and public firms, and the impact of new enterprises on the financial performance of existing enterprises. This committee will only agree to establish a Law 159 company if unanimous approval is granted by all of its members, a very difficult task. Similar bureaucratic difficulties exist for approval of Law 43 projects.

Regulations Concerning Private-Sector Output

Once a private commercial enterprise is established in Egypt, government intervention in operations is still a major constraint. The government intervenes directly in determining the output level and its composition for private firms. One type of intervention is to set output targets which private firms cannot exceed. Another intervention is to fix a firm's ability to change its product mix.

The GOFI and the Investment Authority also maintain the right to disapprove any expansion in a private firm's production capacity. All expansions in capacity must be approved by either GOFI or the Investment Authority. In addition, GOFI and the Investment Authority maintain the right to interfere in product-mix decisions. For example, if a private firm producing plastic manufactures buckets in two sizes, it must seek GOFI or Investment Authority approval if it wants either to introduce a third size or to switch over to the production of a somewhat differentiated product.

Many economists in Egypt believe that the controls on the establishment of private firms and their product mix remain in place to protect ailing SOEs from additional private-sector competition and infringement of their market share.[29]

THE GOVERNMENT OF EGYPT'S STAND ON INDUSTRIAL REFORM

Today, public officials are finding it more and more difficult to justify to taxpayers why their tax revenues are being directed to companies who produce products like corn flakes, bubble gum, and chocolate at low or negative financial returns instead of improved healthcare, the establishment of new public hospitals, and better public education. Public officials are also finding it immensely difficult to explain to taxpayers why the state continues to support SOEs producing nonessentials that have private-sector substitutes which are in many cases cheaper in price than the commodities produced by the state. A serious debate has now erupted over ways to reform existing SOEs.[30] The following summarizes the current debate within the Egyptian government over dealing with SOE financial failure.[31]

No Additional Expansion in SOE Operations

The Egyptian government has already reached the consensus that SOEs should be confined to their existing limits, while the private sector should be encouraged to grow around a well-defined set of incentives and regulations.

Liquidating Failing SOEs

President Hosni Mubarak, the Council of Ministers, and the head of the ruling National Democratic Party, Minister of Agriculture and Deputy Prime Minister Dr. Youssef Wali, have all clearly stated on various occasions that liquidation of SOEs is not on the government's agenda for economic reform and will not be considered as an option for dealing with ailing SOEs.

Reforming SOE Operations

The Egyptian government in coordination with the World Bank is developing a new performance-appraisal system for SOEs. Under this new appraisal system, firms will be allowed a larger role in setting their own production levels, determining their product mix, and setting their salary and incentives levels. The government is keenly interested in developing mechanisms that will encourage SOEs to behave like commercial establishments rather than to resort to either liquidation or privatization.

Joint Ventures and Mergers

The practice of merging troubled firms into joint ventures, widespread in many countries, offers an interesting lesson for Egypt. Both the Council of Ministers and the ruling National Democratic Party assert that definite possibilities exist for utilizing this strategy to reform ailing SOEs. Financially successful SOEs could take charge of weaker units and restore their health. This practice has been used to form joint ventures between successful and ailing SOEs in holding companies like those operating in the food-processing sector. Transforming ailing SOEs into joint ventures with a domestic private-sector firm has to date never taken place.[32]

Fully Liberalize Sectors Where SOEs Are Operative and Allow for More Private-Sector Competition

In theory, the private sector has had the freedom since Law 159 was passed in 1981 to invest in the sector of its choice (although certification by GOFI is still required). This law, though, has not been implemented as was originally envisioned. The government has learned from experience that liberalization can take a serious toll on SOE profitability.

The GOE is worried that liberalization, even though it could add to production and efficiency, may further detrimentally affect the financial performance of state industries in many sectors at a time when the government is still undecided over concepts like liquidation and privatization. State industries were created and have grown in an environment which allowed them to behave as if they were monopolies. When faced with private-sector competition many SOEs have been unable to keep their market share either because managers are ill-trained in dealing with competitive situations or because government controls have prevented firms from behaving like their private-sector counterparts. Many GOE officials now identify liberalization with financial disaster for state firms who, for various reasons, find themselves incapable of behaving like profit maximizers and are unable to adapt to new and more competitive situations. Thus, the government still maintains controls on private investment in areas where ailing state enterprises are heavily active, and liberalization, even though encouraged by the GOE, is moving slowly.[33] Nevertheless, there are indications that the government intends to implement greater liberalization of the sectors in which SOEs operate in the near future. The MOI affirmed in April 1990 that GOFI is prepared to approve any project requested by the private sector, including those that will manufacture goods for which local production has already achieved self-sufficiency according to GOFI analyses. This policy is intended to foster competition in the market, which in turn will lead to higher quality standards, appropriate prices, and encourage exports. If this policy is implemented, it will represent a significant change over former procedures.

Selective Transfer to Private Ownership

The ruling National Democratic Party maintains that a wholesale transfer of SOEs to the private sector would be politically unrealistic. The Egyptian government has chosen to pursue a more pragmatic policy of selectivity. Based on this strategy, the government has reviewed carefully all existing SOEs, examined the rationale for their formation and existence, and critically surveyed their performance levels. The Egyptian government, though, has to date not privatized, in part or in full, the assets of any industrial SOE.

By April 1990, the priorities for privatization of public-sector entities were announced. The majority of holdings of the various governorates would be privatized first through lease, sale, or liquidation. Second, out of 250 joint-venture companies operating under Law 43, the government expressed readiness to sell its share in only 150 of them. The MOI has estimated that the market value of the governorate holdings plus its share in the 150 joint-venture companies is LE 4.0 billion, or 30 percent of the total assets of the public sector. The third category for privatization involves increasing private-sector share ownership in the capital of joint-stock companies of the public sector up to 49 percent.

The government has formed a special Committee on Privatization, headed by presidential aide and former Minister of Defense, Mohammad Abdel Halim Abu Al-Ghazala. Other members include the ministers of Planning, Agriculture, Finance, Economy, Interior, Emigration, Cabinet Affairs, and Supply, the Governor of the Central Bank, and the General-Secretaries for the Cabinet and for Local Government. The committee has been charged with studying the means to implement the sale or lease of the governorate holdings as well as with investigating the legal considerations involved in selling the public-sector shares of both Law 43 joint ventures and public-sector firms to the private sector. In contrast to a great deal of intragovernmental debate over the selection of entities to be privatized, there is unanimous agreement that the large public-sector companies in textiles, iron and steel, chemicals, and other strategic industries will not be put on the agenda for any type of privatization.

By examining two cases of SOE performance, we are able to better visualize the need for reform of industrial enterprises in Egypt. The two cases to be examined are Misr Dairy and General Batteries.

CASE ONE: MISR DAIRY

Financial Performance

One curious example of continued government support for an ailing SOE is Misr Dairy, which produces a variety of cheeses, one type of yogurt, packaged milk, and ice cream. Misr Dairy was established in the late 1960s with start-up capital of 17 million Egyptian pounds. Misr Dairy's capital is now virtually obsolete, and little has been invested over the last decade in depreciation because of the firm's negative returns. For this reason product quality for all of Misr Dairy's products is extremely low.

As of June 1, 1989, Misr Dairy's total liabilities amounted to 103 million Egyptian pounds, and its accumulated losses in FY 1988-89 alone were 15 million pounds. By financial standards Misr Dairy has been insolvent since 1982.[34]

Pricing and Financial Controls

This company's negative financial returns are by no means associated with its pricing policy because Misr Dairy has regularly been allowed to set its prices at will. In fact, Misr Dairy's products are relatively more expensive than those of its private-sector competitors. Misr Dairy is heavily dependent on imports of raw materials from abroad for virtually its entire product line. Exchange-rate devaluation has increased tremendously the price of its inputs, causing prices for its products to rise. The lack of backward linkages to support this firm has had serious negative impacts on its financial position. Backward linkages have not developed due to Egypt's inability thus far to develop a livestock industry to support firms like Misr Dairy. High prices, low quality, and the availability of substitutes have all taken their toll on demand for Misr Dairy products.

Production Quotas and Product-Mix Regulations

Misr Dairy is forced to produce large amounts of packaged milk for the domestic market due to the Holding Company for Food Processing's view that this firm must not allow any shortfall of pasteurized milk to take place. This forced production quota has not allowed Misr Dairy to concentrate on the production of its fast-moving items, like white cheese, and to lower or drop slow-moving items, like pasteurized milk.

Liberalization and Barriers to Entry

Misr Dairy is a prime victim of the government's liberalization policy which began in the mid-1970s. Misr Dairy in the early 1970s had a virtual monopoly on the production of packaged milk, processed cheese, and ice cream. But by the early 1990s, and after more than sixteen years of liberalization, the food-processing sector has been flooded with a wave of new private producers that now compete with Misr Dairy across its entire product line. Private companies like Milkyland, Dallah, Dolce, and Tonsi are now all common household names, producing high-quality dairy products that are in many cases cheaper. As a result, private-sector dairy producers have acquired up to 80 percent of what once was Misr Dairy's market share.

The Government of Egypt's Stand on Reform

Even though Misr Dairy has been insolvent for several years, the government continues to absorb all of its annual outstanding current liabilities and is, in fact, investing a considerable amount of money to insure that Misr Dairy not be declared bankrupt. The government has refused either to liquidate or privatize Misr Dairy or to give the firm more flexibility in shaping day-to-day operations away from central government intervention. Misr Dairy is one of many SOEs that were created and grew in an environment which allowed them to behave as if they were monopolies. When faced with private-sector competition, Misr Dairy was unable to keep its market share primarily because management was ill-trained in dealing with competitive situations and because government controls have prevented firms from behaving like their private-sector counterparts.

CASE TWO: GENERAL BATTERIES

Financial Performance

A second curious example of continued government support for a losing Egyptian SOE is the General Battery Company. The General Battery Company lost 8.1 million Egyptian pounds in FY 1986-87, almost half of its start-up capital. In addition, General has been unable to meet its interest obligations to two state-owned commercial banks on an outstanding loan of approximately 5.5 million Egyptian pounds.[35] General lost roughly 39 million Egyptian pounds since 1980 despite the fact that the government has been pursuing a very stringent battery-import ban. The government now prohibits the import of dry batteries, but protection has done very little to improve the firm's weak financial position.

Pricing and Financial Controls

The state enforces no price controls on this firm and has always given General the flexibility to set its own prices in accordance with only minimal guidelines set by its holding company. General's batteries are cheaper than their domestic private-sector substitutes, but because of its low level of quality control, the firm has lost significant market share. General, like Misr Dairy, is heavily dependent on imports of raw materials from abroad for virtually its entire product line. Exchange-rate devaluation has virtually doubled the price of its inputs, causing prices for its products to rise significantly. Like Misr Dairy, the lack of backward linkages to support General's operations has had serious negative impacts on its financial position.

Production Quotas and Product-Mix Regulations

The government has tried to minimize General's losses by slowing down production by about 50 percent. In 1989, General produced only 20 million batteries a year instead of its full capacity level of 55 million batteries. Even though General has been insolvent since 1985, the government has prevented it from closing down its operations altogether, primarily because of labor concerns.

Liberalization and Barriers to Entry

General operates in a sector which became open to private-sector investment about six years ago. General, which was once a monopoly, competes with two major private-sector producers that now control approximately 85 percent of what was General's market share.

The Government of Egypt's Stand on Reform

As is the case with Misr Dairy, the government continues to absorb all of General's annual outstanding current liabilities to avoid it from being declared bankrupt. The government has also refused to liquidate or privatize General, but it has given the firm more flexibility in determining its own level of output. Despite the greater flexibility, General has been unable either to improve its financial position or to keep its market share.

CONCLUSION

Both Misr Dairy and General Batteries are major examples of what has happened to SOEs in Egypt as the sectors in which they operate were liberalized. These two companies, along with a host of other Egyptian SOEs, suffered severe financial losses in the face of greater private-sector competition and in the absence of regulatory reform, which would allow them to compete in a liberalized environment. In addition, many of these SOEs are performing poorly financially because they operate in areas where Egypt enjoys no comparative advantage.[36] The financial burden from SOEs has forced the Egyptian government to consider more than ever the possibilities open to it for reform in the industrial sector.

The thrust of industrial reform efforts in Egypt in the last seventeen years has been to permit liberalization of various sectors in which SOEs operate but to refuse to liquidate or privatize industrial enterprises. It is clear that the general policy of liberalization will continue, evidenced in part by the government's new unified investment law. These new regulations will streamline the approval process for private-sector projects and unify the incentives for private-sector investment.[37] Yet, in the absence of reform of the regulations governing the operations and management of SOEs to allow them to compete in a liberalized environment, the financial status of the SOE sector is not likely to improve.

The need for further reform in the SOE sector continues to fuel debate over the possibility either of implementing some form of privatization as the solution or of removing constraints on SOE operations. Compared to other sources contributing to the national budget deficit, the SOE sector may be the most politically viable area for lessening state involvement. However, prostatist interests, including strong concern for the status of the public-sector labor force, continue to be a significant force opposing any reduction in the size of the state sector. As such, the Egyptian government has been unwilling to liquidate or privatize SOEs on a large scale as a means to lower the budget deficit quickly.

Nevertheless, privatization of SOEs on a smaller, more selective scale remains on the policy agenda. In other sectors of the economy, the government is pursuing various types of privatization measures designed to increase the returns to the central budget from publicly owned resources. In the tourism sector, private management contracts have been used to run government-owned hotels since the 1960s, and their use has increased in recent years as part of the Ministry of Tourism's bid to turn around unprofitable hotels.[38] In addition, of considerable recent interest is the use of Employee Stock Ownership Plans (ESOPs) as a means to raise enterprise productivity and workers' incomes and to reduce the budgetary burden on the state at the same time. The first such experiment in ESOP use is currently underway outside the SOE sector in tire manufacturing, but government officials are also interested in the potential of ESOPs for reforming ailing enterprises in the SOE sector.[39] Whether or not these and other possible reforms of SOEs occur any time soon depends on a large number of factors that this chapter has not attempted to address. However, given the importance of budgetary reform in Egypt today, it is likely that SOEs will increasingly be at the center of the debate.

Notes

1. State-Owned Enterprises (SOEs) are defined in this article as being only those commercial enterprises producing a wide range of consumer durables or nonessential food products (e.g., chocolate bars, bubble gum, beer, corn flakes). The largest group of SOEs are found in the engineering (electronics) and food processing industrial sectors. This definition distinguishes SOEs from Public Enterprises (PEs) in heavy industries such as steel or automotive as well as from state monopolies of key services such as electricity, telephone, and railways. The national public-enterprise sector as a whole is made up of 360 enterprises. On the public sector generally, see: Isma'il Sabri 'Abd Allah, *Tanzim al-Qita' al-'Am* (Organization of the public sector) (Cairo: Dar al-Maarif, 1969); Nazih Ayubi, *Bureaucracy and Politics in Contemporary Egypt* (Ithaca, N.Y.: Ithaca Press, 1980); Mahmoud al-Maraghi, *Al-Qita' Al-'Am Fi Mujtam'a Mutaghayyur: Tajriba Masr* (The public sector in a changing society: The experiment of Egypt) (Cairo: Dar al-Mustaqbal al-'Arabi, 1983).

2. The net rate-of-return calculations were estimated based on the financial statements for SOEs operating in the engineering (electronics), food processing, and textiles sectors during the periods 1980-81 through 1987-88. Average inflation figures are derived from *Current Trends* reports published by the United States Embassy during the same period.

3. Estimates of the impact of SOEs on the national fiscal deficit were calculated from

the 1987-88 end-of-year actual-budget-expenditure submissions by the Ministry of Finance to the People's Assembly (Parliament) and from 1987-88 end-of-year income-statement submissions by SOEs operative in the engineering (electronics), food-processing, and textiles sectors.

4. Export estimates are only for SOEs operative in the engineering (electronics), food-processing, and textiles sectors.

5. GDP figures were derived from the International Monetary Fund's *Recent Economic Developments Report* (Washington, D.C.: IMF, 1987).

6. This fact is well documented in *Issues of Trade Strategy and Investment Planning* (Washington, D.C.: World Bank, 1983), chap. 9, Sec. 9.3.

7. Ibid. For additional background on the history of industrial policy in Egypt, see Eric Davis, *Challenging Colonialism: Bank Misr and Egyptian Industrialization, 1920–1941* (Princeton: Princeton University Press, 1983); Robert Tignor, *State, Private Enterprise, and Economic Change in Egypt, 1951–1952* (Princeton: Princeton University Press, 1984); Charles Issawi, *Egypt in Revolution* (Oxford: Oxford University Press, 1963); Bent Hansen and G. Marzouk, *Development and Economic Policy in the UAR* (Amsterdam: North-Holland Publishing Co., 1965); Patrick O'Brien, *The Revolution in Egypt's Economic System* (Oxford: Oxford University Press, 1966); ʿAli al-Gritli, *Khamsa wa ʿIshrin ʿAman: Diraasa Tahliliyya li al-Siasaat al-Iqtisaadiyya fi Masr* (Twenty-five years: An analytic study of Egypt's economic policies 1952–1977) (Cairo: General Book Organization, 1977); Robert Mabro and Samir Radwan, *Industrialization of Egypt 1939–1973* (Oxford: Clarendon Press, 1976); and John Waterbury, *The Egypt of Nasser and Sadat: Political Economy of Two Regimes* (Princeton: Princeton University Press, 1983).

8. Estimates were derived from balance sheets and income statements of the above mentioned firms (1984 through 1987) by consent of the Ministry of Industry. It should be emphasized that the implicit subsidies for fuels, electricity, foreign exchange, some raw materials, and services were not factored into the financial calculations of these six firms. Undoubtedly, if these implicit subsidies were taken into account, all of the six firms would have a higher degree of insolvency than what is currently depicted.

9. World Bank, *Egypt: Review of the Finance of the Decentralized Public Sector* (Washington, D.C.: World Bank, 1987), pp. 42–44.

10. Comparisons of estimates of rates of return for PEs versus SOEs can be constructed by reviewing the findings of the World Bank's study, *Egypt;* chap. 2 presents rates of return on assets estimates for organizations like the Egyptian Electricity Authority, the Railways Authority, and a large group of other PEs.

11. See ibid., chap. 2, for additional information on financial returns to public enterprises.

12. The declining rates of returns by SOEs during the periods 1980 through 1986-87 correspond with virtually identical declines in rates of returns in PEs over the same period. See World Bank, *Egypt,* pp. 46–53.

13. Between 1980 and 1987-88, the increase in SOEs' arrears corresponded closely to an increase in arrears in public enterprises. See World Bank, *Egypt.*

14. See World Bank, *Egypt,* pp. 35–42, for an analysis of overall changes in prices of industrial products versus rates of inflation from 1973 through 1984.

15. Managers in public enterprises also constantly use price controls as a way of trying to justify to the public their minimal returns and their inefficiency.

16. World Bank, *Egypt,* pp. 38–42.

17. Ibid., pp. 42–46.

18. This was done by charging as an expense item a relatively large sum of money which shows up in the budgets as "provisions other than depreciation."

19. In the case of loans of less than one-year maturity, approval is not required from LEDD but from the Foreign Relations Department of the Central Bank.

20. A cabinet committee now regulates all types of foreign loans with maturity of over one year. In principle, short-term borrowing remains flexible, constrained primarily by the scarcity of supply due to considerations of credit worthiness.

21. International Monetary Fund (see n. 5), pp. 46–49.

22. See Bent Hansen and Karim Nashashibi, *Foreign Trade Regimes and Economic Development* (New York: National Bureau of Economic Research, 1975).

23. Under Law 43 of 1974 (revised in Law 32 of 1977), foreign investors and their Egyptian counterparts enjoyed substantial incentives in the areas of exemption from taxes and customs duties, access to foreign currency, rights to repatriate profits, as well as other incentives. Companies established under Law 43 are legally considered part of the private sector.

24. Chap. 2 of the Central Agency for Organization and Administration, Law 48 for 1978, the "Civil Service Law."

25. In a study undertaken by Khaled Sherif in the food-processing sector for the Ministry of Cabinet Affairs and Administrative Development, it was found that six out of every ten middle managers in the SOEs operating in this sector had never received any formal management training.

26. Charles Richter, *The Energy Problem* (Cairo: Agency for International Development, 1984).

27. Ibid.

28. Law 159 of 1981, the "Companies Law," was enacted as part of the state's legislative efforts to revitalize the Egyptian private sector. It repealed the old companies law, replacing it with a completely new law. Both Egyptian and foreign investors may establish a company under Law 159. Law 159 differs from Law 43 in many respects, the most important of which is that Law 159 does not contain a guarantee for profit remittance. For a succinct comparison of the two laws, see Michael H. Davies, Esq., "Foreign Investment in Egypt: Laws 43 and 159 Compared," *Middle East Executive Reports* (June 1986): 9–17. A new, unified-investment law which will supersede these two laws was promulgated in Egypt in 1989.

29. See Lames Emery, *The Draft Investment Law: Review of the Proposed Legislation* (Cairo: Agency for International Development, June 1989).

30. For a summary of the debate over SOE reform and privatization in Egypt, see Khaled F. Sherif, "The Politics of Liquidation and Privatization in Egypt" (Master's thesis, Department of Political Science, American University of Cairo, 1988); Said Al-Naggar, "Prospects and Problems of Privatization: The Case of Egypt" (paper presented to the 13th Annual Symposium, "Egypt '88: Critical Decisions," Washington, D.C., Center for Contemporary Arab Studies, Georgetown University, 14–15 April 1988); Ibrahim al-Issawi, "Nathra Tanmawiyya lil-mas'ala Bi' Mashru'aat al-Qita' al-'Am al-Masri (A development view of the issue of selling enterprises of the Egyptian public sector) (paper presented to the 13th Annual Conference of Egyptian Economists, "The Role of Private Investment in Achieving the Goals of the Development Plan," Cairo, November 1988); Gamal Zayda, "Tarah Ashum Ba'd Sharikaat al-Qita' al-'Am lil-Qita' al-Khas" (Presenting shares of some public-sector companies to the private sector), *Al-Ahram Al-Iqtisadi,* no. 1061, 15 May 1989, pp. 14–20, and no. 1062, 22 May 1989, pp. 66–72.

31. This summary is based on the stated policy options of the ruling National Democratic Party (NDP), which were presented to the Council of Ministers in October 1986.

32. See, for example, Gamal Amin, "Al-Indimaj: Hal Yihull Mashakil Sharikatina?" (The merger: Will it resolve the problems of our companies?), *Al-Ahram Al-Iqtisadi,* no. 1050, 27 February 1989.

33. This statement was confirmed by the Minister of Industry, Dr. Mohammed Abdel Wahab, in a luncheon discussion with members of the Egyptian American Chamber of Commerce, Cairo, 12 March 1989.

34. See Aly El Azabi, "Ila Mata Tistamirr Khasa'ir Al-qita^c Al-^{c}Am" (Until when will we support losing public companies), *Al-Ahram Al-Iqtisadi,* no. 1060, 8 May 1989, p. 6.

35. See "Mezaniat El Batraiat El Amma" (General Batteries' financial position), *Al-Goumhouraya,* 10 May 1989, p. 3.

36. A recent World Bank Study on Egypt, *Review of the Finance of the Decentralized Public Sector* (Washington, D.C.: World Bank, 1987), emphasized that the pattern of public investment in industry between 1974 and 1984-85 showed that over 60 percent of the invested resources were devoted to the promotion of noncomparative–advantage-type industries.

37. For a succinct discussion of the new law, see Khaled F. Sherif, "Qanun al-Istithmar al-Jadid" (The new investment law), *Al-Ahram al-Iqtisadi,* no. 1062, 22 May 1989, p. 44; and "Al-Tafasil al-Kamila . . . li-Mashru^c Qanun al-Istithmar al-Jadid" (The complete details of the new investment law), *Al-Ahram,* 24 April 1989, p. 9.

38. See chaps. 4 and 5 of Sherif's *The Politics of Liquidation and Privatization in Egypt* for a discussion of several controversial attempts to transfer state-owned assets to the private sector, including the aborted sale of the San Stefano Hotel and the failed joint venture involving General Motors.

39. For details of the ESOP project involving the Alexandria Tire Company, see ibid., chap. 4; Regina Soos, "Alexandria Tire Company: An Experiment in Privatization," *Business Monthly* 4, no. 2 (February 1989): 28–29; Ayman Mustafa, "Tamlik Wasa'il al-Intaj lil-^{c}Amaliin" (Ownership of the means of production by the workers), *Al-Ahram,* 21 April 1989, p. 7; ^{c}Abd al-Rahman ^{c}Aql, "Tawsi^c Qa'idat al-Milkiyya . . . Tajriba Dakhalit Da'irat al-Ikhtibar" (Widening the basis of ownership . . . The experiment enters the sphere of practical experience), *Al-Ahram,* 23 April 1989, p. 9; and Mahmoud al-Hadari, "Ta'ajiil Diraasa al-^{c}Ard al-Amriki bi-Bi^c al-Qita^c al-Am" (Study of the American proposal to sell the public sector to be delayed), *Al-Ahail,* 3 May 1989, p. 1.

CHAPTER

5

LABOR AS AN OBSTACLE TO PRIVATIZATION: THE CASE OF EGYPT

Marsha Pripstein Posusney

Touted as a means of improving industrial efficiency and reducing burgeoning public deficits, privatization schemes are currently the rage in many developing countries. That such programs can actually be successfully implemented on a wide scale, however, remains in question. The selling of parastatals threatens vested interests in both the state and society, in particular the managers of the publicly owned enterprises and the workforce they employ. It is likely that one or both of these groups will resist privatization efforts, posing political problems for governments seeking to shed or at least shrink their public sectors. The first attempts to sell parastatals in Egypt occurred as early as 1974, and privatization attempts have been a source of conflict both within the government and between it and various societal forces since that time.

This chapter focuses on one central aspect of the controversy over privatization in Egypt: the opposition of organized labor. It will demonstrate that over the course of sixteen years, resistance from the labor movement has been instrumental in defeating or considerably modifying a number of different proposals for selling public-sector firms. While labor opposition alone cannot account for all of the impediments to privatization in Egypt, the success of labor's efforts there has implications for the future of state sell-offs in countries with similar economic and political configurations.

Given the state corporatist structure and legal environment regulating Egyptian labor,[1] comparative theory might lead us to expect that labor was highly active during the ISI (Import Substituting Industrialization) period only to be emasculated by the regime in the 1970s and 1980s, which would have made it unable to challenge privatization and the other liberalization measures associated with it. In fact, much the opposite is the case. The leadership of the Egyptian Trade Union Federation (ETUF)[2] had been strictly supportive of Nasir's economic policies, and the formal union movement had lost much of its raison d'être during that period.[3] By threatening the gains workers had made in the 1960s, *infitah* brought the labor movement into conflict with the government and breathed new life into the union organizations.

Besides dismantling the notion that regimes can render workers powerless through manipulation of the corporatist union structure, this chapter will show how variations in labor's response to different privatization schemes affect the outcome of its bargaining with the state. Of course, labor is not the only societal force involved in the privatization controversy, and there are also factors internal to the state which contribute to the final resolution of conflicts over privatization. Nevertheless, it is possible to show that those policies which elicited, or threatened to elicit, the widest and most unified resistance from workers were the ones most readily abandoned by the government involved. This suggests that the commitment of Egypt's ruling elite to privatization has been strongly tempered by its fear of a political challenge from labor.

THE EARLY INFITAH YEARS: 1974 TO MID-1977

At the time of Egypt's turn to economic liberalization, the Egyptian trade union movement was characterized by sharp political and ideological divisions. Salah Gharib, who was chosen president of the ETUF in 1971, had been promoted by Sadat as a reward for the critical role he had played in helping the latter to consolidate power. However, Gharib's candidacy to the ETUF executive committee had been challenged by several different groups of Nasirists and communists from among the delegates to the nominating convention; out of the twenty-one candidates chosen, he was ranked only sixteenth. His subsequent election as president was facilitated by the support of some of the communists, principally Ahmad al-Rifaʿi, then president of the General Union of Agricultural Workers. His was the largest federation in the ETUF, and al-Rifaʿi himself had ranked first in the executive-committee elections. Some members of al-Rifaʿi's leftist circle had also assisted Gharib in blocking the candidacy of other prominent unionists for federation office. Two years later Gharib, apparently with the blessing of Sadat, turned on the communists and ousted them from the executive committee. The Nasirists whom they had betrayed in 1971 failed to support them against Gharib now. However, the Nasirists and other leftists who remained in leading positions continued to object to Gharib's pro-regime orientation.[4]

It was within this context that the trade union movement confronted the economic-liberalization measures which followed the October 1973 war.

Labor and the Infitah

The ETUF initially adopted a dualistic position on the *infitah*. A fall 1973 statement recommended that constraints be placed on the opening process so that it would not affect the socialist path or place the country "under the control of world monopolies." There was, however, no outright rejection of foreign capital. The report calls for issuing laws to protect foreign and Arab capital seeking to invest in Egypt, widening the scope for international economic agreements and expanding licensing for oil exploration and joint ventures in petrochemical manufacturing.[5]

While voicing the ETUF's concern for protecting the public sector, the statement said it would welcome "any initiative from private local, Arab, or foreign capital to participate in the projects of development plans on the condition that such projects are coordinated in the framework of the general national plan and under the umbrella of existing laws."[6]

There was also no official ETUF response to Law 43 of 1974, even though the law exempted foreign firms from including certain benefits to workers incumbent on the Egyptian private sector. The working class did react to the wave of inflation that quickly followed the passage of Law 43. The years 1975 and 1976 saw a militant strike wave, as well as a small riot on January 1, 1975, that erupted out of a labor demonstration. During these protests workers expressed their outrage over the increasing manifestations of class divisions in the society. But this cannot necessarily be equated with opposition to the lifting of barriers to foreign trade and investment per se. New imports and the products of foreign-owned firms did find a market among workers.

Leftists in the union movement, some of whom helped to organize the January 1, 1975, demonstration, pushed for a stronger confederation stance against the *infitah* afterwards. The result was an ETUF conference on the Economics of Labor, held from April 6 to 9 of that year. It was opened by Gharib, who presented a statement favorable to the concept of *infitah*. The conference then heard papers on the economic opening from a number of academics and other intellectuals. Among the critics who addressed the gathering was the Islamic nationalist ʿAbd al-Mughni Said, a long-time Labor Ministry functionary and friend of the labor movement, who had published one of the early critiques of *infitah* in the leftist journal *al-Katib*. Another critic, Dr. Hassan Zaki Ahmad, argued that *infitah* was in contradiction with socialism. This position was challenged by Dr. Mustafa Kamil Lutfi and Dr. Mahmoud Samir Tubar, who both cited moves toward economic opening in a number of Eastern bloc countries. All the speakers concurred, however, that the influx of foreign capital into Egypt should be subject to control and supervision in the context of national development plans and priorities.[7]

The committee charged with formulating resolutions (*tawsiyyat*) on the *infitah* adopted a unifying position. While recognizing "the necessity of *infitah* for economic growth," the committee insisted that *infitah* should serve the development plans, and not vice versa. Further, they said, the opening should be planned, all entering foreign capital should be productive, and Arab capital should be given preference over foreign capital. Other resolutions called for the preservation of workers' rights and maintaining the public sector as the key to the economy.[8]

These points were ultimately formalized in the Code of Ethics for Union Work (*Mithaq al-Sharaf al-Akhlaqi lil-ʿAmal al-Niqabi*), approved by the general assembly of the confederation in October 1976. The statement expressed support for the *infitah* only so long as it "does not disturb the socialist principles on which our economic and social system is based, nor contradict the national interest."[9]

The story of its evolution indicates that the Code of Ethics represents a compromise acceptable to the various forces in the trade union movement. Nevertheless, the reservations about *infitah* which the code expresses are much stronger than the confederation's original statement, indicating that opposition to *infitah* in the unions had grown during the three years which elapsed between the two policy statements. Leftists and Nasirists in the ETUF interpreted the new position as essentially a rejection of government policies, and considered it a victory. Similarly, Egyptian scholars of the trade union movement have seen the document as fundamentally in opposition to *infitah*.[10]

To Sell or Save the Public Sector?

Egyptian economist Fuad Sultan, later minister of tourism, proposed publicly, shortly before the 1973 war, that the government shed failing public-sector enterprises. In December of that year, the Parliament's Plan and Budget Committee recommended partial privatization of successful parastatals. Charged with reviewing the budget presented by Finance Minister 'Abd al-'Aziz Higazi, the committee expressed fears that the deficit financing implied in the budget would be inflationary. But Egypt need not choose austerity as an alternative, their report said, if it could woo investment from neighboring Arab countries awash in surplus capital. Bemoaning the fact that Western nations placed fewer restrictions on Arab investment than did Egypt, the committee called for allowing up to 49 percent ownership of public industry to devolve to Arabs, slipping in the idea of private domestic participation in this context. The report went on to argue that joint ownership would benefit labor by making parastatals more profitable, thereby directly increasing workers' profit shares, and would enable them to gain even more if they became private shareholders.[11]

The proposal sparked widespread debate in the ensuing months. In February 1974, the ETUF's executive committee strongly denounced the idea in a formal statement. Charging that the public sector was the embodiment of the socialist principle of collective ownership of the means of production and that sharing ownership with private individuals negated this concept, the statement warned that "the millions of workers will not permit any attempt to threaten the socialist gains brought about by the July Revolution." Under the din of this and related objections from other quarters, the committee's proposal was never approved.

The ETUF leadership thus moved more rapidly, and more decisively, around this issue than they had around *infitah;* the majority of union leaders were seemingly more adverse to denationalization than liberalization. It is not surprising, however, that this should be so; diminution or elimination of the public sector threatened to take away benefits that workers had already realized. Furthermore, even union leaders not genuinely concerned with their rank and file's welfare had cause to be wary of denationalization. Since the majority of the ETUF's membership, especially in the industrial unions, came from the parastatals, shrinking the state sector could threaten the membership base of the confederation.

Moreover, though it is not clear to what extent this particular ETUF statement grew out of discussion through the ranks of the confederation, union leaders were under pressure from below to defend the parastatals. Workers had good reason to fear the dissolution of the public sector. At the time of this proposal, wages were comparatively higher there, raises and paid holidays were more frequent, insurance and pension benefits were better, and there was much more job security (see table 1). *Rose al-Yusef, al-Tali'a,* and *al-'Ummal,* the newspaper of the ETUF, featured occasional exposés on private business in the 1970s; a frequent accusation was that employers were refusing to give workers full-time contracts and were lying to authorities about the number of workers they employ. These practices gave them more freedom to fire employees. In addition, because some labor laws apply only to companies with fifty or more full-time workers, they facilitated evasion of workers' representation in management and made unionization more difficult as well.[12]

According to both statistics and workers' testimonials, the wage differential between the two sectors reversed in the late 1970s, largely as a result of worker migration from Egypt. But the objectionable practices in the private sector persisted, and, despite the wage gap, the overwhelming majority of workers interviewed in this research preferred public-sector employment because of the continued disparities in benefits and job security. Almost all of those working in the private sector expressed a desire to switch once they had "established themselves" (i.e., married, found and furnished housing). This implies that it is not so much the issue of wages but of insurance and job security that is behind the rank and file workers' concern to preserve the public sector.

The fight against privatization intensified in 1975. In his remarks to the economics conference in April, Gharib affirmed that "socialism is the only solution for progress," and added that "we all agree that the public sector must remain the leader of progress in all realms, and carries the main responsibility for the development plan, and this requires that it be supported and provided with all it needs to enable it to undertake its pioneering role, assuring through this the control of the people over all the means of production."[13] There was, nevertheless, struggle within the confederation leadership over opposition to privatization, with Gharib and a group around him somewhat more sympathetic to the proposed new orientation. In a *Rose al-Yusef* article that year, Fathi Mahmoud, president of the Commerce Workers' Federation, charged that Gharib had obstructed more widespread distribution of the February 1974 ETUF statement. It had appeared originally just in the confederation's paper; only through independent action by left-wing unionists was it reprinted, several months later, in *al-Tali'a.*[14] Mahmoud made these charges while his federation was embroiled in two significant fights against privatization in the commerce sector, both of which Gharib failed to support.

The first of these battles began at the end of 1974, when the manager of the publicly owned United Wholesale Textile Trading Company (UWTTC) signed a

TABLE 1

**Public/Private Sector Wage Ratio Blue Collar
Workers, All Sectors[a]**

Year	Pub. Sector Eg. Pias./Wk	Pri. Sector Eg. Pias./Wk	Ratio Pub/Pri[d]	% Ch[d]
1970	419	281	1.49	
1971	423	303	1.40	−6.0
1972	460	409	1.12	−20.0
1973	491	421	1.17	4.5
1974	556	432	1.29	10.2
1975	576	473	1.22	−5.4
1976	663	596	1.12	−8.2
1977	813	744	1.09	−2.7
1978	897	842	1.06	−2.7
1979	1,054	1,022	1.03	−3.7
1980[b]	1,289	1,204	1.07	3.9
1981[b]	1,576	1,418	1.11	3.7
1982	1,928	1,671	1.15	3.6
1983	2,271	2,120	1.07	−7.0
1984	2,613	2,569	1.02	−4.7
1985[c]	2,800	2,800		
1986[c]	3,100	3,100		
1987[c]	3,400	3,400		

Source: Annual Survey of Employment, Wages, and Hours of Work (SEWHW), CAPMAS. I am grateful to Ragui Assaad for providing me with these data.
[a]Blue collar is defined by CAPMAS to include all hourly (as opposed to salaried) workers. Only establishments employing more than ten workers are covered in the SEWHW.
[b]Considered estimates by CAPMAS.
[c]Figures rounded to the nearest pound by CAPMAS; ratios not computed.
[d]Calculated by author.

contract to sell two small factories owned by the company to the private-sector Cooperative for Workers of the Delta Spinning and Weaving Company. UWTTC was a large company formed by the successive nationalization of private stores in the 1960s. The two small factories, ʿAzizu and Nublis, had belonged respectively to the Hano and Salon Verte stores, supplying them with ready-made clothing and other textile products. When these stores were nationalized the factories became part of the UWTTC.

The UWTTC manager, Dr. Ali Sabri Yasin, negotiated and signed the sales contract without consulting either his management committee (which, like all public-sector companies, had elected representatives from the workers) or the union local. The workers claimed they were told the factories were merely being transferred to the jurisdiction of a public manufacturing company. Upon learning the truth, they refused to work for their new owner and sent an urgent memo to the commerce federation. The federation hired lawyers and raised a court case against Yasin, seeking to invalidate the sales contract; this was the first court case challenging the sale of public-sector assets. In their deposition, the lawyers argued that the sale violated those provisions of the constitution which call for the protection and preservation of the public sector and socialism as the basis of the Egyptian economy. Concerning the workers, they argued that the transfer would deprive them of numerous benefits associated with public-sector employment, in particular, periodic raises and promotions, annual vacation, and sick leave.

Several months later, Minister of Commerce Zakariyya Tawfiq ʿAbd al-Fattah decided to fully or partially privatize the publicly owned stores. Shares in the largest enterprises would be sold, and the smaller units were to be sold outright to private entrepreneurs. Once again, it was workers in the commerce federation who were to be affected. When the plans were announced in the spring of 1975, the executive committee of the federation took a position against them and sent an urgent memo to the ETUF board seeking assistance. The federation decided to sponsor weekly meetings with locals of the stores involved, to invite all the labor delegates in Parliament to a general meeting to discuss the issue, and to plead their case with other government officials. Mahmoud contacted *Rose al-Yusef,* which publicized the plans via an interview with ʿAbd al-Fatah, followed by a lengthy rebuttal from the unionist.[15]

The commerce federation kept up the pressure on the minister through the summer and fall, and in late October, ʿAbd al-Fatah contacted Mahmoud and offered to rescind his plans in exchange for an end to the campaign against him; he agreed to a request by Mahmoud to announce his decision at a general meeting of the Commerce Federation. Thus, one of the first concrete proposals to transfer public assets to the private sector was defeated by concerted union action. But Mahmoud had not had the full backing of the confederation during this victorious campaign. The antipathy of Gharib (and other confederation leaders close to him, such as ʿAbd al-Rahman Khidr) to the activities of the Commerce Federation was reflected in the complete absence of coverage of these events in the confederation's own newspaper. Mahmoud found more sympathy at *Rose al-Yusef,* and Amina Shafiq, labor reporter for the official newspaper, *al-Ahram,* helped him to publicize the issues elsewhere.

Differing attitudes over privatization among the ETUF and federation leaders were also reflected in the response to presidential decree 262, which was issued by Sadat early in the summer of 1975 and which authorized the use of share subscriptions to increase the capital of public-sector firms. This was followed in July by the passage in Parliament of Law 111, which abolished the General Organizations that had been responsible for guiding the performance of public-sector firms. The law formally made the parastatals autonomous, allowing for the presence of "experts" from the private sector on their individual management boards. Law 111 also set terms for share subscriptions, specifying that they were to be offered first to workers in the affected companies. However, the state's overall share in these joint firms could not be reduced through the subscriptions, although the role of private shareholders in their management was expanded. At the time, there were 32 such joint companies, as compared to 341 that were strictly state-owned.[16]

The addition of clause 10 to the law indicates that there was resistance to privatization within the government in spite of Sadat's personal support for it. It is not clear to what extent union leaders serving in Parliament played a role in this. The ETUF did promptly form a committee to study the new laws and their implications for workers. Its work, according to Said Gum'a, president of the General Union of Electrical, Engineering, and Metal Workers (EEM), was to be guided by the slogan, "No new capitalism at the expense of the public sector." The committee's report, released by the confederation in August, noted with satisfaction that subscription was to be limited to those parastatals which already had private-sector participation, because "public sector companies are not for sale nor for the participation of the private sector." Moreover, the confederation called on the government to ensure that the share of the state in joint companies would not be reduced by stock sales, and that the system of workers' participation in management would not be tampered with in these companies. The statement also upheld the idea of giving workers the first opportunity to purchase shares in them.[17]

The report clearly departed from the views of the hard-line opponents of privatization in the labor movement, such as Mahmoud and Gum'a; the latter had earlier told al-'Amal that workers would rather have their rights in the public sector than the opportunity to buy shares in companies where they worked at the risk of someday being reclassified as private-sector employees. Because the confederation's statement did not condemn subscription sales outright, it was denigrated by Fuad Mursi, a prominent leftist economist and outspoken critic of liberalization, as "the greatest surrender possible." Nevertheless, as Qandil points out, the ETUF report was fundamentally in opposition to the drift of Sadat's government.[18]

In November 1975, there was a coup in the Commerce Federation, as members of the executive committee voted to withdraw confidence from the office committee (the seven leading members of the executive committee responsible for day-to-day running of the union). Gharib recognized the action within twenty-four hours, issuing a new list of officers and orders to change the signatures on the federation's bank account. He then used his powers as president to launch an investigation into the finances of the federation. The move caused a stir of protest within the ETUF, and an investigation by the new minister of labor, 'Abd al-Latif Bultiya. But the change was not rescinded. Mahmoud believes that his outspoken opposition to privatization was one reason for his ouster and that higher authorities acquiesced to Gharib's actions against him. One of the first acts of the group which came to power in the federation afterwards was to withdraw the legal case against the UWTTC, thus making the sale of the two small factories final and forestalling a constitutional challenge to privatization.

This account demonstrates that labor played a key role in beating back the drive toward privatization. It clarifies how the role of different forces within the labor movement is significant. The activity of the Commerce Federation played a key role in defeating the proposed sale of the publicly owned stores; conversely, it was the disunity within the confederation which paved the way for the sale of the two small factories. To the best of my knowledge, these were the only direct sales of parastatals which have occurred in Egypt.

The January 1977 Riots and the Transition to a New Union Leadership

In the union elections of 1976, Gharib was not returned to the presidency of the textile workers confederation, and did not run for confederation office. The ETUF presidency went to Said Muhammad Ahmad of the General Union for Food Industry Workers (GUFIW). On the issues at hand, Ahmad was considered a moderate; he had not played a significant role on either side of the battles within the confederation. His candidacy was apparently endorsed by the inner ruling circles. However, Ahmad had a long history as an active trade unionist. During the 1960s, the GUFIW under his leadership had been virtually the only federation to seriously attempt to organize private-sector workers.

Those leftists who had previously held federation positions were generally returned to their spots. Moreover, progressive elements did extremely well at the local level; overall, the newly formed leftist party, known as *Tagammuʿ*, fared far better in the union contests than it had in the 1976 parliamentary elections.[19] Thus the leftist pole in the union movement was strengthened by these elections. It was a short-lived phenomenon, however, as the battle against subsidy reform soon led to a crackdown on union militants.

Subsidies became an issue for labor at the end of 1976, when Egypt entered into negotiations with the IMF and rumors began to circulate that the agency was pushing for their removal. At its December 1976 conference on wages and prices, the ETUF passed a resolution calling on the regime to maintain the subsidies as vital to the health and welfare of Egypt's workers. On January 17, 1977, the government announced cuts in subsidies on many items, and prices skyrocketed. On January 18 and 19, Egypt erupted in rioting which left 79 dead and 1,000 wounded, with widespread destruction of property and between 1,250 and 1,500 arrests. The rioting ended only when the government rescinded the decision and reinstated the subsidies.[20]

The protests were initiated by workers and students. In Helwan, they began at the Harir plant, where workers left their jobs and marched to nearby factories, drawing out others. The workers then tried to march north to Cairo, but they were turned back by security forces at Tura. Rocks were placed on the train tracks linking Cairo to Helwan, disrupting transportation.

After the riots, the regime cracked down on militants among the rank and file and in local leadership. The government particularly targeted union officials associated with the *Tagammuʿ* Party. As a result, hundreds of the *Tagammuʿ* members who had just been elected to local leadership resigned from the party over the next few years.

But the response of the government to the top union leaders was quite conciliatory. The ETUF leadership had viewed the decision to raise prices so soon after their December conference as a political insult. In an emergency meeting held the night of January 18, they issued a strongly worded denunciation of the government's actions and demanded to meet with Sadat. Husni Mubarak, then vice president, met with the ETUF executive committee shortly thereafter, and on January 21 Sadat acceded to the unionists' request for a dialogue. This was his first formal meeting with ETUF leaders since before the 1973 war.

The union leaders used the occasion to press a number of longstanding concerns, such as the demand for regular and structured channels of communication between the ETUF and the government and for implementation of a 1976 labor law giving the ETUF consultative rights on all draft legislation affecting workers. In addition, the unionists pushed for revival of the tripartite production committees that had existed in plants in the 1960s, with representatives of labor, management, and the ASU.

Over the next several months, Sadat agreed, at least in principle, to all these demands. The ETUF did, in return, make one important concession to Sadat during the meeting—scrapping the possibility of forming a separate workers' party. That Sadat sought guarantees against this, after retracting a key component of his economic liberalization scheme in the face of the strong labor protest, indicates the depth of his desire to prevent a unified political challenge from the union movement.

THE ADVANCED STAGE OF INFITAH: 1977–1987

The repression of the leftist activists in the lower levels of the union movement after the 1977 riots meant less pressure from below on confederation leaders to oppose liberalization. At the same time, Ahmad followed a more democratic style of leadership, seeking to ameliorate rather than exacerbate conflict. Although left and right poles continued to exist within the confederation leadership, the combination of these factors meant that it was a somewhat more moderate and considerably more unified labor movement that confronted the economic liberalization policies of the late 1970s and 1980s.

The Push toward Privatization

In 1978, some wholly owned state firms received authorization to sell shares, in spite of the limitations set in Law 111. In addition, two public-sector paper companies were given private-sector status as part of an agreement for World Bank assistance in their development, and one joint company was granted private-sector privileges at the request of its shareholders. There is no record of specific labor activity with regard to any of these developments. The reasons for this are unclear, but they probably reflect both the small number of workers affected and the changes in the confederation discussed above.

The confederation did respond rapidly and strongly, however, to a more substantive threat when Sadat appointed a new minister of industry in 1980. Taha Zaki promptly introduced a new scheme for selling shares in the public sector, which would have allowed the state to reduce its share in public-sector companies to 51 percent. Ahmad himself had endorsed a version of the proposal that spring, supporting the sale of 49 percent of failing parastatals through subscription. But Zaki's proposal was angrily denounced by most federation leaders in a meeting held October 13. Amid calls for convening an emergency general assembly of the ETUF, Ahmad proposed that the issue be decided at the upcoming confederation conference on "Promoting Production in the Peacetime Economy."

The other union leaders agreed, and although the conference had been in planning for well over a year, this issue became its main focus. After what was generally described as hot discussion, the overwhelming majority of participants rejected Zaki's proposal "in form and content, in the name of all Egyptian workers." The conference opposed "any trend toward selling the public sector or having private sector participation in it." Ahmad publicly announced the ETUF's position on television at the close of the conference.[21]

In October 1982, several ministers met with confederation leaders to discuss a new proposal for subscription in the public sector. The leaders concerned agreed to support the plan, which called for private participation to be limited to 49 percent of the shares in any company, with some modifications: the share price would be 100 pounds, not 1,000 as originally proposed; and the federations would have the right to appoint the Workers' Representatives to the Management (WRM) committees of the jointly owned companies, rather than having them elected by workers. This latter criterion, though obviously a step backwards for workers' democracy, would resolve the historic objection of some union leaders to the fact that the unions were not formally connected to the WRM system. However, some federations, such as the EEM, immediately objected to the new proposal. The left did also, and it was able to publicize the plan and advocate its opposition through *al-Ahali*, which had been given permission by Mubarak to resume publication in the summer of 1982. Leftists in the trade union movement pressed for meetings of locals and federations to discuss the scheme, and denunciations were reported in *al-Ahali*. Rejections came from a confederation regional meeting in Aswan, two large textile locals in Helwan, and five regional meetings of the Oil and Chemical Workers Federation. Then, it was quietly set aside.[22]

After this, there was a temporary respite in government-initiated schemes for direct sale of publicly owned assets. On May Day, 1983, President Mubarak committed himself to "no diminution and no sale of the public sector," a pledge he has repeated on numerous occasions since, and the issue faded for a while from the union and leftist press. By the end of 1985, though, public-sector advocates began to feel pressure from a new source, the recently formed and increasingly powerful private-sector businessmen's associations. Proclaiming the need for "awakening and preparation to confront the vicious campaign that some business-men are launching," the ETUF's executive committee charged that the entrepreneurs were pushing for the sale of inefficient parastatals and were seeking both to undermine workers' gains, especially the principle of WRM, and to diminish the role of unions in the public sector. In February 1986, the ETUF held another conference on the public sector, affirming its support for the parastatals and calling for the strengthening of the WRM system.[23]

The businessmen and the IMF revived proposals for selling the parastatals in 1987. This happened first at a conference on developing the public sector sponsored by the National Democratic Party (NDP). The opposition parties had essentially boycotted the meeting, making it, in effect, an NDP affair; selling some public-sector assets was one of the conference resolutions. Two months later, a new plan for subscription sales, this time involving the banks, was under preparation. Then, over the summer, Tourist Minister Fuad Sultan advocated subscription sales to Egyptians as well as foreigners in a magazine interview. A prominent journalist subsequently wrote that most ministers, especially then Prime Minister 'Ali Lutfi, supported Sultan's idea but were afraid to say so publicly. The ETUF itself did not issue a condemnation; the new acting ETUF president, Mukhtar 'Abd al-Hamid, expressed fear that such an action would have adverse consequences for the confederation.[24]

The immediate clamor over Sultan's proposal was quieted when Mubarak once again stated, in two separate speeches, that he opposed the sale of public-sector industry. Sultan pushed ahead with various methods of privatization in the tourist industry (see below). However, it seems fair to say that, through 1987, the opponents of selling parastatals had beaten back its advocates and that the labor unions have been a particularly important force in protecting the public sector. The left, of course, also deserves some credit for this, but labor's voice appears to have been taken more seriously by the ruling elite.

The Controversy over Joint Ventures

A subtle form of privatization, introduced through the *infitah* laws, is the involvement of parastatals in joint ventures with private concerns. Prior to 1974, any company which had partial state ownership was considered part of the public sector and subject to its laws; there were, as we have seen, thirty-two such companies at the time. Law 43 specified that any new joint ventures created with foreign firms would be considered part of the private sector. Public-sector firms could thus privatize part of their assets by entering into a joint venture with a Law 43 company (often referred to as investment companies).

Through the end of the 1970s, the Investment Authority approved 956 investment firms, mostly in the areas of agriculture, livestock, and building materials. The total capital of these projects was LE 3.1 billion, with public participation of about 30 percent. The number of Law 43 firms had increased to 1,281 by June 1984, with joint ventures involving the public sector representing just under 20 percent of the total; public participation in capital had fallen to an average of 27 percent. In industry, joint ventures involving the public sector have represented about 16 percent of all projects, with public capital contribution averaging 34 percent.[25]

Joint ventures created under the auspices of Law 43 were subject to the same exemptions from WRM and WSP (Workers Share in Profit) as fully private foreign firms. Thus, in those cases where a parastatal's entry into a joint venture involved a transfer of labor, the affected workers would lose benefits. And for the workforce as a whole, the rapid creation of joint ventures attenuated the philosophical principle that WRM and WSP are crucial to industrial development. The spread of joint ventures thus meant a direct loss of rights for some workers, and a more abstract takeaway for Egyptian labor as an aggregate.

Over time, the joint ventures became a lightning rod for criticisms of the *infitah* itself. Besides the diminution of labor's rights, leftists and nationalists (and some unaffiliated economists) charged that the schemes were undermining the national economy, citing cases where foreign firms had made their participation in projects contingent on cessation of local production of competing products. In other cases, the joint ventures' products shrunk the market for similar goods produced by parastatals or wholly Egyptian-owned private plants, causing them to run into the red. Critics also argued that many of the new ventures were ill-conceived and nonprofitable and that state participation in them was an unnecessary drain on the Treasury.

Labor was critical of the joint ventures for similar reasons. The confederation formed a committee to evaluate the experience of the projects late in 1979. One year later, at its 1980 conference on the peacetime economy, the ETUF passed a resolution calling for the participation of parastatals in projects with Arab and foreign investors to be limited to new capital creation (i.e., the involvement of existing public-sector capital in such projects was rejected). In practice, however, the ETUF did not undertake any campaigns against those projects which violated these stipulations; opposition to specific projects came from locals or federations rather than the ETUF leadership. At least in part, this would seem to reflect the fact that an individual project's real or potential effect on labor was limited to a circumscribed group of workers as opposed to subscription sales, which could "privatize" a large segment of the working class at one time. However, leftists within the union movement also see the ETUF's inactivity as a sign of the leadership's conciliatory attitude toward the regime.

The campaigns against individual projects met with mixed success. The first project which elicited a reaction from labor was a large textile scheme known as al-ʿAmiriyya, approved by the Investment Authority in 1977. With a workforce of 37,000, the $1.3 billion project was to produce yarn, polyester, fabric, and knitwear from a location near Alexandria. The Egyptian participant was the state-owned Bank Misr; the foreign partners were to be the Chemtex Co., an American firm, and the Misr-Iran Textile Company, itself a Law 43 concern. The Textile Workers' Federation prepared a detailed report opposing the project on the grounds that the current production of these goods was already sufficient to meet domestic and export demand. The new venture would therefore either drive existing textile firms out of business or find no market for its own wares, thus squandering the state's investment in it. In addition, the report argued, there was an insufficient supply of skilled textile workers to meet the labor demands of the project.

The project was opposed by other powerful forces as well, including the Ministry of Industry, the Ministry of Economy, the Federation of Egyptian Industries, and the World Bank. The objections raised by these groups led the Supreme Investment Committee to suspend the project's authorization in August 1978. A special parliamentary committee was formed to investigate, and it ultimately ruled in favor of the project, albeit with some revisions; but by the end of 1980, all but the polyester-production aspect of the proposal had been scrapped.

After ʿAmiriyya, all of the controversial projects were in the engineering sector, thus involving the EEM federation. The concentration of opposition there may in part reflect the fact that firms in this sector were entering joint ventures in proportionally greater numbers than other industries: at the end of 1981, a study prepared for the Consultative Assembly reported that while 25 percent of all parastatals were involved in or planning to join a new joint venture, a full 33 percent of the state-owned companies in engineering had already entered new joint-venture schemes.

EEM's opposition to joint ventures also reflects the presence of a nationalist/leftist tendency in the leadership of the federation and its associated locals. As will be recalled, Said Gumʿa, who has served as president of the EEM since 1971, was one of the militants in the earlier battles against privatization; and Niyazi ʿAbd al-ʿAziz, who served as the union's cultural secretary from 1976 until 1987, was a leader of the Tagammuʿ in its early years.[26] The party maintains a strong presence in a number of locals in the federation.

The first project challenged by the EEM was a proposed joint venture between the French-owned Thomson company and Egypt's Ideal, a parastatal producing refrigerators and washing machines. Approved by the Investment Authority in 1978, the proposal called for Ideal to contribute one of its plants to the new project, in which it would hold 49 percent ownership. The contract prohibited Ideal's other plants from manufacturing or marketing products which would compete with the output of the joint venture. Critics charged that this latter clause would lead to the idling of these plants and ultimate bankruptcy of Ideal. They also maintained that the proposal essentially meant selling an Ideal plant to Thomson, thus violating Law 111.

Between 1978 and 1980, the general assembly of the Ideal company rejected the proposal six times, but it was kept alive by the Investment Authority and the Ministry of Industry.[27] During this period the EEM prepared a report detailing its objections to the proposal. Aside from the dangers to the remaining Ideal plants and workforce, the report charged that workers at the plant to be transferred would lose up to two-thirds of their pay, since the contract called for maintaining their basic wage but not their incentives, bonuses, and profit shares; these, the report argued, amounted to 200 percent of the workers' basic salary. The proposal was finally brought up for what proved to be a heated discussion in Parliament in the spring of 1980, and the project eventually died there.

The dangers to Ideal predicted by opponents of the joint venture were not mere conjecture but were, in fact, based on experience elsewhere. Later in 1980, workers in the Alexandria Metal Products Co. (AMPC), an EEM local, sent an urgent memo to officials calling for intervention against a joint venture involving that firm with the Wilkinson Blade Company. That project was already underway, and it had entailed transfer of two of AMPC's plants to the joint venture. The workers charged that rather than modernize the plants, Wilkinson had deliberately allowed the existing machinery to deteriorate and then closed the factories, while flooding the market with imported blades manufactured by its plants in Great Britain. The idled workers were transferred to AMPC's other plants, but the company began to incur losses due to the competition from Wilkinson. In this case, there was apparently no action taken by officials against the project.

The most militant and enduring struggle around a joint venture has been over the Chloride Egypt project, a merger of the British-owned Chloride company with Egypt's General Battery Company (GBC) and a small amount of private capital. The project was initially proposed directly to Sadat by Chloride's president when the former visited Great Britain in 1975, and Chloride Egypt was formally established by the Ministry of the Economy in 1980. GBC consisted of two dry battery factories and one liquid battery plant located in ʿAmaraniyya. Under the agreement, the latter plant, which employed 600 workers, would be closed, and the two partners would open a new liquid battery factory. The accord called for 480 of ʿAmaraniyya's workers to be transferred to the new plant; the remainder would receive one year's severance pay. Chloride stipulated that the import of liquid batteries into Egypt be banned.[28]

The GBC local, upon learning of the project in the late 1970s, sent inquiries to the unions of Chloride workers in other countries seeking information about the company. The responses they received indicated that Chloride was not a successful firm. When the agreement was signed, the local, in conjunction with the EEM federation, raised a court case against it, relying in part on this information. The suit further charged that there was no technical necessity for the project. However, the court ruled that it was not empowered to decide the issue, effectively allowing the scheme to proceed.

The issue remained dormant until the fall of 1982, when the new factory was ready to open. Chloride Egypt announced that it would only accept 360 of ʿAmaraniyya's workers, 120 less than specified in the agreement, but nevertheless expected the old plant to be shut. The new factory would take some of ʿAmaraniyya's equipment, and the rest was to be sold as scrap. The local met and rejected the integration and closure orders. Some workers scheduled to be transferred resisted the orders; the management threatened them by refusing to release their incentive pay. Workers also tried to stop the closure of the ʿAmaraniyya plant. Several were arrested, and security forces were called in, under emergency laws, to close the factory at the beginning of 1983.

The local continued to fight after the closure. They challenged the government to let them take over the plant, and vowed to produce more than Chloride had proposed if provided with one million pounds for modernization. Finally, in the spring of 1983, the Ministry of Industry agreed to reopen the ʿAmaraniyya plant, transferring ownership and the remaining workforce to the National Plastics Company. The plant resumed production of liquid batteries, albeit on a much lower scale. Chloride opposed this arrangement. Former Prime Minister ʿAbd al-ʿAziz Higazi, who had assumed the management of the joint venture in 1982, charged that the government had yielded to labor pressure.[29]

Even after this victory, the joint venture has remained an issue, apparently a stalemate. The GBC local has continued to press for ʿAmaraniyya to be returned to GBC and for GBC to pull out of Chloride Egypt. Meanwhile, GBC began to incur losses and debts, and early in 1986 its president suggested eliminating it. The local charged that the company's poor performance was due to deliberate mismanagement by executives loyal to Chloride. (The president of GBC had been co-opted onto the management committee of Chloride Egypt, with a 400 percent increase in salary.) Local leaders frequently complain that the domestic price of liquid batteries rose from twenty-six to sixty-four pounds after Chloride assumed the bulk of their production. Chloride, for its part, continues to object to the resumption of liquid battery production at ʿAmaraniyya.

Among the most famous projects to generate controversy was a proposed joint venture between Egypt's Nasr Car Company (Nasco) and General Motors. At the time of the deal, Nasco was producing a small passenger car modeled by Fiat; the company also made trucks and tractors. Egyptian officials had sought the participation of a multinational car firm to upgrade Nasco's facilities for passenger-car production at its Helwan plant. GM was one of several bidders, proposing to produce a car based on designs by Opel, its West German subsidiary. The project had a cost of $700 million, of which $200 million would be for plant modernization; the remainder was for the establishment of twelve feeder plants to make parts for the auto. Financing was to come from the Misr-Iran Development Bank, Chase Manhattan Bank, US AID, and Egypt's new Export Development Bank.

The Tagammuʿ was the first to attack the project, accusing the United States of pressuring Egypt into accepting GM's bid. *Al-Ahali* charged that the company had twice declared that the proposal had been accepted before an actual agreement was reached, the first time coinciding with a visit by Mubarak to the United States and later during a visit by Assistant Secretary of State for Middle East Affairs Richard Murphy to Egypt. The choice was finally announced on June 16, 1986, when Defense Minister Abu Ghazzala was in the United States negotiating a military aid pact. Abu Ghazzala was head of the committee to select among the bids for the project, a break from previous procedure in which the Ministry of Industry and Investment Authority decided. The newspaper charged that the United States had made certain aid provisions contingent on Abu Ghazzala's acceptance of GM's bid.[30]

The Nasco workers had become increasingly concerned as an agreement grew near. Before GM's selection was announced, officials of the EEM met with the Nasco local and its elected workers representatives and formed a standing committee to study the project. They requested to receive all the documents pertaining to it from the Ministry of Industry. According to *al-Ahali,* the minister, angry at his own exclusion from the selection process, was initially hostile to GM and agreed to supply the papers. However, after the choice was made public, he reversed himself and reneged on his commitment. The local then sent telegrams to Parliament, to the cabinet, and to the minister, protesting the decision. When GM invited Nasco's management committee to the contract signing, the elected workers' delegates refused to attend.

The EEM council scheduled an emergency meeting for July. In the meanwhile, Nasco's managers, who had also not been consulted earlier about the choice, met to evaluate GM's proposal. On July 14, the managers gave conditional approval to the project, voicing nineteen reservations to which they expected GM to respond. The reservations concerned the speed with which the new venture would move to actual automobile manufacturing, rather than just assembly, decision making on imported inputs, the penalties to GM in case of contract violations, the responsibility for payment of foreign salaries, and the name to be placed on the autos. The federation endorsed these conditions. Then, at the general assembly of the EEM in October, the union members rejected the GM project "in form and content."[31]

The precise effect the project would have had on Nasco's labor force is unclear. *Al-Ahali* charged that GM planned to use robots on the assembly lines, which would render more than half the workers on passenger-car production lines superfluous. Mr. Rifaʿat A. Rahman, the director of government relations for GM Egypt, stated that there was so much excess employment at the factory that many workers actually moonlighted during working hours. Of 12,000 employees at the plant, he said, only about 2,500 were really necessary. He attributed the workers' hostility to the project to this; he stated that, even though those who would work for the joint venture would receive higher wages, all the workers were concerned about losing their jobs. However, Mr. Rahman did not actually state that GM would lay off workers, and the union did not explicitly raise this as a central concern.[32]

Between July and December, there were negotiations between GM and Egyptian officials over Nasco's terms, and no work on the project was begun. Nasco threatened to renew production of Fiats if the delays continued, and Nasco had resumed negotiations with the unsuccessful bidders on the project. When no work had begun by the end of December, the agreement with the Investment Authority became inoperative. Misr-Iran bank applied for and received a renewal, but in January GM announced that it wanted to review the agreement. The company cited the fall in the value of the Egyptian pound, changing conditions of production in Egypt, and restrictive laws on operation and expansion. This request was rejected by the Cabinet, which agreed to reconsider the contract only after work on the project had begun.

Al-Ahali reported on March 4 that Nasco officials, with the support of the Ministry of Industry, refused to conduct any further negotiations with GM and were set to resume Fiat production. Two weeks later, the paper said that GM had submitted a new proposal to the Investment Authority, prompting Nasco to formally request abrogation of the contract between Egypt and the multinational. The final cancellation of the project by the Ministry of Industry was not celebrated by *al-Ahali* until October 21, 1987. However, the *Middle East Economic Digest (MEED)* reported on June 20 that the scheme was "frozen," and on August 29 that it had "collapsed." The left attributed the defeat of the proposal to the opposition of labor and Nasco's managers; GM's reservations were portrayed as a smokescreen to deflect attention from the unpopularity of the project.

The full story of GM remains ambiguous. It does seem likely that in this case *al-Ahali* exaggerated the importance of labor's opposition to the project. At a minimum, the part played by Nasco's managers seems more important; it also appears that there was growing resistance to the project from the Ministry of Industry. Indeed, while it may have been GM, rather than Egypt, that ultimately withdrew from the agreement, there is some evidence that the tide among Egyptian officials has turned against joint ventures involving public-sector industries. In October 1986, the Ministry of Industry warned public-sector managers against such schemes and set restrictions limiting the companies to technical participation only, and only on the condition that the project's products not compete with the output of existing public-sector firms, except in food production.

On the whole, then, the record of labor opposition to joint ventures is mixed. At least some projects which violated the ETUF's stipulations did not encounter resistance from labor, and the confederation itself did not play a key role in the battles which did occur. Given this, it is difficult to give labor full credit for this recent restriction of joint ventures. On the other hand, the story of 'Amaraniyya and the projects challenged by the engineering federation do show that labor resistance, where it did occur, was able to at least modify the plans for certain projects and protect some of the rights of threatened workers.

Privatization in the Tourist Sector

The overwhelming majority of Egypt's large hotels are actually owned by public-sector companies, of which the largest is the Egyptian Hotel Company (EHC). Until the mid-1980s, the most successful of these were managed by private hotel companies under long-term leasing arrangements. Since Fuad Sultan became Minister of Tourism in September 1985, he has stressed the need to privatize the management of state-owned hotels; he made the like-minded Bahi al-Din Nasr chairman of EHC. Together they have aggressively sought to lease the EHC hotels to foreign companies, under contracts that require the lessee to renovate the facilities during an initial grace period.[33]

When Nasr took over the EHC, the company had 7,200 employees, with a ratio of employees to room of approximately 3.5:1. The new leasing arrangements commit the foreign firms to maintain a ratio of 1.4:1, about the world standard. The arrangements thus promised to cause layoffs. Before the first deals were concluded, Nasr and other Ministry of Tourism officials met with leaders of the General Union of Hotel and Tourist Workers (GUHTW), and they reached an agreement whereby workers laid off under new management agreements can remain on the payroll of the EHC. They continue to receive their basic salary, but they do not get incentives and bonuses; their pay thus amounts to about 66 percent of previous earnings. Nasr also offered early retirement to about 1800 workers.[34]

The EHC reports that its workforce has declined to 3,500, including 500 workers on basic salary, and that it has realized considerable savings from the employee reduction. For its part, the GUHTW feels that its agreement with the EHC has protected its members from job loss due to privatization. Nevertheless, the federation remains opposed to the leasing deals, in part because the EHC is now required to keep unproductive workers on its payroll; in a personal interview Ibrahim Mustafa, president of GUHTW, charged that this renders the deals unprofitable for the parastatal. Union leaders also told me both that the EHC undervalues the property it leases and that the land's worth is increasing dramatically over time. In summary, Mustafa stated, "Our opposition to privatization is not based on workers' rights. It is based on economics and on nationalism."

The agreement between the GUHTW and the Ministry will also apply in the case of direct sales of hotels to private concerns. As of 1991, Sultan has overseen the sale to private investors of the Hurghada Sheraton, a joint venture between Sheraton Hotels and the public-sector Misr el-Kubra Hotels Company, the San Stefano in Alexandria, and the Cairo Meridien.

On the whole, privatization appears to have proceeded more rapidly in the tourist sector than in manufacturing. In part this would seem to reflect a greater commitment to it from the Mubarak regime; the president's selection of Sultan, known as a fierce advocate of privatization, to head up the Ministry is indicative of this. But even here, there were limits to how far the regime was willing to go in confronting opposition from labor, nationalists, and leftists. The sale of the San Stefano in Alexandria was temporarily blocked, and the government's deal with the GUHTW attenuated the benefits of the leasing deals for the state treasury. This again demonstrates that the ruling elite's commitment to economic reform is strongly tempered by a desire to avoid alienating organized labor.

CONCLUSIONS

The pace of privatization in Egypt has been slow. To be sure, the economy has been transformed since 1974: Western imports abound; the private sector plays a larger role in investment; and Western firms have penetrated the country. In some areas, such as construction and banking, the growth of domestic private and foreign enterprise has been dramatic. Still, the public sector remains the dominant force in the economy, and precious few firms have actually changed from public to private sector ownership.

From the preceding pages it should be clear that opposition from labor has been a formidable roadblock on the path to privatization. There are, of course, other factors involved; advocates of further liberalization often cite mismanagement and bureaucratic inertia. There is also the obvious economic problem that private investors will be reluctant to take over parastatals that are losing money, while there is little justification for the state to shed successful enterprises. The role of state managers in the controversies over privatization needs further clarification.

It is not possible to determine to what degree labor resistance, as opposed to these other factors, has been responsible for the lack of further change. There are, however, important differences in the way labor has reacted to the separate policies associated with liberalization, and in the outcome of the disputes. By identifying and evaluating these differences, it is possible to draw some conclusions as to the ways in which labor opposition has influenced policy decisions.

Labor's response to the various types of privatization can be compared across several different dimensions of what might be considered the overall *strength* of opposition. The first of these concerns the *degree* of rejection: was it outright or only partial? Second, there is the *breadth* of opposition: was the entire union movement involved, or only certain sections or strata? Third, is the *unity* of the reaction: was there general consensus on the issue among those actors involved, or were there important divisions? Finally, we must consider the *militancy* of the opposition, which could range from merely public denunciation of a policy to a general strike or riot.

Among the schemes studied here, privatization through subscription sales ranks first in overall strength of opposition. At the outset, the ETUF's rejection of the policy was not complete; disunity within the ranks of the confederation leadership stood in the way of a firmer stance. But even the ETUF's watered-down statement on Law 111 insisted that subscription sales should not lead to public-sector firms being reclassified as private concerns, which would adversely affect the security and benefits of the workforce. After Gharib's ouster, the confederation's rejection of subscription sales was more unified. In both periods, the depth of opposition was great; the ETUF's position reflects the concerns of rank and file workers in both sectors of the economy. There has not been any visible militancy on this issue per se, but that must be put in the perspective of the lack of implementation of the policy itself; the fear of widespread militancy could well have been behind the regime's decision not to pursue these plans.

Proposals for the direct sales of public enterprises were limited to the commerce sector. Since only a circumscribed group of workers were threatened by this, the breadth of reaction was small relative to the above issues. Among those affected, the degree of opposition was complete, and the workers involved exhibited a moderate level of militancy; there were strikes at the two small textile factories and a considerable degree of mobilization and public agitation on the part of the commerce federation. However, disunity outside the federation, in particular within the ETUF executive committee, prevented a complete victory for the federation's campaign.

The degree of opposition to joint ventures has been only partial, with the ETUF's official policy rejecting only those projects involving existing (as opposed to new) public-sector capital or competing with public-sector firms for the local market. Like direct-sale proposals, each individual joint-venture project affects only a relatively small group of workers. Accordingly, the breadth of resistance to these projects overall has not been great. As we have seen, the confederation essentially left opposition to joint ventures to the locals and federations involved, and some projects never became a source of controversy. Where labor has opposed specific projects, however, it has been with a moderate degree of both militancy and success.

Labor's overall opposition was weakest with regard to the *infitah*. Although some leftists in the confederation pushed for a stronger stance, the consensus position of the union movement was essentially to oppose denationalization of the economy only in so far as it threatened the public sector. Some federations did take a stand against particular imports or foreign investments, but there was no mass activity and apparently little agitation behind these declarations. Although the effects of the opening have been uneven across different sectors of the economy, on the whole the *infitah* has progressed more rapidly than subsidy reform or privatization. Labor opposition does not appear to have been more than a small stone among what roadblocks the opening has encountered.

It thus appears that labor pressure has been the most effective where it has been the broadest and most unequivocal (i.e., on the issue of privatization through subscription sales). Conversely, the government has been more successful in implementing those policies where resistance has been more circumscribed (i.e., joint ventures and direct sales of parastatals). But even there, militant reactions from labor have been able to defeat or modify some proposals. The *infitah,* where labor opposition has been weakest, has been the most successful of the liberalization policies studied here.

Given this, it is difficult to avoid the conclusion that Egyptian policy makers are fearful of labor unrest. Repression has been used to suppress outbreaks of militancy, as with the Chloride workers and the 1977 food riots, but it has been used in conjunction with conciliation; the regime appears to recognize that force alone can at best temporarily offset insurgency from discontented workers. In short, both the Sadat and Mubarak governments have been ready to back off of schemes for economic reform in order to prevent a unified political challenge from labor.

The long and rocky road which Egypt has traveled in its privatization attempts augurs poorly for those countries which are just embarking on a similar course. So long as the public sector is providing workers with jobs and benefits that the private sector cannot or will not offer, labor will resist the sale or dismantling of parastatals; protests against privatization are apt to become as commonplace as bread riots. The militancy may not be as violent or as widespread, particularly where governments pursue a phased approach rather than attempting one massive sell-off. And, as with subsidy removal, some regimes will be able to manage the conflict better than others. Nevertheless, privatization in the Third World on the whole appears destined to be politically problematic until its proponents recognize the need to protect the interests of the public-sector workforce that is threatened by these policies.

Since the research for this chapter was concluded, the agencies involved in Egypt's privatization effort appear to have moved in this direction: recent IMF and World Bank agreements with Egypt reportedly included a special "social fund" to ameliorate the detrimental effects of liberalizing reforms on workers and the un-employed. The Egyptian government has also apparently sought to attenuate labor opposition to privatization by adopting a phased approach which targetted smaller plants outside of Cairo, where unions are weakest. These measures, however, fail to address the underlying sources of labor opposition to privatization, which re-volve around the disparities in working hours and conditions, health and accident insurance, pensions, vacation, and job security between the public and private sectors; as mentioned earlier, in many cases these differences are the result of the evasion of labor laws by private concerns. This suggests that ultimately, if the government wants to remove itself from the productive sphere without suffering a substantial loss of public support, it will need to expand its activities in the realm of regulation.

Notes

This chapter grew out of field research conducted in Egypt between June 1987 and July 1988, which was generously funded by the American Research Center in Egypt, Inc., Ful-bright-Hays, and the Social Science Research Council. Personal interviews with several dozen rank and file workers, as well as leftists active in labor affairs, contributed to the information and analysis contained here. I would like to thank Thomas M. Callaghy, Iliya Harik, John Waterbury, and Robert Vitalis for helpful comments on earlier drafts of this chapter; any remaining errors are, of course, my own.

PERIODICAL ABBREVIATIONS USED IN REFERENCES

A   *al-Ahram*, main official newspaper
Ah   *al-Ahali*, newspaper of the opposition Tagammuᶜ Party
AI   *al-Ahram al-Iqtisadi*, official weekly economics magazine
Am   *al-'Amal*, monthly magazine of the Ministry of Labor
RY   *Rose al-Yusef*, leftist weekly magazine
SA   *Sawt al-ᶜAmal*, nonperiodic rank and file magazine

T   *al-Tali'a,* leftist monthly journal
TS   *Tali'at al Sina'a,* monthly magazine of the EEM federation
U   *al-'Ummal,* weekly newspaper of the ETUF

1. See Amani Qandil, "sun' al-qarar fi Misr" (Policy making in Egypt) (Ph.D. diss., Dept. of Economics and Politics, Cairo University, 1985); Ahmad Faris 'Abd al-Munim, "jama'at al-Masalih" (Interest groups), in Ali Al-Din Hilal, ed., *al-Nizam al-Siyasi* (The political system) (Cairo: Arab Center for Research and Publication, 1982); and Mustafa Kamil al-Sayyid, *al-Mujtama' wa al-siyasa fi misr: dur jama'at al-masalih fi al-nizam al-siyasi al-misri, 1952–1981* (Society and politics in Egypt: The role of interest groups in the Egyptian political system) (Cairo: Arab Future Publishing House, 1983); Robert Bianchi, *Unruly Corporatism: Associational Life in Twentieth Century Egypt* (Oxford: Oxford University Press, 1989).

2. This is the English translation of *al-Ittihad al-'amm lil-Naqabat 'ummal Misr* used by that organization. However, different translations which have been used by other scholars, such as the Egyptian Trade Union *Confederation,* or the *Confederation of Egyptian Trade Unions,* are technically more accurate; the organization is in fact a conglomeration of (a variable number of) federations. I use the official translation here in deference to the organization, but I will also refer to it in text as "the confederation." Each of the federations which make up the ETUF is known in Arabic as *niqaba 'amma,* which is translated by these organizations as "General Union." As with the ETUF, I use these organizations' own literal translations for their formal names, but refer to them in the text as federations.

3. For more details, see Posusney, "Workers against the State: Wage Protest in Egypt 1952–1988" (paper presented at the annual meeting of the Middle East Studies Association, Los Angeles, 1988).

4. This story is based on extensive interviews with current and former labor leaders, union functionaries, leftists of various tendencies, and labor historians. For more details, see my Ph.D. dissertation, "Workers against the State: Actors, Issues and Outcomes in Egyptian Labor/State Relations, 1952–87" (University of Pennsylvania, 1991).

5. Muhammad Khalid, *al-Haraka al-Niqabiyya bayn al-madi wal-mustaqbal* (The union movement between the past and present) (Cairo: Institute of the Cooperative House for Printing and Publishing, 1975), pp. 88–91.

6. Ibid, p. 105.

7. Sayyid 'Umar, "al-niqabat al-'ummaliyya wa al-sulta al-siyasiyya ma'a dirasa tatbiqiyya 'ala al-ittihad al-'amm li-niqabat 'ummal misr, 1957–86" (Workers unions and political authority, with an applied study of the ETUF) (Master's thesis, Political Science Dept., Assiut University, 1987), pp. 249–61.

8. *U,* 14 April 1975, pp. 5–7.

9. The influx of foreign capital "should not take control over the basic structure of our national wealth, and must be in accordance with our development needs." The remainder of the document committed the union movement to struggle for the protection of the "workers' gains of the July Revolution." ETUF, 1977, pp. 93–94.

10. Personal interview with 'Abd al-Rahman Khair, October 1987; Qandil, *Sun' al-Qurar,* p. 459; al-Sayyid, *al-Mujtama'* p. 81.

11. John Waterbury, *The Egypt of Nasser and Sadat: Political Economy of Two Regimes* (Princeton: Princeton University Press, 1983), p. 139; Khalid, *al-Haraka,* pp. 95–103. The committee report was reviewed in a lengthy article by Said Sonbol, in *Akhbar al-Yom,* 9 February 1974 (reprinted in Khalid, *al-Haraka).*

12. For example, one law requires joint-stock companies with more than fifty employees to have a consultative committee with 50 percent workers' representation.

13. Sayyid 'Umar, *al-niqabat,* pp. 249–50.

14. Fathi Mahmud Mustafa, "sharkh fi ittihad al-'ummal" (Fissures in the workers' confederation), *RY,* 15 September 1975, pp. 18–19, and personal interview, July 1988; *T* (May 1974): 113–14.

15. *A,* 2 June 1975; Mahmoud interview, July 1988; *RY,* no. 2450, 26 April 1975, pp. 3–6, and no. 2451, 2 May 1975, pp. 14–17.

16. Fuad Mursi, *Hadha al-infitah al-iqtisadi* (Cairo: New Culture House, 1984) (2nd printing), pp. 151–59; Mahmud al-Maraghi, *al-qita' al-'amm fi mujtama' mutaghayyar: tajrubat Misr* (Cairo: Arab Future Publishing House, 1983), pp. 82–92; 'Issam Rif'at, *"Bi' ishum al-qita' al-'am: tanmiyya am tasfiyya?"* Al no. 481, 1 September 1975, pp. 6–8; *RY,* no. 2706, 5 May 1980, pp. 8–11.

17. Rifa'at, pp. 6–7; Qandil, "sun'," p. 460; *A,* 2 June 1975; *U,* 9 June 1975.

18. *Am,* no. 146, July 1975, p. 14; Qandil, "sun'"; Rifa'at, *Bi',* pp. 6–7.

19. For details on the formation of union platforms and their evolution into political parties, see Waterbury, *Egypt of Nasser and Sadat,* pp. 364–73. This account of the unionists' political affiliations is based on numerous interviews, especially with: Niyazi 'Abd al-'Aziz, then cultural secretary of the EEM and head of the Tagammu' labor bureau; 'Aisha 'Abd al-Hadi, then and still an officer of the chemical workers' federation; Muhammed Gamal Imam, a longtime ETUF functionary, now retired; and 'Abd al-Hamid al-Sheikh, current head of the Tagammu's labor bureau.

20. These figures are from Raymond Hinnebusch, *Egyptian Politics under Sadat: The Post-Populist Development of an Authoritarian-Modernizing State* (Cambridge: Cambridge University Press, 1984), p. 71; and Raymond Baker, *Egypt's Uncertain Revolution under Nasser and Sadat* (Cambridge, Mass.: Harvard University Press, 1978), p. 165. See also Muhammad Heikel, *Autumn of Fury* (London: Corgi Books, 1984), pp. 116–17; Heikel says that 5,000 were arrested and tried.

21. *RY,* 26 March 1987, p. 4, and 10 November 1980, p. 7.

22. *Ah,* 1982: 3, 10, 17 November; 1, 8 December.

23. Amani Qandil, "Jama'at al-masalih wa tatawwur al-nizam al-siyasi al-Misri." Paper presented at the Conference of the Faculty of Economics and Political Science, Cairo University, April 2–3, 1986; *AH,* 1986: 8 January, 26 February; 'Umar, *al-Niqabat,* p. 246.

24. *Ah,* 1987: 21 January; 4 March; 2, 9, September.

25. Not all such projects involve the participation of a state-owned industrial firm. In many cases, the public participant is a bank or insurance company. There are also projects in which the state's contribution is real estate. See al-Maraghi, al-qita', pp. 94–95. However, there are at least five industrial joint ventures which compete with the very parastatals that participate in them. 'Adil Harun and Samia Sa'id, "Ma zal sinariyo tasfiyya al-sina'a al-wataniyya wa istinzaf al-mal al-'amm mustamiran," *Al* no. 914, 21 September 1986, p. 65.

26. After leaving the party, 'Abd al-'Aziz went on to become a founding member of the not-yet-legalized Nasirist Socialist Party. In the 1987 elections, he moved up to general-secretary of the federation, while Gum'a retained the presidency.

27. The general assembly is literally a meeting of shareholders. In wholly publicly owned companies, the shareholders consist of the company's management and various other officials appointed by the Minister of Industry. The assembly normally meets once a year to approve the production plan for the factory. Samir Youssef, *System of Management in Egyptian Public Enterprises* (Cairo: AUC Press, 1983), pp. 128–29.

28. The Chloride story is compiled from the following sources: interviews with 'Abd al-'Aziz Higazi, president of the Chloride-Egypt management council, 30 January 1988, and Fayyiz Mahmud al-Karta, president of the GBC local, 7 February 1988; *Sowt al-'Amal,* no. 4, (January 1986), and no. 5 (May 1986); *Awraq 'Ummaliyya,* no. 2 (May 1985); *RY,* no. 2715, 23 June 1980; *AI,* no. 617, (10 November 1980; and *Al-Ahali,* from successive issues, 29 September 1982 through 19 May 1983, and 6 June 1985, 12 February 1986, and 27 November 1986. Discrepancies in the accounts, where relevant, are noted.

29. Higazi said that workers' salaries were doubled when they transferred to the joint venture, and claimed that it was only leftists among the workforce who opposed the project.

30. *Ah,* 1986: 19 March, 16 June, 2 July.

31. *Ah,* 1986: 2 July; 15, 29 October; *TS,* no. 21, July 1986, pp. 4–5, and no. 22, December 1986, p. 17.

32. Interview with Rifaʿat A. Rahman, January 1987.

33. *Business Monthly* (magazine of the American Chamber of Commerce in Egypt), December 1987, p. 46.

34. Ibid; and interview with Mustafa Ibrahim Mustafa, president of the GUHTW, July 1988.

CHAPTER

6

CONSTRAINTS TO PRIVATIZATION IN TURKEY

Marcie J. Patton

Since the adoption of liberalizing, export-oriented economic reforms in Turkey in 1980, a widespread consensus has developed on the need to reduce the public sector's share of economic activity and, correspondingly, to increase the participation and contribution of the private sector in the economy, particularly in the export arena. Both of these goals have been apparent in the post-1980 agenda of privatization which, fashioned under the leadership of Turgut Ozal, has included ambitious plans (although few offerings) for the sale of state-owned economic enterprises, and a complex system consisting of as many as five export-incentive regimes designed to stimulate and sustain an export drive by Turkish private manufacturers.

Privatization in Turkey has moved along these two tracks: the transfer of state-owned productive assets to private ownership, and the development of incentives to encourage and sustain an export drive propelled by large export trading companies in the private sector. Over time, however, results have lagged behind state intentions. Changes in the public-private mix have not been dramatic, and barriers to rapid privatization have emerged.

The purpose of this chapter is to offer some insight as to why the public-private division of labor remains so resistant to change, insight gained by assessing the record of privatization and by analyzing obstacles that have blocked the progress of reform.

CONTINUITIES IN THE PRIVATE-PUBLIC DIVISION OF LABOR

Since the establishment of a mixed economy and the creation of State Economic Enterprises (SEEs) over a half century ago, the question of an appropriate balance between the public and private sectors has remained politically controversial. In the early years of Turkish industrial development, state entrepreneurship was re-garded as imperative for the establishment of an industrial base. During the etatist period in Turkey (1933–38) an institutional and legal framework for direct state intervention in the economy was established, and the state was assigned a strategic role in developing infrastructure and basic industries. However, the private sector was not de jure excluded from similar activities. Although the public sector quickly established dominance across a wide range of industrial activities, the private sec-tor has registered steady growth and expansion, particularly during the years of planned import substitution industrialization (1960–80).

While the participation of the public sector in the economy does not appear to be shrinking, within the parameters of a mixed-economy framework, there has been a consistent and continuous secular trend showing movement of the private sector into a leading role in the production of consumer and investment goods. Since 1980, the private sector has shouldered primary responsibility for the man-ufacture of Turkey's principal exports while the state has focused on such support services as: developing Turkey's infrastructure (roads, railroads, irrigation, and en-ergy); providing key intermediate inputs (petrochemicals, steel, cement, paper) to private industry; offering export rebates; and promising to provide special facilities to assist exporters (by converting the State Investment Bank to an Eximbank and establishing marketing centers abroad). However, this division of labor is quite similar to that which prevailed during the period of import-substituting industrial-ization.

THE CHARACTER OF INDUSTRIAL DEVELOPMENT

The importance of industrial development can be seen in the rather dramatic shift in emphasis from agriculture to industry. The share of GDP (Gross Domestic Prod-uct) contributed by agriculture began to fall swiftly in the sixties[1] when planned import-substitution industrialization was introduced. In terms of the rate of GDP growth, since the 1960s when industrialization was begun in earnest, industry has tended to make a more substantial contribution to GDP than both the agricultural and services sectors.[2] Of particular note is that until the period of economic stag-nation and crisis in the latter half of the 1970s, the rate of increase in GDP by agricultural production fell well behind the contribution of industry.

After 1980, industry surged ahead as the leading economic sector contributing to the growth rate of GDP between 1980 and 1984 at nearly triple the difference from agriculture (compare 7.2 percent with 2.5 percent). Since 1984, agriculture has grown only half as fast as industry. From the tables it can be seen that, re-gardless of whether the strategy of either import-substitution industrialization or export-promotion industrialization was preferred, rapid expansion of the industrial sector has clearly been the focus of development efforts in Turkey.

STRUCTURE OF THE MANUFACTURING SECTOR

The principal beneficiary of the industrial development drive in Turkey has been the manufacturing sector, with mining, energy, housing, tourism, and banking services tending to attract greater investment attention only of late. There has been a clear secular trend in the direction of emphasizing production of intermediate and investment goods over consumer goods. Changes in the distribution of the labor force across sectors reflect this trend as well. In the early phase of Import-Substitution Industrialization (ISI), consumer goods accounted for over half of value added in manufacturing (51.1 percent in 1963). However, during the deepening phase of ISI in the 1970s, the contribution of consumer goods to value added declined, falling to 33.4 percent by 1980 while the contribution of intermediate and investment goods to value added increased significantly.[3] While consumer industries still carry substantial weight in the manufacturing sector, Turkish manufacturing has undergone considerable diversification and deepening in the direction of more technologically advanced and specialized branches of production. It is important to recognize that these transformations in Turkish manufacturing pre-date the introduction of the liberalization reforms and emphasis on exports of manufactured goods.

ECONOMIC PERFORMANCE OF THE PUBLIC AND PRIVATE SECTORS

A comparison of the public and private sectors shows an interesting divergence in concentration of manufacturing activity (see table 1). The state sector exhibits a strong preference for holding on to consumer-goods industries over time, but has shifted its production emphasis to its intermediate-goods industries. The private sector, in terms of production, employment, and value added, evidences a transformation away from consumer towards intermediate- and investment-goods industries with a pronounced movement towards investment-goods industries at the expense of consumer industries. However, both the state and private sectors are converging in their emphasis on intermediate goods production.

Structural changes in private as compared to public manufacturing in Turkey are shown in the following tables. Table 2 uses the number of firms in each sector as an indicator of the concentration of ownership. Three significant observations emerge: First, contrary to assertions that capital was becoming increasingly concentrated throughout the 1970s, the number of privately owned firms more than doubled between 1971 and 1980 with all sectors (except for tobacco) multiplying in number of firms.[4] Second, this trend is dramatically *reversed* after 1980 when the number of private-sector firms within a short period of three years falls to below the number existing in 1971. This reflects the huge number of bankruptcies

TABLE 1

The Structure of Manufacturing in the State and Private Sectors, 1955–83 (percent)

	1955	1963	1971	1980	1983
		Firms			
State Sector					
Consumer goods	54.3	55.8	55.3	63.7	60.8
Intermediate goods	28.6	30.4	25.7	26.2	26.8
Investment goods	17.1	13.8	18.8	10.0	12.2
Private Sector					
Consumer goods	58.5	59.6	46.0	37.8	38.3
Intermediate goods	35.3	26.6	30.8	34.3	34.6
Investment goods	6.2	13.8	17.8	26.3	25.1
		Employment			
State Sector					
Consumer goods	60.8	55.8	51.9	52.0	48.9
Intermediate goods	18.5	24.6	31.6	35.6	37.6
Investment goods	20.7	19.6	16.3	12.4	13.3
Private Sector					
Consumer goods	72.8	60.5	47.7	43.3	44.4
Intermediate goods	23.5	26.7	28.5	30.9	29.5
Investment goods	3.7	12.8	20.6	24.9	25.1
		Value Added			
State Sector					
Consumer goods	78.0	50.2	49.0	30.1	32.4
Intermediate goods	13.2	37.6	44.9	62.4	61.6
Investment goods	8.1	11.7	5.6	7.5	6.0
Private Sector					
Consumer goods	63.8	52.2	39.6	35.6	34.5
Intermediate goods	30.5	28.4	36.6	39.4	38.3
Investment goods	4.7	18.0	21.9	24.4	26.5

Sources: Robert Bianchi, *Interest Groups and Political Development in Turkey* (Princeton, N.J.: Princeton University Press, 1984), p. 48; State Institute of Statistics, *Turkiye Istatistik Yillig 1985* (Ankara: Devlet Istatistik Enstitusu Matbaasi, 1985), pp. 256–67.

which occurred following the introduction of the 1980 reforms. Third, up to 1980 privately owned firms multiplied in the intermediate and investment fields, and public-sector firms increased in consumer- and investment-goods industries; however, in the early 1980s, the number of public-sector firms rose in the intermediate- and investment-goods industries such that there was an overall increase in the number of public-sector firms from 1980 to 1983. The same trend towards increasing concentration on intermediate and investment goods is apparent in the private sector when a comparison is made between 1971 and 1983; the number of consumer-goods firms is down but intermediate and investment industries have picked up.

In table 3, firm size as determined by the number of workers is presented. Of particular note is that public-sector firms employ many more workers per firm than their counterparts in the private sector (with the exception of furniture, leather and rubber products). Overemployment in the public sector has been an oft-noted political patronage device that the 1980 reforms attempted to curb, and judging from table 3, a modest degree of restraint has been exercised. Using 1980 as a threshold, the public-sector firms have trimmed and scaled back the number of their employees whereas the private sector, while halving the number of firms, has doubled the average number of workers per firm.

However, even after 1980, the scale of industry remains comparatively larger in the public than the private sector. Since 1980, the larger public-sector firms are in the intermediate-goods industries while incremental growth in the size of private-sector firms appears to be favoring the investment-goods sector. This division of labor suggests that the state remains an important supplier of industrial materials to the private sector (especially petrochemicals, nonmetallic minerals, and metal products). It also suggests that the private sector is expanding its scale of production in the capital-intensive sectors of transportation equipment and heavy machinery as well as doubling firm size between 1980 and 1983 in most of the consumer goods industries.

Productivity of the private and public sectors increased markedly after 1970. Most remarkable is the more than tenfold increase in value added per worker in *both* the private and public sectors (with the exception of state manufacturing of consumer goods) between 1971 and 1980, given that negative growth rates were experienced in the late 1970s. Between 1980 and 1983, there is a two- to threefold increase in value added per worker for both sectors.[5] The public sector leads productivity in intermediate goods while the private sector is clearly making significant strides in investment goods and appears to be closing the gap with the public sector for consumer goods.

Among the consumer-goods industries, the private sector shows much greater productivity (except for beverages) than the public sector, which has a higher worker per firm ratio.

Since 1980, there appears to be strong sectoral competition between the state and private sectors in most consumer industries (with the exception of clothing and beverages), but a more scattered picture emerges when the intermediate and investment industries are examined. Paper, rubber, nonmetallic minerals, and metal products appear to be competitive intermediate industries, as are metal products and nonelectrical machinery products in the investment industries. There appears to be a tacit division of labor in which the private producers have opted for man-

Concentration and Productivity in Manufacturing, 1955–83
(number of firms by industrial sector)

	State Sector					Private Sector				
	1955	1963	1971	1980	1983	1955	1963	1971	1980	1983
Food	24	63	103	164	167	1,271	822	1,093	1,552	633
Beverages	13	18	18	23	24	33	24	55	66	43
Tobacco	18	27	29	28	27	188	40	31	18	28
Textiles	23	22	30	41	31	856	689	812	1,143	654
Clothing	2	2	3	4	5	20	32	115	362	247
Wood	10	18	23	26	24	233	76	144	195	82
Furniture	—	—	—	—	5	33	40	109	131	46
Paper	2	2	6	8	9	12	24	61	133	80
Printing	4	6	9	10	7	108	115	190	216	87
Leather	—	—	—	—	—	53	63	92	138	71
Rubber	—	—	—	1	1	72	99	113	535	232
Chemicals	9	13	11	18	19	475	153	250	417	217
Petrochemicals	3	6	7	7	7	2	1	8	31	23
Nonmetallic mins.	5	18	22	26	27	388	119	282	570	362
Basic metals	9	9	7	11	13	58	29	162	481	252
Metal products	11	14	12	6	8	88	209	320	779	349
Nonelec. mach.	3	3	19	17	20	102	80	227	597	288
Electrical mach.	—	1	2	5	9	8	47	125	409	215
Transport. equip.	11	15	29	13	14	55	40	148	396	202
Other[a]	—	—	—	—	1	—	—	—	133	83
Total	156	237	330	408	418	4,106	2,775	4,571	8,302	4,194
Consumer goods	80	132	183	260	254	2,368	1,607	2,106	3,141	1,605
Intermediate goods	42	72	85	107	112	1,434	719	1,411	2,847	1,452
Investment goods	25	33	62	41	51	253	376	820	2,181	1,054

Sources: Robert Bianchi, *Interest Groups and Political Development in Turkey* (Princeton: Princeton University Press, 1984), pp. 50–53; State Institute of Statistics, *Turkiye Istatistik Yillig 1985* (Ankara: Devlet Istatistik Enstitusu Matbaasi, 1985), pp. 256–67.
[a]Not included in calculation of consumer, intermediate, and investment breakdown.

ufacturing consumer and investment goods and the public sector has focused on intermediate goods. Even within these branches of industry (consumer, intermediate, investment), there are clearly certain sectors reserved to each. Hence, in spite of the promises of the new economic model to radically restructure the private-public balance, the diversification of manufacturing still reflects a tacit compartmentalization of the public and private domains.

THE STATE AS A PRODUCER

The economic policies adopted soon after the War of Independence in 1923 reflected the "liberal," procapitalist orientation of the indigenous business community. State intervention in the economy took the form of fostering the development of the private sector through the granting of virtual monopoly rights to private entrepreneurs, the establishment of the Business Bank (Is Bankasi), and other sundry incentives. However, the advent of the Great Depression strengthened proponents of stronger protectionist controls, proponents who were responsible for introducing the etatist policies of the 1930s. Between 1933 and 1938, a number of public enterprises were founded in the banking, manufacturing, agriculture, transportation, mining, and energy sectors. During the late 1930s, the state emerged as the major producer in the economy in addition to dominating investments.[6]

The initial motivation for establishing SEEs was to accelerate economic development and to contribute to the development of the private sector. The SEEs, however, were quickly subject to political interference. Every ruling party in Turkey has used the SEEs as a patronage device to distribute benefits to its supporters. While by law the SEEs were promised administrative and financial autonomy, over the years the hiring and promotion of SEE managers was governed by partisan considerations, as was the practice of overemployment. Managerial control of SEEs was further undermined by the power of the cabinet to fix the prices of basic goods and services. Because the prices of SEE products were not market determined but served sociopolitical objectives (such as supplying cheap raw materials and intermediate inputs to the private sector, and inexpensive goods and public services to the populace), the SEEs were not self-financed. Financially the SEEs drew on public funds (transfers from the Central Bank and Treasury funds) to cover their losses as well as their need for investment credits.

During the foreign-exchange and debt crisis of the late 1970s, the number of SEEs reporting losses and the size of these losses ballooned. Despite the adverse impact of global oil-price increases in this period, SEE investment programs were expanded, militant wage demands of public-sector workers were met, excessive hiring practices were continued by weak coalition governments, and SEE prices of energy and other basic products continued to be subsidized. Consequently, the financial burden of the SEEs on the Treasury rose rapidly, worsening the deterioration in the economy and contributing to the view that SEE reform was essential.

The post-1980 privatization plans for the public sector have been targeted at

Concentration and Productivity in Manufacturing, 1955–83
(workers per firm by industrial sector)

	State Sector					Private Sector				
	1955	1963	1971	1980	1983	1955	1963	1971	1980	1983
Food	495	460	374	353	322	16	43	41	42	89
Beverages	207	217	256	246	219	15	29	94	94	153
Tobacco	792	515	890	1,795	1,589	160	70	203	142	153
Textiles	1,120	1,380	1,050	807	1,040	59	105	118	116	215
Clothing	850	1,150	735	583	607	10	19	40	37	91
Wood	210	200	182	203	257	10	19	40	44	78
Furniture	—	—	—	—	78	12	23	26	26	67
Paper	1,700	3,450	2,200	1,523	1,362	17	25	49	43	80
Printing	125	150	189	248	285	23	35	43	37	90
Leather	—	—	—	—	—	19	32	40	30	59
Rubber	—	—	—	53	53	72	60	67	41	84
Chemicals	200	415	663	783	861	21	30	67	71	108
Petrochemicals	167	300	542	1,064	1,087	10	20	100	84	136
Nonmetallic mins.	200	316	441	431	418	28	120	98	84	131
Basic metals	890	1,185	3,320	4,505	3,789	10	31	67	52	99
Metal products	530	650	550	418	376	31	57	73	44	97
Nonelec. mach.	330	400	205	735	692	13	49	79	58	117
Electrical mach.	—	100	550	430	478	25	119	103	70	132
Transport. equip.	1,170	1,000	712	1,428	1,161	11	55	89	74	168
Other[a]	—	—	—	—	482	—	—	—	34	66
Total	605	590	600	704	671	34	65	72	61	124
Consumer goods	710	600	558	574	540	42	70	74	70	144
Intermediate goods	405	490	735	956	941	22	68	66	55	105
Investment goods	780	840	520	871	733	19	62	82	58	123

Sources: Robert Bianchi, *Interest Groups and Political Development in Turkey* (Princeton: Princeton University Press, 1984), pp. 50–53; State Institute of Statistics, *Turkiye Istatistik Yillig 1985* (Ankara: Devlet Istatistik Enstitusu Matbaasi, 1985), pp. 256–67.
[a]Not included in calculation of consumer, intermediate and investment breakdown.

making the SEEs financially self-sufficient, with a view to reducing the number of SEEs in the long run. There are in effect two purposes at work: to reduce the burden that SEEs deficits place on the central government's budget, and to improve the productivity as well as financial performance of individual SEEs in order to make them attractive for sale. The principal mechanism used both to ready the SEEs for sale and to enhance their profitability and competitiveness in the economy has been the reform of SEE pricing policy. The SEE practice of selling goods and services at subsidized prices has been abandoned. To cover operating deficits and to generate new funds for investments, the prices of SEE products have been decontrolled. In short, overpricing SEE products has proved to be a quick way to ensure an operating profit.

EFFORTS TO REFORM PRICING AND IMPROVE PRODUCTIVITY OF SEES

Financially, the performance of SEEs between 1980 and 1986 improved considerably. By raising prices, SEEs not only began registering an aggregate profit in 1984, but, in addition, the SEE's share of the public-sector borrowing requirement was lowered. However, the financial performance of SEEs is still governed by political considerations. National and local elections in 1987 and 1988 caused delays in price increases for public-sector goods as well as in the passage of a huge wage increase for public-sector workers.[7] As a result, SEE losses rose, and the SEE borrowing requirement, which had been falling, climbed from 4.3 to 4.7 percent of GNP in 1987. The central government had to meet the operating losses of the SEEs with large budget transfers. The pricing policies of SEEs have been manipulated to serve the ambitions of political leaders. The SEEs continue to be blamed as a major source of high inflation and as an important contributor to the public-sector deficit, much as they were in the 1970s.

While improvements in the financial performance of the SEEs have come primarily through price hikes,[8] efforts to improve the productivity of SEE's have been handicapped by bloated employment rosters and antiquated equipment. Although measures to reform employment practices (by requiring the hiring of new personnel based on term contracts) were instituted in 1987–88, the SEEs continue to be overmanned by 10 to 25 percent. In addition, huge investments are needed to modernize the outdated facilities and equipment of SEEs. As the decision to make a telecommunications company, Teletas, the first candidate for privatization indicates, plans to privatize SEEs hinge on selling off modernized, profitable firms.[9] The amount of financing that the SEEs have utilized for their investment programs shot up by nearly 400 percent between 1984 and 1988. Unfortunately, the overall financing requirements of the SEEs have gone up at the same time that the government is concerned with reducing public investments to control inflation.

OBSTACLES TO PRIVATIZATION

The actual progress of selling off enterprises has been slow. The task is enormous. The SEEs account for approximately 40 percent of Turkey's industrial production and 60 percent of fixed investments. However, the more insuperable obstacles are not economic but political. Public awareness of and disgruntlement with the inflationary costs of preparing the SEEs for sale, by hiking prices and spending to invest in modernizing plants, has kindled a political debate over the way in which state assets will be sold and how the proceeds of selling off state assets will be spent. While there is popular resentment over the inflationary effects of SEE reforms, there seems to be little controversy over the desirability of state intentions to turn loss-making enterprises into economically efficient, rationally run, profitable concerns. Rather, the focus for popular discontents is the second phase of the privatization program, the selling off of state enterprises. At issue is whether these enterprises should be sold, and to whom.

In 1986, a legislative framework for privatization was instituted. Once a SEE is designated for privatization, it automatically becomes a corporation and its shares are placed under the managerial control of the Mass Housing and Public Participation Administration (MHPPA) whose board consists of eleven ministers under the chairmanship of the prime minister. As of September 1989, two SEEs, eleven subsidiaries, five banks, and the state shares of thirty-eight public companies had been transferred to the MHPPA.[10] The first privatization was launched in February 1988 when 22 percent of Teletas, a 40 percent state-owned telecommunications company, was sold through a public offering. However, because of stagnation in the Istanbul Stock Exchange throughout 1988, the government turned to sales of block shares to foreign investors. The opposition parties on the left as well as the right in Turkey have registered strong opposition to this method of sale.

In 1989, the government sold block shares of five cement plants belonging to the state-owned Citosan to France's SCF (Société des Ciments Français) for $105 million and 70 percent of USAS (Turkish Air Catering Service) to SAS Partner, a subsidiary of Scandinavian Airlines System, for $14.5 million. In early 1990, the opposition True Path Party and Social Democrat Populist Party challenged the legality of the sales in separate cases brought before administrative courts in Ankara. The plaintiffs argued that a 1987 government directive required that privatized firms be offered first to Turkish nationals and then to foreigners. The court in turn annulled both deals and also rejected maneuverings by the government to revise its directive, allowing for block sales to foreigners and to make the changes retroactive. Ozal's government has argued the benefits of block sales to foreigners by asserting that they attract investment capital to Turkey and bring in technology and managerial expertise.[11] They also point out that capital markets are weak in Turkey and that the conditions of sale to foreign companies have included provisions for delayed public offerings.[12]

Nevertheless, the privatization program has come under growing criticism for selling national assets to foreigners. Members of the opposition had earlier made an issue of plans for selling a state-owned air charter and cargo company to a foreign company at what was regarded as too cheap a price. The sale was dropped. Challenging block sales to foreigners is a major challenge to the privatization program. The government must again discuss the privatizing alternative of returning to the sale of public shares on the stock market. Resort to this method, however, due to the underdeveloped state of capital markets in Turkey, is likely to slow the process of state disinvestment.

The controversy over transferring state assets to foreigners has also increased public sensitivity to the issue of who will benefit from the sale of SEEs. Opponents of privatization claim that the state will sustain losses of income in the future from having sold off the more efficient SEEs. They can easily find examples to support their position. The announced decision in spring 1990 to commence privatizing the state tourism company, Turban, starting with the sale of Turban's marinas, caused considerable consternation as the marinas are the most profitable of Turban's assets. By privatizing the marinas, insiders predict that the company will be headed for heavy losses in the coming years. Moreover, critics of the sale of state assets have argued that privatization amounts to nothing more than a debt-payment mechanism whereby the revenues of the shares sold will be used to service the Turkish debt. Proceeds from the sale of state assets are supposed to be deposited with the MHPPA and the Treasury, but the government has been accused of using the revenues from these sales to cover shortfalls in the budget. In fact, President Ozal was recently quoted as saying: "If the state wants to close its budget gap then it has to sell shares of its enterprises on the exchange."

Opposition to privatization has become more clamorous, particularly as the sale of the giant state conglomerates Petkim (petrochemicals), Erdemir (iron and steel), and Sumerbank (textiles) moves to the top of the privatizing agenda. What was an issue of the domestic repercussions of market-based, economic reforms is being transformed into a hotly contested political debate over the highly sensitive issues of dependency on foreign multinationals and the denationalization of Turkey's industrial base.

PASSAGE TO A COMPETITIVE MARKET ECONOMY

Since 1980, the Turkish economy has turned in an impressive performance based largely on export-led growth. Growth rates climbed to 8.0 percent and 7.5 percent in 1986 and 1987 respectively, and the country's exports have soared from $2.9 billion in 1982 to $11.43 billion in 1988. Where once the main export was hazelnuts, over three-fourths of the 1987 exports were industrial goods, with agricultural goods accounting for only 18 percent of the total. In addition, the current account deficit, an important barometer for international bankers, has been falling.

Heavily indebted in 1979, Turkey by the mid-1980s had become the leading recipient of World Bank B-loans, signifying that the international financial community not only has restored Turkey's creditworthy status but also had confidence in Turkey's economic performance into the foreseeable future. However, the transition to a competitive market economy has not been smooth.

ENGINES OF THE EXPORT DRIVE: THE FOREIGN TRADING COMPANIES

Former Prime Minister, and now President, Ozal and his handpicked coterie of technocrats manning key government posts in banking, planning, treasury, and foreign-trade spheres had envisioned reliance on Turkey's top holding companies for leadership in adapting to export-oriented competition. The clearest manifestation of this has been Ozal's own pet project, the creation in 1983 of general trading houses to which special export privileges were granted. The idea was borrowed from the Japanese style of state-business collaboration, as exemplified by the Sogo Shosha trading companies, and was intended to be of advantage to Turkey's large industrial capitalists. Specifically, "Turkish exporters who realized an annual export volume of $30 million of which at least 75 percent consisted of manufactured, and processed foods were granted the title of Foreign Trade Corporate Company [with] special credit facilities, interest-rate reductions, and tax rebates."[13] In April 1988, the Turkish government raised the export requirement for FTC (Foreign Trade Company) designation to $50 million. The most important of the special incentives granted to the FTCs have been a 6 percent tax rebate over export volume and exclusive permission to import from and engage in special barter (countertrade/buy-back operations) with Eastern bloc countries.[14] Among the anticipated and desired consequences of offering extra export incentives to these trading companies has been the concentration of private-sector exporting power in the hands of a few as most of the trading houses constitute an arm of the top Turkish holding companies in the private sector.

Have the FTCs lived up to expectations? In 1981, these foreign trading companies accounted for only 9 percent of Turkey's exports, but by 1985 this figure had soared to 36.0 percent and continued climbing to over 50 percent in 1988. However, while these trading companies are considered to be the primary engines of the export trade, they have been highly dependent on the government for an array of special export subsidies and incentives. Moreover, there is little indication that the government has been able to wean these companies from the continued reliance on its favors.

In early 1987, the Foreign Trade Department of the Treasury admonished a number of the large export companies for accepting incentives in 1986 but then falling short of requirements to export $30 million of merchandise to qualify for special privileges. The Foreign Trade Department went on to remonstrate these companies further for not meeting the requirement that at least 75 percent of their exports be composed of industrial goods.[15] In fact, because most Turkish exporters appear to be strongly responsive to subsidies and incentives, the government has become apprehensive about reducing export credits, fearing that this would likely precipitate a fall in exports. Indeed, it is with this concern in mind that the government—in view of the need to eliminate overt subsidies on exports by the end of 1988 (due to signatory agreements with GATT and with an eye toward Turkey's impending membership in the EEC)—decided to switch to a system of indirect export incentives in 1989. The main features of the new incentives to encourage exports are cheap Eximbank credits, subsidized energy, and premium payments out of the extrabudgetary Support and Price Stability Fund.

RELUCTANCE OF BIG BUSINESS TO ADJUST

Owners of the largest holding companies in Turkey, most of whom belonged to the pre-1980 coalition of import-substituting interests and on whom Ozal's strategy to a large extent has relied, have been protesting since 1980 that adjustment to the new economic rules of a competitive marketplace takes time and that Ozal's policies push them too far, too fast. On a number of occasions, leading businessmen have mobilized to oppose Ozal's policies. In 1982, a contingent of key businessmen travelled to Ankara to pressure the military government to remove then Deputy Premier Ozal and to relax Ozal's economic policies, including abandonment of his tough opposition to governmental bailouts of bankrupt firms. Ozal was subsequently fired by the generals. Following his dismissal, Ozal founded the Motherland Party and was returned to power as Prime Minister after the 1983 return to democracy elections. However, Ozal's policies remain controversial among businessmen concerned about the rapid reduction in state protection. Prior to the 1987 elections, newspapers reported significant campaign contributions from big businessmen being made to support the True Path Party, led by former Prime Minister Demirel who is regarded as a strong supporter of industrialists favoring continued government subsidies and other forms of protection.

In a 1988 interview with Euromoney magazine, Yusuf Ozal, brother of Turgut Ozal and at the time minister for planning, treasury and foreign trade, commented that for Turkish industrialists the pre-1980 business climate had meant, "High protection, high profit, easy money. Export led growth, however, means competition, it means selling outside of Turkey in a difficult environment. Not all businesses have managed to turn round to exports. They are still doing import substitution."[16] With the exception of a few holding companies whose activities are concentrated principally or solely in the textile and construction sectors, Turkish industrialists have not abandoned their ISI-orientation.[17] Many of the top Turkish exporters continue to produce largely for the domestic market. For example, Turkey's two largest industrial conglomerates, Koc and Sabanci Holding companies ". . . exported only about six percent of their turnover in 1986 and are largely oriented to the home market."[18] And yet, Koc Holding owns the trading company Ram and Sabanci Holding owns Exsa, which ranked third and fifth respectively among the top ten exporting groups of 1986.

A study published in 1986 by the Istanbul Chamber of Industry suggests that many of Turkey's large firms have been finding it difficult to adjust to the new competitive market rules. An increasing number of the Fortune 500 companies of Turkey have been experiencing net losses, 35 in 1984 and 55 in 1985. And while inflation in 1985 was averaging 45 percent, real average earnings of these companies came to 42.6 percent—an overall decline in real average earnings.[19] The scaling back and elimination of export subsidies in 1989 and continued high inflation (70-plus percent) are not likely to brighten prospects for high profits in the future.[20]

In spite of the policy preferences of the state technocrats, the transition to a competitive market economy is not exclusively the province of the big holdings. Export success is not simply a function of firm size.[21] In fact, a comparison of the 500 largest firms with firms in the economy as a whole reveals an interesting trend with respect to exports.[22] Whereas the Fortune 500 Turkish firms accounted for 63.7 percent of industrial exports in 1983, this figure had dropped to 45.1 percent by 1987. Even in terms of total exports, the Fortune 500 firms generated 42.8 percent of the total in 1983 and 36.9 percent in 1987. It would appear that Ozal's project of establishing foreign trading companies has proved to be an expeditious method for getting exports up by encouraging the output of smaller businesses to be consolidated with that of the big export houses. The FTCs have been useful as a marketing outlet for the products of small- and medium-sized enterprises. However, the above figures also suggest that the largest firms in the Turkish economy are not wholly converted to manufacturing exportable goods. More often than not, the large industrial groups (including those linked with a FTC) have a foot in both camps—producing mainly for the domestic market and trading exportable goods, some of which may be produced by a subsidiary and the rest acquired from smaller manufacturers in order to take advantage of the sizeable export subsidies and rebates.

The Ozal government has recognized that the FTCs are more trading entities than outlets for the exports of Turkey's big industrial producers, but is not sure how to alter this. After direct tax rebates were discontinued at the end of 1988, officials introduced a package of export incentives directed at the manufacturers of export goods. This approach failed to bring up exports in 1989. Incentives for 1990 were directed once again at the entities doing the actual exporting, namely the FTCs.

The export-led growth model has generated a variety of support groups, especially from those with a proven ability to compete in world markets. Nonetheless, given that the business community in Turkey has been accustomed to producing under an umbrella of state protectionist measures, it should not be too surprising that even as sectoral successes are reported, many industrialists (including ISI-oriented holdings) are still inclined to look to the state to provide incentives to ease the transition. Nor is it unusual that those who are insistent that the state continue to offer incentives also support Turkey's application for full membership in the EEC.[23]

The most significant change that the post-1980 reform measures have wrought is a change in private-sector attitudes. Businessmen accept that the transition to a competitive market economy is not reversible and that they must seek ways to make their enterprises competitive. For most industrialists, however, the preferred and least painful way to survive in a more competitive environment is for the state to help shoulder the cost of adjustment. Hence the issue of to whom the state should offer export incentives and subsidies remains a subject of unresolved debate.

CONCLUSION

The post-1980 privatization program in Turkey has been aimed at redrawing the boundaries between the public sector and the private sector. Yet, while the intended purpose of the post-1980 policy reforms was to bring about a radical structural transformation in the participation and contribution of the private and public sectors to the Turkish economy, a major redivision of labor is not in evidence. A comparison of the economy before and after 1980 showed continuation of preexisting patterns and trends and evidence of incremental rather than radical structural change. The Turkish case is illustrative of the difficulties of bringing about a redivision of labor in a mixed economy.

An examination of the principal privatizing strategies for rolling back the public sector showed that while some progress has been recorded, there has emerged a ground swell of popular opposition to the sale of enterprises to foreigners and concern over how proceeds from sales will be applied. Mounting criticism over the sale of state assets is likely to restrain rapid privatization along this track. In addition, efforts to induce the private sector, especially the large holding companies, to increase exports have been frustrated by the reluctance of many of these business interests to abandon import-substituting interests and turn seriously to exports. Businessmen have been insistent and effective in ensuring that export incentives be continued. By turning the debate from whether incentives should be offered to the question of the type of incentives which should be offered, business has effectively compelled the state to retreat from rapid privatization along this track. Contrary to optimistic predictions that the barriers to privatization will dissipate once public opinion and businessmen accept that a realignment of the public and private sectors is necessary, the Turkish case shows how the strategies chosen for shifting a mixed economic system in the direction of a private-sector-led economy are shaped by policy debates that can redefine privatizing ends as well as means.

Notes

1. The Economist Intelligence Unit, *Turkey, 1989–90,* p. 16.
2. Union of Chambers of Commerce, Industry, and Commodity Exchanges of Turkey, *1923–1982, Cumhuriyet Doneminde Istatistiklerle Turkiye* (Ankara: Union of Chambers, 1982), table 18; State Institute of Statistics, *Turkiye Istatistik Yillig 1987* (Ankara: Devlet Istatistik Enstitusu Matbaasi, 1987), p. 92.
3. Whereas intermediate goods accounted for 32.5 percent of value added in 1963 by 1980 they accounted for 48.7 percent. By 1980 investment goods contributed 17.6 percent of value added as compared to 14.6 percent in 1963.
4. Of course, just because there was a growth in the number of firms does not mean that ownership was dispersed. Indeed, there is considerable evidence that a small number of holding companies control the firms which dominate industrial production in Turkey.
5. Robert Bianchi, *Interest Groups and Political Development in Turkey* (Princeton: Princeton University Press, 1984), pp. 50–53; State Institute of Statistics, *Turkiye Istatistik Yillig 1985* (Ankara: Devlet Istatistik Enstitusu Matbaasi, 1985), pp. 256–67. Bianchi, *Interest Groups,* pp. 50–53; State Institute of Statistics, *Turkiye,* pp. 256–67.
6. Not only has the state remained influential in the post-1980 economy by virtue of its sizeable ownership role, but the share of the state in fixed investments remains high. Since 1980, the state has directed its investments primarily to sectoral investments in energy, in transportation and communication (for infrastructure-related projects), and in decreased investment in manufacturing. Yet, the state still contributes at least 25 percent of total investment in manufacturing. State investment in manufacturing stood at 31.0 percent of total investment in manufacturing in 1985 and 26.0 percent of total in 1986 (Turkish Industrialists' and Businessmen's Association, *The Turkish Economy, 1987,* p. 13). Moreover, a special survey on Turkey pointed out that via an extra-budgetary fund financed by special tax levies the state contributes to fixed investments in housing even more than is actually recorded; see "Getting Ready for Europe," *Economist* (June 1988): 12.
7. To woo rural voters, generous increases in agricultural commodity support prices were also approved in 1987.
8. A portion of the increased profitability of SEEs can be attributed to managerial improvements which include changes in personnel and greater decisional autonomy. However, SEE managers are by no means insulated from politics.
9. According to Cengiz Israfil, formerly in charge of the privatization program, "Citosan's cement business looked to be a good first candidate but when we looked at it from a marketing point of view, we realized it was hard to get people excited about a cement plant with old equipment when we had Teletas which was selling high technology" (*Euromoney,* Special Supplement, May 1988: 21).
10. *Finance* (September, 1989): 34.
11. Between 1954 and 1979, the value of foreign investment in Turkey amounted to only $228 million. Between 1980 and 1986, a total of $1575 million in foreign investment entered Turkey. However, approximately one third of this consisted of unsecured commercial loans. The remainder of this investment amount represents actual capital inflows, which for the most part have been directed to augmenting existing holdings. In spite of the tremendous reduction in the bureaucratic red tape pertaining to foreign investment regulations and application procedures since 1980, political uncertainties and inflationary pressures throughout the 1980s have dissuaded interested investors from embarking on major new undertakings.

12. For example, according to the sale agreement with SCF, 40 percent of the shares of one of the cement factories to be acquired would be sold to the Turkish public within five years.

13. Foreign Trade Association of Turkey, Brochure, 1984, p. 5.

14. SEE's also shared in this exclusive privilege of trade with the USSR and East European countries. The share of COMECON countries in Turkey's total exports was 4.2 percent in 1985 and 5.2 percent in 1988, and their share in Turkey's total imports was 5.8 percent in 1985 and 7.7 percent in 1988 (Istanbul Chamber of Commerce, *Economic Report,* 1989:72, 81).

15. *Diplomatic Pulse,* no. 4625–274, 6 April 1987.

16. *Euromoney,* Special Supplement, May 1988: 28.

17. Businessmen in the textile and construction industries became active in selling their goods and services outside Turkey during the 1970s. Even with the exchange-rate bias against exports during the late 1970s, the large firms (Mensucat Santral, Altinyildiz, and Narin Mensucat in textiles; Kutlutas and ENKA in construction) continued to seek export opportunities.

18. *Financial Times,* Survey of Turkey, 16 December 1987: 2.

19. This is if the two largest state-owned companies are omitted from the Fortune 500 list.

20. Naturally the Gulf War has had a devastating effect on the Turkish economy; however, the focus of this paper is on the prewar period 1980–90.

21. Indeed, adjustment to producing for export, across sectors, has been uneven. Four commodity groups (textiles, iron and steel, leather, and chemicals) account for just over 50 percent of Turkish exports.

22. "Turkey's 500 Large Industrial Establishments," *Journal of the Istanbul Chamber of Industry* (October 1988): 40.

23. In a joint declaration signed by members of the Turkish business community concerned about the too rapid removal of protectionist measures, a number of the preparatory conditions for Turkish membership proposed by European members are criticized as "asking for too much without promising anything tangible in return"; see *Turkey Monitor,* no. 41, 20 October 1989: 8–9.

CHAPTER

7

DIVERGENT MODES OF ECONOMIC LIBERALIZATION IN SYRIA AND IRAQ

Fred H. Lawson

By the fall of 1987, economic liberalization programs in both Syria and Iraq had reached a state of crisis. The Syrian regime found itself faced with growing shortages of foreign exchange, aggravated by the virtual evaporation of economic-assistance funds coming into the country from other Arab states. Meanwhile, imports of basic foodstuffs continued to increase: wheat and maize imports jumped almost 50 percent between 1986 and 1987, while total cereal imports stabilized at around 13.7 million metric tons. More significantly, the country's trade deficit grew by just over 25 percent from 1986 to 1987, despite a series of measures designed to cut back the quantity and value of manufactured imports and continuing supplies of subsidized petroleum from Iran, which allowed the government to avoid having to purchase the oil it needed at prevailing world-market prices. As a result of these trends, state officials cut the 1987 budget's current spending by almost 5 percent and drastically curtailed government subsidies on selected foodstuffs and fuel.[1]

At the same time, the Iraqi regime confronted sharply escalating levels of foreign indebtedness: the country's total external debt was estimated at around $50 billion in August 1987, a "sharply increasing portion" of which was coming from private commercial banks charging nondiscounted interest rates.[2] In addition, the local economy was suffering persistent disruptions in the flow of crucial capital goods and spare parts coming in from the outside as a result of the continuing Iran-Iraq war; difficulties in maintaining the productivity of local factories led to the forced resignations of the ministers of the interior and of trade at the end of the summer. And the Iraqi economy remained burdened by the diversion of scarce resources into the war effort as well as by intermittent shortages of locally produced food and consumer goods.

These two regimes responded to the growing difficulties associated with their economic liberalization programs in markedly different ways. Syria retained a considerable degree of state control over the country's internal and external economic affairs. In particular, the regime in Damascus maintained the drive to clamp down on black-market currency transactions and smuggling that it had initiated in the fall of 1986. Sixty-five prominent businesspeople and middle-level bureaucrats were sentenced to death or to long terms in prison by the economic security court in early September following their convictions on charges of smuggling, corruption, forgery and embezzlement.[3] Furthermore, the government continued to subsidize the cost of staple foodstuffs and fuel for domestic consumption, running up sizable budget deficits in the process. State officials also negotiated a barter arrangement with Jordan whereby Syrian debts, worth some $40 million, could be offset by shipments of agricultural products and light manufactures produced in government factories; they also signed an industrial cooperation agreement with Romania providing for assistance from Bucharest in expanding the state-run tractor factory in Aleppo and other modernization projects.

Iraq, on the other hand, responded to the crisis of 1987 by implementing a wide-ranging program of privatizing public enterprises in virtually all sectors of the local economy. Government officials leased agricultural lands from the state farms to private landholders and supported the activities of the new lessees with low-interest loans from the Agricultural Co-operative Bank. They opened the country's domestic market to private importers and commercial agents and doubled the capital of the semi-autonomous commercial bank in an effort to expand its lending and investment operations. In early February 1988, the minister of trade announced a 22 percent increase in state allocations to fund private sector imports, along with a 13 percent increase in funds available for the importation of new capital goods by both private and public sector firms. The trend toward privatization was reinforced by a presidential memorandum circulated that fall that encouraged greater competition on the part of private entrepreneurs; in early October, the regime announced that new private industrial investments would be exempt from both taxation and participation in employee profit-sharing arrangements for their first ten years in operation.

This divergence between Syrian and Iraqi economic policy has continued to grow in the years since 1987. The regime in Damascus has persisted in using the central administration to orchestrate, if not actually to direct, the course of Syria's internal and external economic affairs, while the regime in Baghdad has sharply accelerated its program of privatization. This chapter will first spell out in some detail the most important differences that have characterized recent economic policy in these two Ba'thi states, and it will then propose an explanation for their divergent political-economic programs in terms of relations between the dominant social coalition and the labor movement in these two countries.

SYRIA'S CONTROLLED LIBERALIZATION

Syrian economic policy since the end of 1987 reflects the regime's difficulties in wrestling with the puzzle of how to introduce a measure of market mechanisms and incentives for private enterprise into the country's economy, while maintaining the coordination and central supervision necessary to prevent a rise in unemployment and the reemergence of the old regime of rich merchants and large landowners that dominated the country's politics prior to 1958. These twin objectives have tended to produce a succession of steps toward greater deregulation of internal and external economic affairs, matched by efforts to improve the efficiency of state administration over these affairs. The result appears contradictory at first glance but illustrates, upon closer observation, a complex and subtle balancing act on the part of the country's ruling coalition.

At the beginning of 1988, deregulation represented the dominant trend in Syria's economic policy. The cabinet appointed in early November 1987 ordered a 70 percent devaluation of the Syrian pound in mid-January as part of an effort to encourage the flow of hard currency into the country. A month later, a group of twelve Syrian entrepreneurs announced the formation of a new agricultural investment company to work some 5,000 hectares of farmland in the Euphrates valley made available by the ministry of agriculture; the new company was formed according to the terms of a 1986 law granting such mixed-sector enterprises substantial exemptions from taxation and customs duties on imported machinery as well as permission to deal in foreign currencies to finance their operations. Such steps generated a significant increase in economic activity within the country, which in turn provided markedly higher levels of income to the government from export taxes and dividends on state-supported investments. Consequently, the cabinet, in mid-July, approved a draft budget that called for a 20 percent increase in total expenditure during fiscal 1988–89 in addition to allocating funds to begin repaying the state's $4 billion foreign debt.

But this turn toward deregulation was accompanied by continued measures to promote central supervision over Syria's economic affairs. In mid-October, the government announced plans to purchase some 14,000 tractors and 400 harvesters for use by the ministry of agriculture and agrarian reform; these new machines were to be dispersed among state agricultural stations throughout the country in an attempt to prevent the spoilage of crops left too long in the fields due to a lack of harvesting equipment. The following month, officials publicized plans for the state-run Syrian National Industrial and Agricultural Company to build a vegetable oil processing plant, metal pipe factory, and first-class hotel in the free-trade zone situated along the Syrian-Jordanian border. At the same time, the government renewed a set of economic cooperation agreements with Romania that laid the foundation for state-run industrial projects in the northern and western provinces.[4] The minister of housing told foreign journalists, in February 1989, that the most likely candidate to win a $70 million contract with the World Bank to construct a modern sewage system for the city of Aleppo was the rehabilitated Military Housing Establishment, a subsidiary of the ministry of defense.

By April 1989, Prime Minister Zuʿbi admitted that the country's scarce supplies of foreign exchange for industrial investment were being severely rationed by the central administration. He told viewers of a televised address that hard currency was being allocated "according to the priorities of operating factories that produce basic and important commodities for the agricultural sector so that some sort of integration can be achieved between the agricultural and industrial sectors" of the local economy. This objective was a key component of the government's fifth five-year plan (1981–85) and had been reiterated at subsequent Regional (Syrian) Congresses of the Ba'th Party.[5] Shortly after the minister's speech, state officials announced a 25 percent pay raise for government employees and personnel in the armed forces and police. This raise was to be financed by a 50 percent increase in customs duties on goods entering local markets.

Later that year, the Military Housing Establishment contracted to carry out improvements to the port facilities and ship repair yard at the state-controlled harbor at Tartus. But other public-sector construction projects fell victim to shortages of investment capital: plans to expand both the Public Establishment of Telecommunications and the General Organization for Agricultural Mechanization suffered repeated delays as funds to finance them were diverted to pay for imported foodstuffs needed to offset shortfalls in local production resulting from persistent drought. Nevertheless, the assistant secretary-general of the Syrian Ba'th, 'Abdallah al-Ahmar, exhorted high-ranking party officials meeting at the Higher Political Sciences Institute in Damascus in late November to remain committed to "our firm course toward building the society of progress and socialism," despite apparent domestic economic difficulties. Four days later, Prime Minister Zu'bi admonished those attending a conference called by the General Federation of Trade Unions to work together to improve production, reduce costs, and maintain discipline at public sector factories. "This giant, strong sector," he continued, "is considered the economy's safety valve which absorbs all shocks. Moreover, it is the power which protects our national economy from any international disturbances or fluctuations."[6] Zu'bi singled out the construction sector as one area of the economy in which foreign firms had been kept at bay by state-supported indigenous enterprises and the goal of economic self-reliance had been virtually achieved.

IRAQ'S WHOLESALE DEREGULATION

Iraqi economic policy has been characterized by a series of moves designed to deepen and accelerate the regime's drive toward privatizing the country's internal and external economic affairs. This program took shape as early as 1985, when forty-two state industrial plants were sold to private entrepreneurs. But it was in 1987, with the sale of an additional forty-seven government firms to private interests, that the drive gained momentum. With the completion of this second set of transactions, the private sector gained a firm foothold in the local heavy-industrial and food-processing sectors, complementing its predominance in light manufacturing, construction, and real estate.[7] The government's commitment to privatization was underscored that fall with the simultaneous replacement of the minister of heavy industry by the director of the multinational Arab Industrial Investment Company and the creation of a new planning agency charged with determining the feasibility of new private enterprises and supervising their establishment within the country. The crisis of late 1987 merely confirmed the regime's support for the comprehensive deregulation of the Iraqi economy.

Throughout the summer of 1988, state officials repealed controls on the prices of a wide range of goods produced by private-sector firms. These moves steadily raised the cost of production for those engaged in light manufacturing, forcing them to charge higher prices for their finished goods. More importantly, the lifting of price controls led to sharply higher prices on such foodstuffs as eggs, chickens, fruits, and vegetables grown on local farms. These price rises prompted the ministry of planning to publish, in early September, guidelines encouraging greater investment in poultry farms, grain and livestock production, and fisheries. Problems associated with inflation took up a substantial portion of the agendas of congresses of the Regional (Iraqi) Baʿth Party and Revolution Command Council the following month; President Saddam Husain emerged from these discussions with a firm warning to private merchants not to engage in price gouging. But price controls were not reinstated, and the warning was soon forgotten.

Privatization picked up speed during the last quarter of 1988. Finance Minister Hikmat ʿUmar al-Hadithi told Western reporters, in early October, that banking and finance would be the next sector of the Iraqi economy to be privatized. The first step in this process was to be the inauguration of a new investment bank to operate on equal terms with the existing Rafidain Bank, thereby injecting a significant degree of competition into local financial affairs. This move was to be followed by the chartering of several mixed-sector banks run by former Rafidain managers, who would be offered attractive terms to retire from their present positions and join the new institutions. In mid-November, state officials announced plans to establish a free zone for industrial enterprises and began soliciting German and Korean firms to participate in joint ventures with local companies. Meanwhile, a new company with a majority private shareholding was established "with the approval of the president's office" to process and export domestically produced dates. This move signalled the demise of the state-run Iraqi Dates Commission, whose operations had already been severely undermined by an earlier decree permitting private traders to purchase dates directly from farmers and thus avoid the regulations imposed by the commission.[8]

In early December, the ministry of industry and military industrialization announced that seventy of its factories would be put up for sale. The enterprises involved were largely concerned with food processing, textile manufacturing and the fabrication of building materials, and they were predominantly small in scale. A spokesperson for the ministry added that the state would continue to manage companies that concentrated on the production of high-technology items or industrial exports, while providing needed raw materials and expertise to the privatized factories. At the same time, the ministry of finance proposed establishing a stock market to facilitate the buying and selling of shares in private and mixed-sector shareholding companies, and it congratulated the Industrial Bank for its efforts to promote share trading. The following spring, the ministry of industry and military industrialization outlined plans to sell off its metal foundries and light manufacturing plants: "There will be no more assembly concept in the ministry's industrial policy," its director told reporters in late April. Instead, the ministry would devote its attention to research and development as well as to orchestrating joint ventures with foreign corporations.[9]

On 20 April 1989, the Revolution Command Council adopted a new law allowing private commercial agents to operate as brokers between government agencies and foreign firms. The measure, known as Law 45 of 1989, removed all restrictions on the type of goods such agents could bring into the country; it also allowed agents to import capital goods worth 100 percent of their commissions and other commodities worth up to 30 percent of their commissions. Three months later, the council approved sweeping changes in the law regulating the number of branch offices foreign companies could operate within the country. The new rules permitted firms to open branches by contracting with local agents instead of with government agencies, significantly expanding opportunities for private commercial entrepreneurs. As a result of these changes in Iraqi commercial regulations, the level of imports coming into the country from the United States jumped dramatically during the first half of the year.

By the fall of 1989, state officials had taken the first tentative steps to privatize parts of Iraq's petroleum industry, a sector of the local economy previously excluded from the privatization drive. The minister of petroleum told reporters on 6 September that his ministry was planning to put oil tankers and trucks to transport natural gas cylinders up for sale "as a further incentive to private operators of petrol stations and gas cylinder distribution centers."[10] New owners would be offered not only the vehicles themselves but also the fuel products they would distribute at concessionary rates spread out over several years. The list of items private merchants were permitted to bring into the country using their foreign-exchange holdings was expanded in early November; furniture, refrigerated trucks, farm machinery, and electrical equipment of various sorts constituted most of the new additions. A further lengthening of the list at the end of the month followed the publication of figures by the State Company for Sales and Trade Services reporting greater than expected activity by private trading houses during the first two-thirds of the year.

One should not conclude from all this that the state has withdrawn completely from Iraq's economic affairs. In early April 1989, a presidential decree reimposed upper limits on the prices of a wide range of agricultural staples. The announcement reaffirmed the government's support for private enterprise, but went on to "remind those greedy people that this policy does not mean leaving their hands free to exploit the consumers."[11] More significantly, three state-run textile enterprises signed an agreement with a Soviet company the following month to supply the Iraqi public sector with modern weaving equipment, a move that set the stage for a more comprehensive economic and technical cooperation pact between the two states at the end of the year authorizing joint ventures in a number of heavy-industrial and capital-goods projects. At the beginning of October, a massive grain-storage project on the outskirts of Baghdad was contracted to Fao State Enterprises, a subsidiary of the government's Military Industries Commission; MIC had just completed work on a smelter capable of producing 1,500 tons of stainless steel per year for use in both the public and private sectors. Nevertheless, the Iraqi regime has remained committed to the institutionalization of a deregulated economic order within the country in the wake of the crisis of 1987. This orientation contrasts sharply with the relatively more deliberate and controlled liberalization program undertaken by the Syrian regime during the same period.

ACCOUNTING FOR THE DIVERGENCE IN LIBERALIZATION PROGRAMS

Differing relations between the regime and the labor movement can provide a useful starting point for explaining the divergent modes of liberalization that have appeared in Syria and Iraq in recent years. More specifically, the Syrian labor movement finds itself in a substantially stronger position vis-à-vis the dominant coalition of social forces within the country than does the Iraqi labor movement. The strength of Syria's industrial workers enables critics and opponents of greater liberalization based in the trade union federation to block or delay implementation of initiatives designed to deregulate the country's economic affairs. Moreover, the government in Damascus recognizes that workers in large-scale public-sector enterprises hold a relatively advantageous position within domestic society in general and within the national network of popular front organizations in particular. Consequently, state officials have considerable incentive to curtail the introduction of market mechanisms in an attempt to forestall or limit conflicts over economic policy between rank-and-file trade unionists and the governing elite.

The comparatively advantageous position of the Syrian labor movement arises in part from the importance of the industrial sector within the country's economy. During the mid-1980s, industrial laborers made up some 15 percent of the economically active population in Syria, with another 16 percent employed in construction. In Iraq, on the other hand, only about 9 percent of the economically active population was engaged in manufacturing, while an additional 10 percent held jobs in construction.[12] Conversely, the petroleum sector accounted for some 63 percent of the Iraqi gross national product in 1979, whereas manufacturing made up less than 6 percent. For Syria, the proportions were 4 percent and 18 percent respectively.[13] Consequently, industrial workers occupy a strategic position in Syrian society; the regime in Damascus is highly vulnerable to any action that might disrupt or slow down production in the industrial sector of the local economy. The relatively larger role played by petroleum and agriculture in the Iraqi economy significantly reduces its regime's reliance upon indigenous industry to generate goods for the local market and revenues for the state treasury.

Labor's relatively advantageous position within Syrian society is reinforced by a crucial but unintended consequence of the economic liberalization measures adopted by the regime in the early 1970s. Two social forces benefitted most from these policies: a "class of new capitalists . . . based on monopolization and commerce" and "a genuine state bourgeoisie made up of the highest level of officials in the state apparatus."[14] The former amassed considerable fortunes by acting as brokers and suppliers to public-sector firms, activities that became particularly profitable in the wake of the jump in regional petroleum prices that took place in 1973–74. Its members parlayed their contacts with high-ranking government and military officers into lucrative commissions from foreign companies looking for access to the Syrian market. By the end of the decade, many of the richest individuals that made up this "new class" had become successful entrepreneurs, investing in transportation, tourism, and construction, as well as in urban and rural land.[15] The latter dominated the industrial sector of the country's economy through its members' control over the state-run heavy-industrial enterprises and public-sector establishments producing textiles, furniture, ceramics, shoes, and consumer durables. In addition to the access to publicly produced goods and influence over investments and licensing decisions entailed by their positions within the central administration, these officials enjoyed entry into such highly prized professions as engineering and medicine. Privileged members of the state bourgeoisie actively collaborated with individuals belonging to the new commercial-entrepreneurial elite to advance their mutual interests in expanding the role of foreign capital and private subcontracting within the local economy throughout the 1970s and early 1980s.

But a third social force besides the "new capitalists" and state bourgeoisie also profited from the growth of foreign trade and from the loosening of government regulation over Syria's domestic economy during these years. Independent tradespeople and shopkeepers in the larger cities and towns took advantage of the inability of public-sector firms to supply adequate quantities of affordable, well-made goods to local markets by setting up workshops and stores of their own to manufacture and sell such items. As early as 1978, Elisabeth Longuenesse observed that

> in the present state of the development of the productive forces and of the functioning of the economy (in particular the public sector . . .), modern handicrafts (since traditional handicrafts are in decline) is not only viable but flourishing and plays an important role in the economy. The petty bourgeoisie . . . is not a class which is condemned to disappear in the short term, as in the developed capitalist countries. Far from it, it is a rising class.[16]

These artisans and traders continued to flourish over the succeeding half decade despite their inability to compete with the richest of the country's mercantile interests centered in Damascus.[17]

Some members of the Syrian petite bourgeoisie did well enough for themselves during the early 1980s to transform their operations into establishments employing a significant number of workers. According to Volker Perthes, one of the most outstanding examples of these new industrialists is Riyadh Seif, a carpenter's son who started working as a street vendor and a packer in order to finance his secondary education. In 1962 he and his brothers bought some sewing machines and started a workshop that in the seventies became a real factory. In 1975 the brothers separated, each of them now having a project of his own, producing shirts, pajamas, and ladies' wear. Riyadh began trading in cloth, too, and directed his own production of ladies' wear to the Soviet Union, which was buying Syrian products in exchange for part of its loans to Syria, thus becoming a golden market for Syrian producers. He successfully enlarged his project, employing about 200 workers in 1980 and controlling a workforce of about 1000 in 1989, in his own factory and others which he holds shares in and manages.[18]

These more successful petit bourgeois industrial entrepreneurs largely fell in with the regime and tolerated its efforts to revive public-sector manufacturing during 1981–82.

Other independent tradespeople consolidated their position in local markets, but without accumulating enough capital to become major industrialists like Riyadh Seif. The growth of these private manufacturers is evident in the Syrian government's figures for gross fixed-capital formation during the 1970s and 1980s. The average annual rate of gross fixed-capital formation in the private sector jumped by some 50 percent across these two decades, while that in the public sector rose by around 30 percent (see table 1). And while private fixed-capital formation showed a steady upward trend during the mid-1980s (the latest period for which figures are available), public fixed-capital formation was stagnating at a level of about 10.5 billion 1980 Syrian pounds.

Artisans and shopkeepers in this dynamic private manufacturing sector not only resented the "new capitalists" and their allies in the central administration, but also shared a deep-seated hostility toward the group of ʿAlawi military officers who occupied top positions within the state apparatus. Furthermore, small-scale manufacturers resented the state-run cooperatives that controlled the distribution of agricultural staples and industrial crops throughout Syria. They were therefore attracted in growing numbers to the country's Islamist movement around the turn of the decade, providing both financial support and cadres for the Muslim Brethren and its offshoots based in the larger cities and towns of the north central provinces.[19] Government moves to expand and modernize large-scale, capital-intensive public-sector plants in the areas around Aleppo and Hamah between 1979 and 1981 exacerbated the conflict between local artisans and traders on the one hand and the regime on the other, precipitating a number of violent clashes between Islamist militants and units of the state security forces. These confrontations culminated in the rebellion that broke out in Hamah in February 1982.[20]

In the wake of the Hamah revolt, state officials stepped up their efforts to improve the efficiency and profitability of public-sector enterprises, particularly in industries related to agriculture. Government planners supervised construction of new sugar refineries at Tal Salhab, al-Raqqah, Maskanah, and Dair al-Zur, and they

offered subsidized loans to farmers who undertook mechanized sugar beet cultivation in the districts around al-Hasakah, al-Raqqah, Dair al-Zur and Aleppo. At
the same time, the state built a series of large-scale spinning and weaving mills in
the districts around Idlib, al-Hasakah, and Dair al-Zur. These plants posed a direct
challenge to smaller, privately owned refineries and workshops in these provinces,
increasing the potential for a resurgence of the Islamist movement that had been
suppressed at such cost earlier in the year.

Faced with a continuing threat from disaffected tradespeople—and confronting
recurrent shortages of investment and operating capital for public-sector firms—
Syria's dominant coalition of "new capitalists" and state bourgeoisie found itself
increasingly dependent upon the continued support of the country's labor movement. Islamist activists focused on this connection in the wake of the insurrection
in Hamah, publishing a series of manifestoes calling for the adoption of a new labor
code to protect workers in private-sector industry, supporting a greater degree of
profit sharing in state-run companies and criticizing corruption and inefficiency in
the public sector.[21] The regime responded to these appeals by orchestrating a
succession of rallies and demonstrations sponsored by the trade-union federation
in the larger cities and towns. There was even a limited campaign to arm and
deploy paramilitary formations composed of members of the popular organizations
to protect party and state officials from further attacks by Islamist militants. But
perhaps out of respect for their underlying vulnerability vis-à-vis the trade unions,
government officers packed these units with members of the Peasants' Union rather
than with personnel drawn from the General Federation of Trade Unions.

By the mid-1980s, the regime's dependence upon the organized-labor movement became more and more evident. Delegates to the eighth Regional Congress
of the Ba'th in January 1985 advocated greater deregulation of internal and external economic affairs as a way both of encouraging the expansion of private enterprise in commerce and agriculture and of generating the revenues needed to support the regime's drive toward "strategic parity" with Israel. But when representatives
of the trade-union federation and other popular organizations countered by advancing the argument that the country's economic difficulties could be solved more
readily by the reinvigoration of the largely defunct Higher Economic Council, the
party's leadership opted for a markedly more restricted program of liberalization.
The closing communique criticized state-run factories for their persistent inefficiency and opened the door to freer exchanges of currency and consumer goods.
But it also reiterated the objectives of the government's fifth Five-Year Plan, which
provided for a substantial degree of state intervention in the domestic economy.
Only after the congress had adjourned did Prime Minister al-Kasm reshuffle his
cabinet, reinstating Muhammad 'Imadi—a noted proponent of greater liberalization—as minister of economy and foreign trade.

State officials continued to collaborate with leaders of the labor movement in
policing the implementation of the liberalization measures adopted by the government in the years after 1985. The president of the Workers' Union joined the
prime minister in attempting to form a Commission for the Rationalization of

TABLE 1

Gross Fixed Capital Formation in Syria, 1975–86

Year	Public Sector			Private Sector		
	Million Syrian Pounds	Index	Percent of Total	Million Syrian Pounds	Index	Percent of Total
1975	6,218	100	72	2,418	100	28
1976	8,298	133	73	3,100	128	27
1977	7,988	128	60	5,325	220	40
1978	7,195	116	62	4,372	181	38
1979	8,452	136	72	3,288	136	28
1980	9,017	145	64	5,099	211	36
1981	8,976	144	62	5,445	225	38
1982	9,268	149	62	5,628	233	38
1983	10,450	168	68	5,007	207	32
1984	10,438	168	66	5,304	219	34
1985	11,382	183	68	5,387	223	32
1986	10,316	166	60	7,021	290	40

Source: Syrian Arab Republic, *Statistical Abstract 1987* (Damascus: Central Bureau of Statistics, August 1987), Table 37/16, p. 558.

Imports, Exports, and Consumption to interpret the terms of a law promulgated in April 1987. The new regulation granted permission to private enterprises to export a wide range of industrial and agricultural goods and apply 75 percent of the profits to further commercial ventures, subject to approval by the Commercial Bank.[22] The authorities have made repeated efforts to curtail the importation of unlicensed goods into the country, and they have also harassed black-market money-changers and precious-metal traders, whose activities help to reduce the buying power of those whose salaries are fixed by the central administration.

In Iraq, on the other hand, the state's program of wholesale liberalization has, for the most part, consolidated the regime by channeling greater resources to forces within the dominant social coalition. As ʿIsam al-Khafaji has demonstrated, the largest proportion of the primary beneficiaries of Iraqi deregulation consists of individuals and groups having close ties to the state apparatus. The construction boom of the late 1970s led directly to the rise of a class of wealthy contractors with intimate relations with government and Baʿth party officials. A report prepared by the local communist party in mid-1977 described the process whereby such building tycoons made their fortunes:

> What does the contractor need? He needs the capital, which he obtains from the state; the machinery, which he also obtains from the state; the raw materials, which are supplied by the state at subsidized prices; and technical expertise, which is available by depleting the state sector of its technicians. When all these facilities are made available to him, he has nothing left but to open an elegant office; and even this may not be necessary.[23]

By the early 1980s, contractors made up the largest single group of families possessing assets valued at more than 15 million Iraqi dinars, and they had begun to supplement their construction operations by investing in transportation, by importing building materials and heavy equipment, and by buying real estate.

Rich merchants and agents for foreign corporations have benefitted almost as much as the contracting elite from their ties to the central administration during the period of extensive privatization. Al-Khafaji notes that he has collected "numerous instances of commissions granted by multinational companies to key figures in the Iraqi leadership, including members of the Revolutionary Command Council, members of the Regional and Pan-Arab Commands of the Baʿth Party, and members of President Saddam Husain's family."[24] The activities of this commercial elite generated a sharp rise in the value of wholesale and retail trade as the 1970s went by; most of the profits from this trade were then invested in real estate, fueling a jump in the value of the service sector of the local economy during these years.

Trends in the country's agricultural sector mirror those in contracting and trade. Robert Springborg notes that

> In 1979 private individuals began to act on opportunities made possible by irrigation, particularly for fruit and vegetable cultivation. Medium and high ranking

state employees and party officials joined private businessmen and professionals in buying or leasing land, especially in the environs of Baghdad. Through the state importation company they were able to purchase pumps, pipes, plastic sheets and the other accoutrements of modern plasticulture and drip and sprinkler irrigation. Returns to these investors have been impressive, particularly when one considers that a large proportion of investment funds are provided by the government on favorable terms.[25]

These mechanized farms, primarily oriented toward producing cash crops for export, profited disproportionately from state subsidies for agricultural produce and the dissolution of government cooperatives in rural districts. Manufacturing, by way of contrast, has suffered as a result of shifts in the local economy over the last few years: Hanna Batatu demonstrates that between 1968 and 1981, "the number of industrial enterprises of both the private and mixed sectors grew by only 3.7 percent and their employees by only 6.5 percent. It is true that the value of their sales increased sixfold but, as the figures for wages suggest, much of the increase could be attributed to the impact of inflation." Batatu concludes from these figures that "the industrial bourgeoisie remains essentially a middle-scale bourgeoisie," largely subordinate to the interests of the central administration and the contracting/commercial elite.[26]

Under these circumstances, the regime in Baghdad has had little to fear from the impact of economic liberalization on social forces outside the dominant coalition. Small-scale manufacturing constitutes a much smaller component of the Iraqi economy than it does of the Syrian economy, and those workshops that do exist are almost totally dependent upon larger public-sector enterprises for their raw materials and other inputs. The seven fat years after 1973 saw a significant expansion of private-sector industrial output as well as the transformation of "hundreds of small businessmen" into "big industrialists." But this development provoked little opposition on the part of the country's craftspeople and shopkeepers. Petit bourgeois acquiescence in the regime's policies was no doubt encouraged by the ruthlessness of the state security services; as al-Khafaji observes, "under a brutal dictatorship like Iraq's, an entrepreneur cannot show the slightest sign of opposition and stay in business. Extra-economic measures come into play: confiscation, arrest, assassination and torture."[27] But it was also a consequence of the fundamentally vulnerable position these smaller tradespeople occupied in the structure of the country's economy.

Throughout the later 1970s, the sheer number of small-scale private manufacturing enterprises in Iraq multiplied steadily. The 26,332 such establishments operating in the country in 1974 jumped to 41,719 three years later, an increase of more than 58 percent. The number of paid employees working in these enterprises rose even more dramatically during this period, from 26,016 to 44,847, while their total output more than tripled in value, from 93.6 million Iraqi dinars to 300.8 million. But few of these firms achieved the level of capital accumulation or scale of operations necessary to insure their continued economic viability: instead, "the overall picture is one of a proliferation of tiny 2–3 man units."[28] Enterprises this small stood little chance of competing successfully with the state-affiliated import-export companies, whose operations inundated local markets with consumer goods manufactured in Europe and Asia during the last years of the decade.

As a result, the early 1980s witnessed a dramatic decline in both the number and the significance of industrial enterprises employing fewer than ten persons within the Iraqi economy. In 1977 there were more than 41,700 such firms operating in the country, making up more than 96 percent of all industrial establishments. By 1980, their number had dropped by almost 18 percent, to just over 34,300, although they continued to account for almost 96 percent of the country's total manufacturing concerns. Only about 30,000 small industrial establishments remained operating in Iraq in 1981, a fall of some 13 percent over the previous year.[29] The decline in the number of persons working in these factories during these years was even more pronounced: in 1977 almost 96,000 paid and unpaid employees worked in small establishments; four years later this total had fallen to 64,400, a drop of nearly one-third. It is thus no exaggeration to say that by the early 1980s the vanguard of Iraqi industry was the small collection of large-scale, capital-intensive firms owned or managed by the state apparatus and its allies in the contracting/commercial elite. The dynamic class of small manufacturers specializing in what Longuenesse calls "modern handicrafts" was severely constricted, creating a situation in which "domestic production has not kept up with demand or reduced imports."[30]

Under these circumstances, Iraq's rulers have faced little or no challenge from forces enriched by deregulation but whose interests stand opposed to their own. The regime has consequently had no incentive to moderate its drive to introduce market mechanisms into the local economy in an effort to retain the support of the country's labor movement. On the contrary, the years after 1978 have seen a concerted campaign by the Ba'th Party and state security forces to seize control of the trade unions and other workers' organizations. Party officials had begun to force activists identifying with the Iraqi Communist Party out of leading positions in the various mass organizations immediately following the creation of the National Front in 1972, when traditional strongholds of the labor movement were "being swamped with migrants from a background with little tradition or experience of working class struggle."[31] This process gained momentum two years later with the dissolution of the Communist Party's local branches within the trade union federation. And by the end of the decade, the expansion of the Ba'th Party apparatus engulfed not only the labor movement but also the federations for youth, women, peasants, and students.[32] By 1980, Iraq's leadership had even stopped paying the usual lip service to socialism in its statements of fundamental Ba'thi principles: President Saddam Husain was quoted by the party daily al-Thawrah to the effect that "Socialism does not mean the equal distribution of wealth between the deprived poor and the exploiting rich; this would be too inflexible. Socialism is a means to raise and improve productivity."[33]

The Iraqi regime's ability to dominate the trade union organizations has been enhanced by the strategy adopted by militants within the labor movement in their struggle against the country's political leadership on the one hand and by two interrelated peculiarities of the industrial labor force on the other. Following the suppression of cadres of the Iraqi Communist Party that took place in the wake of the Ba'thi coup d'etat of February 1963, party militants joined forces with Kurdish partisans in the northern provinces. Leaders of the Communist Party maintained their support for the creation of an autonomous Kurdistan over the succeeding seventeen years, despite periodic rapprochements with the Ba'thi-led regime. With the signing of the 1975 Algiers accord and the subsequent defeat of the Kurdish separatist movement, the Ba'th pointed to the Communist Party's policy toward the Kurdish issue as justification for its moves to eradicate members and support-ers of the party beginning in 1978. The party's Central Committee riposted with a manifesto demanding an end to the program of Arabizing Kurdish areas in the north, the formation of a popularly elected national assembly and the adoption of more doctrinaire socialist economic policies.[34] The publication of this document prompted widespread arrests of alleged party members, particularly among the armed forces. By mid-May 1979, this anti-Communist campaign had resulted in a situation in which

> all Communist party offices have been closed down in all provinces; the central organ of the party has been banned; the party no longer has representatives, either in the Cabinet or in the Patriotic Front, and with that the very existence of the Front has come to an end and our party is no longer bound to any decision taken in the name of the Front.[35]

The remaining party cadres then completed their demarche by reestablishing their ill-fated tactical alliance with the Kurdish national movement, leaving the country's trade unions too weak to resist becoming subordinated to the Ba'th.

Moreover, expatriates and younger women made up a larger proportion of the industrial workforce in Iraq during the 1980s than they did in Syria. Most of the former immigrated into the country following the outbreak of the Iran-Iraq war. As young Iraqi males were inducted into the regular and reserve armed forces in growing numbers, unskilled workers from the other Arab states were offered at-tractive wages to take their place. By 1984, informed observers estimated the size of the Egyptian expatriate community at between 500,000 and 1 million men; these workers were for the most part engaged in agricultural labor, but they moved into jobs in the manufacturing and services sectors of the local economy as the war dragged on.[36] At the height of the war effort in the summer of 1986, Egyptian and other expatriate laborers were earning some $4 billion a year of Iraq's increas-ingly scarce controvertible funds, an amount equalling roughly one-third of the government's total revenues from oil exports for the year.

Both Syria's and Iraq's Ba'thi regimes encouraged women to train themselves for technical and professional careers as part of their programs to overturn the exploitative relations that characterized their respective prerevolutionary societies.

In Syria, this drive resulted in women's representing almost one-quarter of the membership in public-sector trade unions by the early 1980s. Female workers made up about the same proportion of employees in large-scale textile mills during these years, and approximately 10 percent of the country's tobacco workers as well.[37] Iraqi women began the decade comprising only about 17 percent of the country's industrial workforce as a whole, "but almost 14 percent of the paid workers in large industrial establishments were women."[38] In addition, some 25 percent of Iraq's laboratory technicians, 31 percent of its medical professionals and 37 percent of its agricultural laborers were women. These percentages shot up dramatically during the course of the Iran-Iraq war: as early as the summer of 1983, *Middle East Economic Digest* quoted a British manager as saying that "Over the last year, the war has had a very significant impact on manpower. Nearly all experienced young men have been drafted, and have been replaced by well-qualified, but inexperienced, young women."[39] The General Union of Iraqi Women projected in the fall of 1983 that 28 percent of the country's industrial workers would be women by the middle of the decade, while the proportion was even greater in some plants: "In one factory producing electric lamps, half of the 400 workers are now women, and half of the men are Chinese!"[40]

Expatriate and female workers in Iraq were generally too weak to resist being dominated by the ruling social coalition. As early as 1983, state officials adopted new regulations limiting the amount of Iraqi dinars earned by foreign nationals that could be converted into hard currency and taken out of the country. When Egyptian laborers began to leave rather than submit to the new rules, Baghdad contracted with the Philippine government for the provision of some 30,000 skilled and semiskilled workers in exchange for a promise to pay more than half of their salaries at the conclusion of the war. Currency transfer regulations were again tightened in June 1989, creating a rush of emigration on the part of Egyptian expatriates who "suddenly found their situation untenable."[41] Women workers found themselves in an equally vulnerable position: by 1983, wages for female factory laborers had been subjected to substantial cuts, while the authorities were deducting sizable "donations" to support the war effort from the paychecks of these workers.[42] At the same time, the growing drain on the country's population resulting from the war sparked a concerted effort on the part of state officials to encourage young women to raise the birth rate, a move which pulled female workers out of the labor force before they could gain either the experience or the seniority to demand pay raises from their supervisors.

THE LABOR MOVEMENT AND THE STATE IN SYRIA AND IRAQ

Organized industrial workers not only differ in terms of the power they exercise relative to that of the dominant social coalition in Syria and Iraq; they also occupy sharply divergent positions with regard to the central institutions of the state in these two societies. In Syria, the trade union federation has been formally incorporated into the institutional apparatus of the regime since the early 1960s. It has thus played a crucial role in mobilizing popular support for the country's Ba'thi leadership and, more recently, in distributing patronage among the party's rank-and-file supporters. Iraq's trade unions, on the other hand, have had a much more antagonistic relationship with the regime during the Ba'thi era. Paradoxically, rather than enhancing the degree of autonomy enjoyed by the state-sponsored trade union federation, the continual jockeying that has characterized relations between organized workers and the party leadership in Iraq has severely limited both the range of activities open to organized workers and the resources available to support collective action on the part of trade unionists.

Syria's organized labor movement has been significantly strengthened by its status as one of the more autonomous institutional pillars of the regime. In an attempt to rally popular support behind greater state intervention in Syria's economic affairs, the Ba'thi leadership embraced the trade unions as partners in the drive to create a nonexploitative social order; the General Federation reciprocated by pledging itself to "help to build the new Arab socialist society by contributing to the technical and political formulation of the workers" at its 1968 national congress.[43]

As the rivalry between Salah Jadid and Hafiz al-Asad intensified after 1968, the faction of the Ba'th allied to Jadid attempted to mobilize radical members of the General Federation of Trade Unions in opposition to the military wing of the party led by al-Asad. The leadership of the federation joined those of the General Federation of Peasants, the General Federation of Women, and several other associations in announcing that "the Popular Organizations insist on strengthening and developing the form of the present regime. They regard retreat from the achievements implemented by the party and the Popular Organizations . . . as the beginning of a painful setback which only serves the counter-revolutionary forces in their ferocious attack."[44] And immediately after the congress adjourned Minister of Defense al-Asad and his allies in the armed forces ousted Jadid and took control of both the party and the state apparatus.

Ten days after seizing power, newly appointed Prime Minister al-Asad called on the offices of the General Federation of Trade Unions to explain his cabinet's political and economic programs to the leadership of this organization. In the wake of his visit, leading trade unionists expressed support for the new regime and al-Asad reciprocated by urging the formation of a National Progressive Front made up of "all national progressive groups and elements" sharing a commitment to national unity, freedom and socialism. More specifically, the prime minister told a rally in the capital in early December 1970:

> We have to stress that the Popular Organizations which represent the widest masses must carry on their tasks in leading the socialist transformation and popular censure of the state apparatus, and in participating in the fulfillment of popular democracy. We shall work in co-operation with the leaderships of these

organizations in preparing the objective action which will enable them to carry out and realize their role.[45]

These moves not only provided the new regime with vital connections to Syria's well-organized labor movement but also opened the door to closer relations between the Ba'th on the one hand and the Syrian Communist Party and Nasirist Arab Socialist Union on the other.

As a result of this early bargaining between the trade union federation and the al-Asad regime, Syria's labor organizations were able to maintain a degree of autonomy from party and government officials throughout the 1970s. Longuenesse reports that Ba'thi nominees usually provided the largest proportion of candidates in the federation's local and provincial elections during these years; but, she continues,

> Sometimes alternate lists, or rather individuals, will present themselves. They are usually activists in the leftwing parties or members of the opposition front of dissident communists and Nasserists, Muslim Brothers or independents. These candidates are rarely elected, but in the fall of 1978 discontent with the deteriorating standard of living was translated into the election of a number of candidates who ran against the official list.[46]

The gap separating the regime from radicals within the trade-union federation narrowed precipitately in the face of more militant opposition on the part of the country's Islamist movement. By the spring of 1980, high-ranking party and state officials were reaffirming their commitment to a program of socialist transformation in general and to the revitalization of the popular-front organizations in particular. The government even encouraged the arming of popular militias recruited from the membership of the workers' and peasants' federations to assist the armed forces in suppressing Islamist activity. Units of the workers' militia participated in ferreting out Ikhwani strongholds in Hamah and Aleppo that April. In the aftermath of these operations, President al-Asad appointed the presidents of the General Federations of Trade Unions and of Peasants to the central committee of the governing National Progressive Front.[47] Such active collaboration between the organized labor movement and Syria's dominant social coalition was greatly facilitated by the institutional linkages Ba'thi leaders forged between the trade union federation and the party in the two decades after 1963. But it also reflects the labor movement's success in resisting total domination by the party-state hierarchy.

In Iraq, trade unions have continued to be marginalized during the years since Saddam Husain seized control of the party-state administration in mid-July 1979. The insignificance of the labor movement to the Ba'thi regime is illustrated by the results of the elections to the new National Assembly held in June 1980: despite the party's official recognition of the proletariat "as the class that together with the 'revolutionary intelligentsia' is supposed to comprise the pioneer-class upon which the revolution relies," only a handful of workers was elected as representatives to this assembly.[48] A somewhat more impressive collection of trade unionists won seats in the second National Assembly elections of June 1984, largely as part of a concerted effort by the regime to prop up public morale in the face of a string of tactical reverses in the war with Iran.[49] But the subordination of the unions to the party apparatus was evident in the local elections held a year earlier; the 1.25 million workers polled in these elections were provided with a single list of candidates drawn up by Baʿthi officials.[50]

In the spring of 1987, the Iraqi regime drastically restructured the country's trade-union system by removing the legal basis for the state-affiliated locals and reinstating labor organizations in private sector firms. President Saddam Husain announced the new policy by telling the leadership of the moribund General Federation of Trade Unions that the term "workers" had been abolished and that henceforth all trade union members would be called "officials." Consequently, he continued, workers' federations could safely be disbanded, "now that all are becoming state officials."[51] The central committee of the General Federation dutifully prepared plans for the organization's dissolution in the weeks following the president's speech. This development marked a crucial stage in the regime's turn toward wholesale privatization: by permitting company unions in the private sector, it added to workers' incentives to move away from inefficient public-sector enterprises and into newly established private firms suffering from acute shortages of labor. And by dissolving the remnants of the overarching labor federation in the state-run companies it removed one of the few potential institutional bases for opposition to its accelerated liberalization program.

CONCLUSION

After pursuing more or less identical programs involving state-led industrialization and state-sponsored efforts to redistribute indigenous wealth and nationalize the local operations of outside firms during the 1960s, the Baʿthi regimes in Syria and Iraq have adopted markedly different strategies to reduce the level of state intervention in their respective economies in more recent years. Syria has largely maintained its extensive network of public-sector holding companies while introducing a greater variety of market mechanisms in an attempt to enhance the efficiency and productivity of these firms; Iraq, on the other hand, has virtually dismantled its public sector through a wholesale policy of privatizing major agricultural, commercial, and light industrial enterprises and by soliciting substantial amounts of foreign direct investment. The divergent modes of economic liberalization implemented by the Syrian and Iraqi regimes illustrate not only the wide diversity that characterizes the general trend away from socialist political and economic orders in the contemporary Arab world but also the importance of distinguishing among countries in this region on the basis of their respective social structures rather than according to the ideological tenets articulated by their respective governing elites.

Three aspects of relations between dominant and opposition forces in Syrian and Iraqi society provide a fruitful and elegant explanation for the difference between the liberalization programs adopted by the regimes in Damascus and Baghdad. In the first place, the Syrian labor movement finds itself in a much stronger position relative to the dominant social coalition than does the Iraqi labor movement. This puts Syrian workers in a relatively advantageous strategic situation in local society, leaving forces within the regime highly vulnerable to threats to disrupt or slow down the industrial sector of the economy. Second, the relatively advantageous position enjoyed by the Syrian labor movement is reinforced by a notable side effect of the liberalization program initiated by the regime during the early 1970s: moves designed to deregulate domestic economic affairs and encourage the expansion of private enterprise disproportionately benefitted Syria's smaller traders and craftspeople, who represented the most powerful challengers to the dominant coalition of state officials and rich Damascene merchants. Consequently, the regime in Damascus became heavily dependent upon the continued support or acquiescence of the trade unions in its struggle against Islamist militants associated with the urban petite bourgeoisie. In Iraq, on the other hand, *infitah* has, for the most part, consolidated the position of the regime by channeling greater resources into the hands of forces within the dominant social coalition, while potential and actual challengers have been undermined or suppressed relatively handily. As a result, the country's rulers have had no need to propitiate the trade unionists and have, instead, undertaken a wholesale purge of radicals within the organized labor movement. This drive has left the workers' federation virtually subordinate to the dictates of the regime and precluded the emergence of opposition to privatization from among the rank and file.

Finally, Syria's General Federation of Trade Unions has maintained a relatively high degree of autonomy vis-à-vis the dominant social coalition, which has enabled its members to resist becoming totally dominated by the party-state apparatus. Its counterpart in Iraq has had no such success: the incorporation of the labor movement into the central administration has left no institutional basis for trade-union opposition to the regime's economic policies. Under these circumstances, the divergence between these two countries' political-economic orders is likely to grow during the 1990s, exacerbating ideological and diplomatic conflicts between their respective Baʿthi leaderships.

Notes

1. *Middle East Economic Digest (MEED)*, 15 August and 14 November 1987.
2. *MEED*, 15 August 1987.
3. *MEED*, 12 September 1987.
4. *Economic Review of the Arab World* (Beirut) (ERAW), November 1988.
5. "Étude analytique de l'économie syrienne: 1981," *Syrie et Monde Arabe* 345 (25 No-

vember 1982): 2–5; Yahya M. Sadowski, "Cadres, Guns and Money: The Eighth Regional Congress of the Syrian Ba'th," *MERIP Reports* 134 (July–August 1985): 5–6.

6. Damascus Domestic Service, 29 November and 5 December 1989 (FBIS); Damascus Television Service, 4 December 1989 (FBIS).

7. Marion Farouk-Sluglett, "Iraq after the War (2)—The Role of the Private Sector," *Middle East International* 346 (17 March 1989): 17–18.

8. *MEED,* 9 September and 4 and 18 November 1988.

9. *MEED,* 26 May 1989.

10. *MEED,* 22 September 1989.

11. *MEED,* 12 May 1989.

12. Phebe Marr, *The Modern History of Iraq* (Boulder, Colo.: Westview Press, 1985), p. 268.

13. Ibid., p. 266; Elisabeth Longuenesse, "L'Industrialisation et sa signification sociale," in A. Raymond, ed., *La Syrie d'aujourd'hui (Paris: CNRS, 1980)*, p. 333.

14. Longuenesse, "The Class Nature of the State in Syria," *MERIP Reports* 77 (May 1979): 9–10.

15. Volker Perthes, "The Bourgeoisie and the Ba'th," *Middle East Report* 170 (May–June 1991): 35–37.

16. Longuenesse, "Class Nature," p. 5.

17. Hanna Batatu, "Syria's Muslim Brethren," *MERIP Reports* 110 (November–December 1982): 16.

18. Perthes, "Bourgeoisie and the Ba'th," p. 33.

19. Batatu, "Syria's Muslim Brethren," p. 15; Raymond A. Hinnebusch, "The Islamic Movement in Syria: Sectarian Conflict and Urban Rebellion in an Authoritarian-Populist Regime," in A. Dessouki, ed., *Islamic Resurgence in the Arab World* (New York: Praeger, 1982), pp. 154–56; idem., "Syria," in S. Hunter, ed., *The Politics of Islamic Revivalism* (Bloomington: Indiana University Press, 1988), pp. 50–51.

20. Fred H. Lawson, "Social Bases for the Hamah Revolt," *MERIP Reports* 110 (November–December 1982).

21. Hinnebusch, *Authoritarian Power and State Formation in Ba'thist Syria: Army, Party, and Peasant* (Boulder, Colo.: Westview Press, 1990), p. 284.

22. Lawson, "Political-economic Trends in Ba'thi Syria: A Reinterpretation," *Orient* 29 (December 1988): 593.

23. Quoted in 'Isam al-Khafaji, "State Incubation of Iraqi Capitalism," *Middle East Report* 142 (September–October 1986): 6.

24. Ibid.

25. Robert Springborg, "Infitah, Agrarian Transformation, and Elite Consolidation in Contemporary Iraq," *Middle East Journal* 40 (Winter 1986): 44.

26. Batatu, "State and Capitalism in Iraq: A Comment," *Middle East Report* 142 (September–October 1986): 11.

27. Al-Khafaji, "State Incubation," p. 8.

28. Farouk-Sluglett, " 'Socialist' Iraq 1963–1978—Towards a Reappraisal," *Orient* 23 (June 1982): 217–18; Celine Whittleton, "Oil and the Iraqi Economy," in Committee Against Repression and for Democratic Rights in Iraq (CARDRI), *Saddam's Iraq* (London: Zed Press, 1986), pp. 67–69.

29. Marr, *Modern History of Iraq,* table 9.2, p. 257.

30. Marr, *Modern History of Iraq,* p. 258.

31. Farouk-Sluglett and Peter Sluglett, *Iraq Since 1958* (London: KPI, 1987), p. 174.

32. Samir al-Khalil, *Republic of Fear: The Politics of Modern Iraq* (Berkeley and Los Angeles: University of California Press, 1989), pp. 39–42.

33. Farouk-Sluglett and Sluglett, "Iraqi Ba'thism: Nationalism, Socialism and National-Socialism," in CARDRI, *Saddam's Iraq,* p. 104.

34. U. Zaher, "The Opposition," in CARDRI, *Saddam's Iraq,* pp. 154–55.

35. *Iraqi Letter,* no. 4 (May 1979), as quoted in ibid., p. 155.

36. Marr, *Modern History of Iraq,* p. 281; *MEED,* 28 January 1983.

37. Longuenesse, "The Syrian Working Class Today," *MERIP Reports* 134 (July-August 1985): 18.

38. Marr, *Modern History of Iraq*, p. 273.

39. *MEED*, 5 August 1983.

40. Farouk-Sluglett, Sluglett and Joe Stork, "Not Quite Armageddon: Impact of the War on Iraq," *MERIP Reports* 125–26 (July–September 1984): 29.

41. Max Rodenbeck, "Egypt and Iraq: Accusations Fly," *Middle East International* 364 (1 December 1989): 11.

42. Deborah Cobbett, "Women in Iraq," in CARDRI, *Saddam's Iraq*, p. 135.

43. Longuenesse, "Syrian Working Class Today," p. 23.

44. *Middle East Record 1969–70*, p. 1155.

45. Ibid., pp. 1163 and 1165–66.

46. Longuenesse, "Syrian Working Class Today," p. 24.

47. *Middle East Contemporary Survey 1979–80*, p. 768.

48. Amatzia Baram, "The June 1980 Elections to the National Assembly in Iraq: An experiment in Controlled Democracy," *Orient* 22 (1981): 405–407.

49. *Middle East Contemporary Survey 1984–85*, pp. 464–65.

50. *Middle East Contemporary Survey 1982–83*, p. 570.

51. *MEED*, 28 March 1987.

CHAPTER

8

ECONOMIC LIBERALIZATION IN OIL-EXPORTING COUNTRIES: IRAQ AND SAUDI ARABIA

Kiren Aziz Chaudhry

The economic recession of the 1980s precipitated economic liberalization and privatization programs in most developing countries, fueling the popular view that capitalism and democracy have been globally recognized as a tonic for underdevelopment.[1] The new orthodoxy of development economics views "the market" as a panacea for the economic crisis in the Third World, yet it fails to explain the severe difficulties confronting almost all economic liberalization programs.[2]

This chapter examines the experiences of two major oil exporters, Saudi Arabia and Iraq, in restructuring their economies during the recession period of the 1980s. It focuses not so much on why or how these policies were initiated but, rather, on what these cases can tell us about the obstacles to market reforms in late developers that, until recently, enjoyed virtually unlimited access to foreign exchange. Privatization and liberalization programs either failed outright in the so-called market economies of Saudi Arabia and the United Arab Emirates or were blocked in the so-called socialist countries of Syria, Libya, and Algeria through the concerted efforts of labor, party members, and bureaucrats. The Ba'thist regime of Iraq, however, emerged from a devastating eight-year war to implement the most wide-ranging privatization program in the Middle East.[3] Because of its apparent success, particularly in comparison with other oil exporters, the Iraqi experience in economic restructuring raises a number of questions about the political, economic, and social prerequisites for privatization and economic liberalization.[4]

On the eve of the reform efforts, Iraq and Saudi Arabia shared important characteristics. Neither country was well equipped to implement market reforms in the 1980s. Heavy reliance on external capital inflows conditioned domestic institutions and the formation of social classes in ways that were antithetical to market reform.[5] The inflow of oil revenues in the preceding decade had forestalled the development of legal, regulatory, financial, and administrative institutions necessary to define property rights, cut transaction costs, enforce contracts, and promote competition. The oil boom of the 1970s diminished the extractive, regulatory, and information-gathering capacities of both bureaucracies while expanding the distributive and productive capacities of the state in Saudi Arabia and Iraq, respectively.

Despite wide differences in the ideological proclivities of the two regimes, the role of the state in the two economies was comparable, suggesting the irrelevance of ideology in determining the scope of government intervention in major oil exporters. The content of this involvement, however, differed. Iraq was a radical socialist state in which all aspects of the economy, including retailing, were dominated if not completely controlled by the government. The state's direct control and ownership of all aspects of the Iraqi economy generated state institutions specializing in self-regulation and production which, nevertheless, lacked the capacity to regulate a private economy. Saudi Arabia, while professing to be a laissez-faire economy, was in fact an almost completely unregulated private economy in which state spending and distribution were the primary sources of capital accumulation. Lacking any resemblance to a market system, the Saudi economy was, instead, a completely open system where the state simultaneously subsidized importers, producers, and consumers through the unencumbered distribution of oil revenues.

The boom years undercut the development of corporate groups necessary for national markets to function smoothly. In both cases, the weak legitimacy of the regimes led the state to deliberately thwart the development of political or corporate groups. The remarkably nonconflictual climate of the boom years undercut the emergence of corporate groups in both cases. In Saudi Arabia, individual rather than group strategies were most successful. Economic conflict between different social groups was minimal, while primordial divisions persisted and were, in many cases, strengthened. As the state mediated the relationship between all incipient classes in both cases, neither the need nor the institutional context for aggregating interests or bargaining developed. In Iraq, the Ba'thist regime penetrated corporate, religious, and even familial groups, deliberately and systematically destroying, by force and repression, all civil institutions.[6] The distributive policies of both regimes, in their direct and indirect guises, were designed precisely to forestall the development of conflict between the government and various groups and among groups in civil society itself. In short, both the "socialist" intrusions of the Iraqi state and the distributive measures of the Saudi government aimed to control the economy to achieve political ends.

In both countries, the complex set of characteristics that one might call "culture of the market" was nonexistent. Confidence in the legal system and property rights was minimal, primordial loyalties were not replaced by "self-interest" as a motive for behavior, and collective group interests were not clearly recognized. In Saudi Arabia, appeal to the ultimate authority of key members of the royal family and the importance of informal forms of access mitigated the acceptance of the broad norms of competition and equality under the law. In Iraq, fear of the arbitrary and pernicious nature of the Ba'thist regime, particularly in light of its previous hostility to private capital, undercut investor confidence. Furthermore, neither regime had been willing to liberalize information: income distribution, the productive capacities of existing industries, and other pertinent information continued to be jealously guarded by the state.

The variation in the initial outcomes of the reforms was the result of the different sources of social opposition to the policies and divergent patterns of business-government relations in the two countries. Historically, both regimes were dominated by sectarian, regional and tribal minorities. Both the Saudi and Ba'thist regimes assumed political power despite the opposition of traditional commercial classes drawn from opposing primordial groups and faced the task of constructing a social base of support while undercutting the economic dominance of their primordial rivals. By the 1980s, both regimes had managed to neutralize the old commercial elites. In Iraq, the economic power of the old Shi'i commercial elites was undermined, if not virtually eliminated, through nationalization, intimidation, and mass deportations. The state directly gained control of agriculture, industry, trade, and services. The Ba'thist regime's main clients were located in the bureaucracy and the army, but broad-based subsidies and wage policies maintained stable standards of living for laborers and consumers. The private sector clients of the Iraqi Ba'th were a very small group of private contractors who controlled over 80 percent of the construction sector in the 1970s and 1980s. In contrast, the Saudi government replaced the old Hijazi elite through state contracts, finance, and patronage, creating a very large new private sector which mirrored the tribal characteristics of the Nejdi bureaucracy. In the recession, as both regimes tried to withdraw the flow of oil wealth from their respective clients in society, the forces of opposition to the liberalization policies were very different in the two cases.

In the initial stages of the market reforms, the absence of an industrial and commercial elite in Iraq (such as the large, protected group in Saudi Arabia), was crucial in allowing the market reforms to be implemented. When combined with the regime's ability to disregard distributional issues, the Iraqi state's unequivocal dominance of the economy in the form of direct ownership was an administrative bonus. Even though the ideological justifications for liberalization policies were firmly entrenched in Saudi Arabia, the existence of a highly protected and pampered private sector in that country forestalled economic liberalization policies immediately.

The contrasting experience of these two countries suggests not only that the absence of a domestic entrepreneurial and industrial class can, in some instances, enhance the initial success of market reforms but that the existence of a large, highly protected economic elite can be an insurmountable barrier to liberalization. In the initial stage, the state's ability to push through disruptive reforms appears to be directly related to existing contours of business-government relations and the cohesion of other social groups that may oppose privatization.

NATIONAL MARKETS AND THE STATE

The difficulties confronted by liberalization programs in oil exporters raise the larger issue of how national markets are constructed and underline the critical role of the state in creating markets. Market reforms initiated after a long hiatus in economic regulation are administratively demanding and politically disruptive in all countries attempting to reintroduce domestic market forces, whether these involve transitions from socialist redistributive regimes, state capitalism, or distributive patrimonial systems. While the importance of institutional transformations has increasingly been recognized,[7] the Saudi and Iraqi cases illustrate the still more complex social, legal, political, and psychological changes that must accompany successful transitions. Because of particularly truncated institutional and social processes related to their status as oil exporters, the experiences of Saudi Arabia and Iraq in the 1980s illustrate the process by which national markets are formed and the administrative, informational, and social rigidities that must be overcome for them to function. When examined in light of these broader processes of state-building, national integration, and the creation of social consensus for radical shifts in economic policy, privatization programs shed light on the conflicting pressures confronting a very special subset of late developers with intimate ties to the volatile global economy.

On the other hand, markets do not emerge full-blown under the pressure of sheer political will. While the comparative analysis of the two oil exporters underscores the high efficacy of certain social groups in forestalling liberalization schemes, the Iraqi case demonstrates the necessity of broad-based institutional and social change before economies dominated by the state can respond fruitfully to "shock therapy."

Finally, Iraq and Saudi Arabia's reliance on oil revenues illustrates the ways in which the external capital inflows to which so many developing countries had access in the 1970s undermine the evolution and impair the capacities of those public and private institutions necessary for the creation of national markets. They highlight, in rather dramatic terms, some of the reasons why the numerous social, institutional, and political prerequisites for the creation of functioning national markets have failed to emerge in the developing world. At a broad theoretical level, these difficulties challenge the key assumption of economics that markets exist in an administrative vacuum and question the notion that "state" and "market" are two alternative modes of economic organization.

INTERNATIONAL ECONOMIC FORCES AND DOMESTIC MARKETS IN OIL EXPORTERS

In the decade between 1973 and 1983 the inflow of wealth to many developing countries in the form of aid, loans, oil revenues, labor remittances, and investment curtailed the need for market reform and expanded state control of the economy. The bulk of these resources accrued directly to the state, but even in countries where the sources of external capital, such as labor remittances, were privately controlled, the institutional response of the state was to shrink regulatory institutions and pursue the most politically convenient regulatory strategies possible. Access to external capital inflows had a profound influence on the institutional, social, and political structures of recipient countries.

These changes are nowhere clearer than in major oil exporters and are crucial to understanding the domestic context in which the liberalization reforms of the 1980s were undertaken. In oil exporters, external capital influenced the structure and functions of the state bureaucracy by undercutting regulatory and extractive institutions and augmenting the role of the state in direct production and distribution.[8] Oil revenues, like state controlled loans and aid, saved the government from having to tax its population directly and enhanced the ease with which the state could ameliorate political conflict through directly distributing resources through gifts, subsidies, loans, and state contracts. Over the 1970s, distribution and direct state ownership of production became the primary, if not the sole instrument through which oil exporters regulated the economy. Along with extractive and regulatory institutions, capital markets, commercial law, banking, and insurance industries remained undeveloped; the old bourgeoisie was eliminated or driven into the lower echelons of the business community and replaced by bureaucratic and private elites with strong links to the state.

The inflow of oil revenues to state coffers in the 1970s expanded the role of the state in major oil exporters to such a degree that even in those countries that professed to have market economies it was difficult to distinguish between the public and private sectors. In Kuwait, Saudi Arabia, Libya, the UAE, Iraq, and Iran, oil revenues comprised over 50 percent of the GNP in the 1970s, giving the government ample funds to simultaneously subsidize producers, importers and consumers. The volume of subsidies was such that market forces in labor, commodity and financial markets ceased to exist. The key difference between countries like Iraq and Libya on the one hand and Kuwait and Saudi Arabia on the other, was not in the extent of state interference in the economy but, rather, in the composition of the client groups. The "socialist" oil states entered directly into production themselves, taking over industry, agriculture, trade, and services, and they used their control to uphold the living standards of a broad base of consumers. The "capitalist" oil states, on the other hand, distributed oil wealth to create clients in society who had strong primordial links to bureaucrats and decision makers.

Through a variety of means, including state contracts and consumption, interest-free lending, and patronage, a class of private sector "commission entrepreneurs" emerged in each country during the boom years. In all but the Kuwaiti case, these groups were distinct from the old merchant classes. While the size of the client groups varied a great deal, oil states uniformly practiced corporatism on a grand scale, using distributive policies to create economic groups as a base of social support on the one hand and to ameliorate conflict between sectoral, occupational, economic, and social groups on the other. Explicitly designed to depoliticize the population, these distributive policies forestalled the emergence of class conflict and public debate about the ends of development and growth. In all cases, the government went about deliberately destroying independent civil institutions while generating others designed to facilitate the political aims of the state. In Saudi Arabia, Iraq, and Libya the government deliberately destroyed the stronghold of the old private sector, although the means employed to this end varied a great deal. The new private-sector elites emerged in a peculiar economic period where quick profits and low risks were the norm. In the highly insulated business environment of the 1970s, these elites failed to develop the entrepreneurial skills that would enable them to withstand either domestic or international competition.

In the recession of the 1980s, when oil exporters faced pressure to cut state spending, rationalize prices, and solicit the participation of the private sector in economies less insulated from risk, none of the social and institutional prerequisites for creating competitive domestic markets existed. The societies and governments upon which the untempered ravages of the international economy were visited in the recession were singularly unprepared for them. In institutional terms, the task facing Iraq and Saudi Arabia in the recession was nothing less than a thorough reform of the public and private sectors. This entailed forging national regulatory, legal, and extractive institutions, as well as their ancillary information-gathering and enforcement agencies, and creating legal, accounting, and disclosure requirements for private-business elites who had yet to experience the burdens of regulation. The hiatus of regulation, conflict, and political debate in the 1970s coincided with the intensification of primordial and regional divisions. The oil state's abundant resources in the 1970s and early 1980s had allowed it to postpone the creation of alternative mechanisms for the expression and reconciliation of conflicting economic claims and interests. The resulting confrontation between state and social forces was particularly stark. The effects of political abstinence and the rise of primordial sentiments were cumulative: the process of liberalization was enmeshed in the struggle between primordial groups vying to protect their exclusive economic interests.

The fiscal crises fast became political crises. Authoritarian governments were confronted with the necessity of withdrawing the distributive policies of the 1970s and overcoming the objections of client social groups that opposed reforms in a political context where granting participation in return for taxes was ruled out at the onset due to weak political legitimacy.[9]

One result of the apolitical years of the 1970s was that in the recession it was unclear who was entitled to bargain on policy issues. The boom years favored individual or primordial group strategies over sector-specific ones and the awareness of convergent or conflicting economic interests remained dormant. Few legal, organized civil groups existed to aggregate and voice collective interests. The recession forced the government to step out of a direct mediating role and to replace the distributive bureaucracy with institutions that would provide a forum for the aggregation of interests and the resolution of conflicting claims. It was in this context that Iraq and Saudi Arabia initiated the reforms of the 1980s.

GOING TO MARKET: IRAQ AND SAUDI ARABIA IN THE 1980S

Emerging from radically different historical experiences, but sharing characteristics common to all major oil exporters, the attempts of both Iraq and Saudi Arabia to encourage private initiative are puzzling. While both regimes are authoritarian, they are formally committed to radically different ideologies. Saudi Arabia, arguably the most conservative monarchy in existence today, has always upheld its commitment to laissez-faire capitalism. Since it was founded in 1932, the Saudi state has proclaimed its adherence to an "Islamic" ideology developed through the teachings of Mohammed Ibn Abd al Wahab, the founder of the ultraconservative version of the Hanbali school of Islamic thought. The Ba'thist regime that has dominated Iraq, on the other hand, is avowedly socialist. Apart from Algeria and the People's Democratic Republic of Yemen, which had genuine revolutionary legacies, Iraq could, until recently, be described as the most radical socialist regime in the Middle East.

The involvement of the state in the economy of both countries had been so extensive as to obscure ideological differences. While neither regime has publicly revised its ideological position, deep ambiguities existed in the stated goals to be achieved by economic restructuring. The arguments by both regimes for expanding the role of the private sector are efficiency-related and reflect little political revisionism.[10] On the eve of the reforms, neither Iraq nor Saudi Arabia had a market economy. The form of state intervention, however, varied. In Iraq, the government dominated foreign and domestic trade, manufacturing and agriculture almost completely. By 1987, when the reforms began in earnest, 96 percent of Iraq's industrial work force was employed in state-owned factories which produced in excess of 84 percent of total industrial output. Government control of foreign trade was complete and its part in retailing was not unsubstantial. Over 50 percent of agricultural land was directly owned by the state. Similarly, the government owned banking, insurance, and other major services. The construction sector alone was the preserve of the private sector. In Saudi Arabia, by contrast, the government's involvement in direct production was limited to the large petrochemical projects, such as SABIC. Still, the role of government in the economy, through subsidies, price manipulation, state spending, interest-free credit, and other distributive measures, was as pronounced as that of the Iraqi government.

These varieties of government intervention resulted in wide differences in the client groups of the two regimes in civil society. Neither country, however, had the social, institutional and political prerequisites for the creation of self-sustaining domestic markets. Both liberalization and privatization policies were pursued by the two countries. Liberalization essentially means allowing prices to rise by curtailing state subsidies; privatization involves divestiture of state assets. Social opposition to liberalization is normally widespread, while privatization can provide a rather painless way of creating client groups, particularly in cases where prices remain subsidized, or labor is imported, or in cases where existing wages and continued employment of workers is a condition of privatization.

PRIVATIZATION AND LIBERALIZATION IN IRAQ

In Iraq, both liberalization and privatization policies were pursued simultaneously. Agriculture was the first to be privatized. While halting attempts to divest state-owned farms and agricultural projects had begun in 1983, privatization began in earnest in 1987 and gained momentum beginning in the fall of 1988, after the cease-fire with Iran was announced. Prompted by the steady decline in agricultural yield since the mid-1970s, which generated a soaring imports bill and created widespread rural to urban migration,[11] the new agricultural policies reflected a radical shift from an emphasis on equity to efficiency, based on production targets set by the Ministry of Planning.

While agricultural reforms have been the most dramatic, privatization of state-owned industries during 1989 was significant. In a single year, the Iraqi government divested seventy factories in construction materials and mineral extraction, food processing and light manufacturing.[12] The government made efforts to privatize specific parts of the service sector by selling small hotels and leasing gas stations to the private sector for a duration of three years.

In addition to divestment, the government adopted a number of policies to remove existing barriers to large industrial investments that had been in place since the nationalizations of 1964. In 1983, the investment ceilings were raised to ID 2 million and ID 5 million for solely owned and limited share companies, respectively. In 1988, the ceiling was lifted completely and private investors were allowed for the first time to invest in any sector. The law against cross-sectoral investment was abolished, allowing for the development of large, vertically integrated industrial, trading and agricultural conglomerates. Most important, previous tax laws, which claimed up to 75 percent of profits and forced large private industries to pay 25 percent of the remaining profits to social security funds for workers were abolished. In 1987, the maximum tax on industrial profits was lowered to 35 percent and then, in 1989, all industries were given a ten-year tax holiday.

While imports were previously completely controlled by the state either directly or through strict licencing procedures, starting in 1987 all imports were liberalized for the private sector provided that they were paid for with foreign exchange held outside the country. Export-promotion policies were also initiated in the form of access to foreign currency at a one-to-one ratio (compared with the black-market rate of ID 3.3/$1), provided that export earnings covered initial investment by 120 percent within two years.

Privatization and liberalization were accompanied by trimming the bureaucracy and the dissolution of the labor unions. Over two hundred general directors and their entire staffs were dismissed. Changes were introduced in the organizational structure of the still large public manufacturing sector, including worker incentives, greater management autonomy, and production bonuses. As a result, production in state-owned factories increased by 27 percent between 1987 and 1988, and labor productivity jumped by 24 percent. Concessions to state construction companies, ostensibly set up to complete "strategic" projects and to compete with foreign contractors in the 1970s, were withdrawn, forcing them to compete with private contractors for government projects.

Dramatic as they appear, the reforms of the 1980s did not signal a fundamental change in the balance between public and private shares in the economy. While private agricultural and industrial investment has grown in recent years,[13] the government's share in manufacturing actually grew. Despite tax breaks, price liberalization, and the new labor laws, total private industrial licenses for 1989 amounted to only ID 33 million for 117 new industrial projects. In contrast, government investment in downstream petrochemical projects alone was $3 billion for the same year. The government continued to control the "commanding heights" of the domestic economy and began work on several large joint ventures in automobile manufacturing, heavy industries, and arms manufacturing. While both public and private fixed-capital investments had declined steadily since 1983, at no point did the state's share fall below 76 percent. Indeed, even in construction, the traditional preserve of the private sector, the share of the public sector increased, while private-sector imports actually declined in 1989.[14]

In addition to its continuing presence in manufacturing and trade, the government's role in pricing policy remained significant. Only ten basic food products retained fixed prices, but the government had to resort to temporary price fixing and emergency imports of foodstuffs twice after commodity prices were deregulated. While price controls were lifted in 1988 on a number of agricultural products, they were reimposed a few months later after prices rose to unacceptable levels, before being lifted again.

In addition to price fixing, the government retains control of the "feed" projects for agribusinesses. Private investors in dairy farms, livestock, fisheries, and poultry remained dependent on the largest agribusinesses retained by the state for inputs of all kinds, including hatching eggs, imported livestock, components of feed, fish, machinery, spare parts, and so on. This was a deliberate policy designed to retain control over the agricultural sector, which is matched in the state's retention of ownership of land leased to the large grain-producing agribusinesses. Thus, while the economic liberalization and privatization policies appear to favor investors over labor and consumers, the government directly controlled agriculture and industry alike by controlling access to capital, machinery, and intermediate supplies.

The administrative problems of monitoring the private sector are far more difficult than anticipated, particularly since cooperation was required between the state and private enterprises. A formidable reorganization of the bureaucracy became necessary, for example, simply to insure that bread reached consumers at the fixed prices. The government subsidized producers and consumers alike, but as the farms, mills, bakeries, and retail outlets were privatized, price fixing required substantial administrative energies. Direct links between either local producers and processing industries or between exporters and producers were nonexistent. Yet, it was the deliberate policy of the government to force many transactions through the bureaucracy. Those agricultural enterprises and food-processing units that were retained by the government for "security reasons" were also responsible for monitoring inputs and prices, supplying spare parts and machinery, and performing a number of activities that involved the government directly in the day-to-day operation of the firms.

Despite these constraints, and what appeared to be exceedingly high social opportunity costs, in terms of pure efficiency, the private sector has performed well. In agricultural products, yield more than doubled. Industry's performance was difficult to evaluate due to absolute declines in production because of raw material shortages. However, labor costs were cut, production methods were improved, and, in many cases, local inputs were successfully substituted for imported intermediate products.[15]

Neither the timing nor the substance of Iraq's reforms can be understood in light of conventional explanations for liberalization and privatization measures, which stress fiscal considerations, external pressure, and the "coming of age" of the local bourgeoisie. The government's lack of an immediate profit motive is reflected in the fact that the total sale price for the seventy privatized industries was only ID 305 million. In most cases the prices paid for these enterprises barely covered the market cost of the land they were built on. In both agricultural and industrial projects, the government allowed the ownership to pass to the private sector with a down payment of 40 percent and an understanding that the remaining funds would be transferred in increments. Agricultural lands were leased at highly favorable rates and under the same deferred payment scheme.

Neither can these policies be explained as the natural outcome of a learning process in economic planning and management coupled with advances in the skills and resources of the private sector. It is incorrect to believe that the Iraqi bourgeoisie was somehow better prepared to assume its rightful place in 1988 than it was in 1964. In contrast to substantial capital stores enjoyed by the old commercial, landed, and industrial elite, after the consolidation of socialist gains of the 1970s, the activities of the traditional private sector were confined to retailing, wholesale, transportation, and small artisan industries and crafts.[16]

Finally, the role of international donors and agencies in pushing through the reforms in Iraq is negligible, if it exists at all. Despite its foreign debt, estimated—before its ill-fated invasion of Kuwait, to be about $30 billion, excluding loans from Arab countries—Iraq has maintained its independence from the West and international agencies alike, and it continues to strictly control the scope of external influence in the economy, even when this has meant foregoing favorable credit arrangements.

THE POLITICAL CALCULUS OF REFORM

Explanations of Iraq's economic policies in the 1990s must take into account the rather stark distributional decisions that these policies embody. First, the regime's choices had been strictly circumscribed by the regional aims of the top leadership, namely, to achieve military parity with Israel and strategic superiority over Iran. At base, the foreign-currency shortage grew directly from the planned outlays for military industries. The choices made by the government in implementing them suggest a rather unique formula of economic transformation in which all political pacts were sacrificed to the national aim of achieving military superiority in the region. In light of this aim, which was not open to debate or question, the government simply took the clearest path to achieve savings in foreign exchange. The speed with which the policies were undertaken, and the sheer impunity with which they were enforced, was not unrelated to the strength of the domestic repressive apparatus of the regime, which has long been strong enough to override, by force if necessary, any opposition.

Given the overarching aim of saving foreign exchange for military spending, the political calculus underlying the Iraqi liberalization policies cannot be understood without a review of their effects on the ability of the private sector to achieve the necessary production levels on the one hand and the impact of the reforms on different economic groups on the other. First, following a pattern reminiscent of bureaucratic authoritarian economic programs, the government began by neutralizing social opposition to the reforms, but it did so by undercutting the traditional sources of regime support in labor, consumers and the bureaucracy. In 1987, Saddam Hussein dissolved the labor union, which had included both private and state sector workers. Workers remaining in public-sector enterprises were turned into regular members of the civil service, while private-sector employees were formally given the right to reconstitute labor unions on their own. The right to form unions applied only to private sector establishments with over fifty workers, a category which covers only 8 percent of the total industrial work force. The membership in the General Union of Iraqi Labor, which had included agricultural, industrial, and service workers in both the private and public sectors, plummeted from 1.75 million to a total possible membership of only 7,794 in 1989.

In short, the government began its program by completely undercutting the bargaining power of labor, removing minimum wages, and opening up the domestic labor market to Arab labor at a time when some 200,000 members of the armed forces are returning to the civilian work force.[17] Unlike Egypt and Algeria, where concern for laborers in state-owned enterprises has been a dominant factor in forestalling privatization, Iraq's leadership did not hesitate to give industrialists full power to restructure employment. Not surprisingly, the first act of almost all of the new owners of industries and agribusinesses was the dismissal of between 40 and 80 percent of the laborers, with the aim of trimming costs as well as replacing Iraqi labor with Arab laborers.

Similarly, the second major source of opposition to privatization, the bureaucracy, was neutralized before the reforms began. Over two hundred "General Directorships," including their entire staffs, were dissolved and the Ministry of Industry was merged with the Ministry of Military Industries.

Consumers were the third group adversely affected by the reforms. Unlike labor and the bureaucracy, consumers lacked organization as well as a formal representative body. Allowing all but the prices of some basic goods to rise completely unchecked, creating inflation rates of over 60 percent by the end of 1989, was a direct consequence of the government's privatization and imports policy.

Ironically, the very factors that guaranteed the initial ease with which these measures were undertaken showed early signs of presaging their failure. At the same time that most food-processing and agricultural enterprises were turned over to the private sector, the government stopped providing raw materials for industry and curtailed state imports of foodstuffs drastically. For a variety of reasons, most notably severe foreign-exchange shortages, which prohibited capacity expansion, raw material imports, and access to spare parts, large-scale shortages of goods were created. Investors, though clearly the most favored group, lacked confidence in the regime's long-term commitment to private enterprise, and they priced goods at the highest possible level to recoup all their costs within two years. Thus, attempts to attract serious long-term investments, such as the sale of the large, government-owned luxury hotels, failed due to domestic and Arab investor's lack of confidence in the government's definition of property rights. The government's desire to retain control of certain companies—through stock ownership as well as representation on the boards of directors—contributed further to private sector uneasiness.

Government policies reflected a flagrant disregard for issues of equity that normally are the focus of debate in drastic economic restructuring programs. Unlike the Soviet Union, Poland, Syria, Egypt, and Algeria, the Iraqi regime felt no compulsion to solicit a public mandate for these policies or even to publicly revise its pronouncements on the redistributive aims of the regime. While in much of the Gulf recent attempts to expand the stock market are based on the explicit desire of the government to attract small investors and provide the poor with a regular source of income, no attempts were made to design policies that would expand ownership in Iraq. The stock market did not emerge as a source of investment capital. The total number of shareholders remained small, and shares in the lucrative "mixed-sector" plants (which have access to government foreign exchange and boast annual profit rates of between 30 and 90 percent) were used primarily as political patronage. Administrative sluggishness and legal restrictions on share-trading curtailed the entry of new investors and discouraged small investors.

RESULTS OF REFORM: COSTS AND BENEFITS

The result of Iraq's privatization and liberalization programs was highly inequitable. Ownership of the newly privatized enterprises was highly concentrated. Thirteen of the seventy factories that were privatized were bought by one family. Not counting agricultural projects, this same family owned thirty-six of the very largest industries and over 45 million square meters of land. The new importers, as well as the investors that bought and leased the large government holdings in agriculture and industry, were not traditional private sector elites; rather, most of them made their fortunes in contracting. Some of the smaller investors were retired army officers, particularly in agriculture. Unlike the old commercial elite, the new private sector emerging from the reforms had strong political, financial, and kinship ties to the regime. The continuing role of the government in determining access to foreign exchange, raw materials, spare parts, and other inputs forced the emerging private sector to maintain close contact with the bureaucracy.

The costs of the economic reforms in Iraq were clearly borne by fixed-income groups, consumers, and labor, who fondly recalled the long years of war with Iran as times of certainty and plenty. Private-sector elites were given wide privileges, but other policies prevented them from meeting domestic demand. In short, while enjoying unprecedented profits and benefits, private investors were hamstrung due to the lack of foreign exchange for capital goods. Furthermore, the institutional and social changes necessary for them to gain enough confidence to invest within the new policy framework showed no signs of emerging. Like other Third World entrepreneurial elites, Iraqi investors perceived free repatriation of capital as the only true guarantee for investments. The reforms failed completely in introducing domestic competition. Wary of one another, the legal system, and the regime's commitment to uphold contracts, new investors attempted to insulate themselves from each other by gaining control of all upstream and downstream activities in a particular product. Without the new investment and competition, the sale of industries to the private sector in Iraq has simply meant the transfer of public monopolies to private monopolies. Even in the best of circumstances, setting up new industries to meet domestic demand and to compete with existing plants requires a lead time of four to five years. In Iraq, where potential investors lack access to foreign exchange, the positive side of market reform will not emerge for the foreseeable future.

For many of the same reasons, foreign capital was equally shy of Iraq. While General Motors and Mercedes had begun construction on joint-venture plants with the government, non-Arab foreign investment was still strictly prohibited. Despite the fact that Iraqi investment laws were in many ways more favorable to Arab investors than to Iraqis themselves, Iraq did not succeed in luring any investors from the rich Gulf states. Palestinian, Lebanese, and Jordanian businessmen who enjoy high levels of mobility used the favorable laws to quickly affect highly lucrative transactions, but most of these were confined to commerce, and neither industrial investment nor investments in the large state-owned hotels was forthcoming. Apart from a handful of large industrial families who appeared to follow signals other than those apparent to outside observers or less well-connected Iraqis, investor confidence was low. Iraqi business, on the whole, was reluctant to sink large amounts of capital into any venture that did not promise a complete return on capital within two years. The government's dismal experience with attempted sales of the hotels attested to this reluctance.

By widely publicizing its withdrawal from the economy and divesting itself of those industries that catered specifically to the needs of the average consumer, the government freed itself from direct responsibility for inflation, shortages, and the mushrooming black market in goods, currencies, and services. Furthermore, by stepping out of its heavy role in mediating the relationship between consumers and labor on one hand and producers on the other, the blame for economic hardships was placed squarely on the shoulders of the newly affluent private industrialists and businessmen. The new terms under which workers or service-sector employees with fixed incomes were to bargain with business were deliberately left undefined. The resentment of the consumers, bureaucrats, and workers who bear the burden of these policies was a political facility that the state could use with impunity against the new entrepreneurs at any time.

Thus, while liberalization and privatization clearly benefitted the new business group in the short term, the private sector that emerged in the late 1980s was hamstrung in several ways. Although there is not enough evidence to prove or disprove the widely accepted view that this group forms a social base of support for the regime, the contradictory economic policies pursued in 1989 and 1990 almost guaranteed the failure of the private sector to import and produce enough to correct market shortages. Foreign-exchange shortages resulting from defense expenditures prevented production levels from rising to meet demand due to difficulty in obtaining raw materials, parts, and new machinery. The regime's reluctance to define property rights in such a way as to produce investor confidence coupled with its refusal to publicly revise its ideology and legitimate the growing inequalities in the cities naturally made investors shy, particularly in light of the historical acrimony between private capital and the state.

While the private sector was given wide privileges and undoubtedly forms a firm base of support for the regime, it bears the political onus of being the target of social discontent. This central fact explains the regime's willingness to divest precisely those factories that cater to the everyday needs of consumers. It is unclear whether even the present regime would be able to protect private capital from broad-based social discontent.

REFORM, OPPOSITION, AND NEW ENTITLEMENTS IN SAUDI ARABIA

Unlike Iraq's far-reaching economic restructuring program, the austerity measures in Saudi Arabia focused primarily on cutting budgetary outlays by imposing new fees and taxes, withdrawing general subsidies on goods and services, and cutting specific subsidies to industrial and agricultural producers. New labor regulations were introduced to force the private sector to relieve the public sector of excess labor, trim foreign labor, and take over social security payments previously covered by the government.

All those policies which affected the entrepreneurial elite—including corporate and individual taxes, *zakat* payments, progressive fees on the consumption of electricity, water and gasoline, the new Labor Transfer Law (requiring businessmen to get authorization for the import of foreign labor), the Saudization Law (requiring businesses to hire Saudi labor instead of foreign workers), the new Social Insurance Law (requiring business to pay social insurance payments previously covered directly by the state budget) and the withdrawal of agricultural subsidies—were successfully opposed through the Riyadh Chamber of Commerce and informal contacts and unceremoniously withdrawn. In contrast, minor fees on passports, document verification, and revised customs duties, all of which affected either low-income consumers or foreigners, were implemented.

Apart from blocking liberalization policies that would have cut into profits, the Saudi private sector united to demand broad-based protective measures against foreign competition in commodities and contracts.[18] Like other dormant pieces of legislation, protective laws already on the books had never been implemented during the oil-boom years and only began to be applied during the recession.[19] To alleviate the burdens of "unfair dumping and competition from foreigners," protective tariffs and indirect subsidies were demanded to enable domestic producers to compete with the prices of foreign goods and capture market shares.[20]

To achieve protection under the "buy Saudi" laws, Riyadh's businessmen advocated the creation of a centralized agency composed of bureaucrats and Chamber representatives to fill government supply needs with locally manufactured products.[21] Some private-sector elites even suggested that the government stop announcing tenders and preselect local factories to purchase goods from, regardless of price differentials![22] Further, in recognition of massive overcapacity in many industries, Saudi industrialists demanded export promotion subsidies so that they might compete in foreign markets. Unlike the Iraqi case, privatization in Saudi Arabia was risk free, both economically and politically: like previous sales of shares in public utilities and other state industries, the privatization of SABIC shares in 1987 were made on the basis of a 15 percent guaranteed rate of return.

Fantastic as these demands were, particularly in light of declining state revenues and the degree of government promotion already enjoyed by local industry, the government formally met all of them. In 1984, strict guidelines were issued, requiring contractors for state projects to use only local products if they were available and to use only local services, transport, insurance, food, and banking. In response to contractors' demands, as expressed in the March 1985 Business Conference in Riyadh, the 30 percent rule (stipulating that foreign contractors subcontract at least 30 percent of their projects to local companies) was expanded to require all contracts to be split into small enough portions for local contractors.[23] To overcome the persisting compliance problems within the bureaucracy, standard forms were issued for government agencies to fill out, certifying the purchase of domestically produced goods and services. The legislation delegated wide-ranging policing powers to the Council of Saudi Chambers to investigate complaints of local suppliers against government agencies and to link up suppliers and subcontractors with specific government projects.[24] In December 1985, an export-promotion agency was set up, with the participation of 160 local businessmen, to study and distribute export subsidies to local manufacturers.[25]

These patterns of opposition and capitulation reveal a great deal about the political priorities of the regime and the efficacy of different social groups in Saudi Arabia. The *ulema,* for example, opposed many of the new banking and legal regulations of the late 1980s but were regularly unable to affect policy change. The most effective group was composed on the new Nejdi business class and the state-created agricultural elite that had benefitted most from the state's distributive policies during the oil boom. In serving the interests of this group, the state was willing to retract its long-standing adherence to Wahabbi Islamic doctrine and to compromise its own fiscal soundness, the preservation of scarce national resources, and the interests of other, much larger groups, such as consumers and the swelling ranks of unemployed Saudi labor.

The successes of the Saudi business elite in defining the terms under which the post-boom economy would function was extensive and directly challenged the stated objectives of the government. Thus, despite the fourth Five Year Plan's repeated endorsements of the need for education and human resource development, the budget for the seven universities in the Kingdom fell from SR 9.84 billion in 1984–85 to SR 4.86 billion in 1988–89, while the budget of the Grain Silos Organization, which bought domestic wheat from local producers at ten times the international price, was increased from SR 2 billion to SR 3 billion over the same period. While overtime for professors and all government employees was abolished in 1986,[26] and salary, housing, and traveling allowances cuts were enforced strictly for civil servants, the government continued to subsidize all inputs and outputs for local industrialists and agricultural companies. On one hand, the government declared a freeze in hiring and promotions, withdrew its guarantee of employment for all Saudi graduates wanting public sector jobs,[27] and ran a deficit that was over 25 percent of the total budget;[28] on the other, shareholders in the electrical companies continued to receive their guaranteed 15 percent return on investments.

HISTORICAL ANTECEDENTS OF FAILURE: STATE-BUILDING AND BUSINESS-GOVERNMENT RELATIONS IN SAUDI ARABIA AND IRAQ

Both the Saudi and Iraqi governments set out to cut state outlays by creating domestic markets following the recession of the 1980s through liberalizing prices and encouraging the private sector to assume a larger role in the economy. Both

failed, but at very different junctures. The Iraqi regime was able to overcome resistance from the bureaucracy, labor, and consumers, succeeding in one year in
privatizing over seventy state factories (almost all agriculture, some services) and
liberalizing trade. In a country where previously all goods were imported, produced, and sold by the state, the highly subsidized prices of basic goods were
allowed to rise, reflecting the regime's abrogation of its long-standing commitment
to protect workers, fixed-income groups, and consumers.

The regime clearly had the political will to push the reforms through. The
smoothness with which these were carried out was enhanced by dissolving the
labor unions and abolishing an entire layer of the bureaucracy before implementing the reforms. In contrast, the Saudi private sector first blocked those liberalization policies that affected them and then successfully lobbied the government to
implement a series of privatization and protective measures resulting in new and
expanded state guarantees of private sector profits.

These two cases illustrate that the political decisions embodied by "liberalization" and "privatization" policies are not difficult to pinpoint. Both sets of market
reforms entailed the state's withdrawal from mediating conflict between economic
groups and the government's abrogation of long-standing commitments to its clients
in society. Although both regimes supported business in the short term, a variety
of factors forced Iraqi investors to assume primary responsibility for the disruptive
transition period. Business elites in Saudi Arabia, in contrast, were given extensive
concessions which absolved them from assuming any of the risks of participating
in a "market economy" while granting them all the benefits. While it is not difficult
to understand why the two governments sought to withdraw from their extensive
roles in the economy, or why the two regimes were no closer to the free-market
ideal after the reforms than before, the differences in their experiences reveals the
importance of existing patterns of state-society relations in setting the parameters
for reform. The differences between these two failed attempts to introduce competition and market forces in the domestic economy center on the differences in
the social basis of the two regimes and the historical evolution of business-government relations.

In both Iraq and Saudi Arabia, the deep primordial cleavages between the state
and business meant that the regulation of business was tightly entwined with pressing
issues of national integration and state building. In Iraq, due to the colonial legacy
and the strength of the private-sector conglomerates, during the mandate, these
were expressed in a particularly stark form. By historical accident, or colonial design, the military was composed of a different primordial group than the business
class, thereby heightening the sense of threat. To be sure, the general insecurity of
the postcolonial reconstitution was an important factor in the behavior of the entrepreneurial elites in Iraq: investors are naturally shy in times of great national
upheaval. But these other factors were important as well. While the populist agendas of the leaders that came to dominate politics were feared, the more basic threat
to the commercial elite was the newly independent government's interest in expanding competition, protecting consumers and undercutting the long-standing

monopolistic pacts that bound domestic commercial elites to the foreign corporations that thrived under colonial rule.

While the initial confrontation between the government of the two oil states and their respective private sectors determined the character of state intervention in the economy in the long term, in the 1970s the enormous inflow of oil revenues expanded the economic role of the state in both cases and allowed both regimes to create new social bases of support in society. In Saudi Arabia, state contracts, loans, gifts, and a variety of formal and informal distributive measures were used to create a large new entrepreneurial elite with strong kinship and business ties to the bureaucracy and political elites. In Iraq, oil revenues expanded the government's role in direct ownership and control of industry, trade, agriculture services, and even retailing. The Iraqi state's core supporters were located in the army and the bureaucracy. Key positions in these institutions, in turn, increasingly became the preserve of individuals from Takrit and its environs, many of whom were related to Saddam Hussain, Chairman of the Revolutionary Command Council. Unlike Saudi Arabia, so acute was the Suni government's sense of threat from the Shi'i commercial classes and their cosectarians that form a majority of the Iraqi population, that the government took every opportunity to eliminate the Shi'i leadership in both the economic and the socioreligious realms through mass deportations, imprisonment, and other, more violent methods. Apart from the top echelons of the Ba'th Party, a group that is hardly characterized by stable tenure, the private clients of the government were confined to a very small, new class of contractors who dominated the entire construction sector and benefitted enormously by winning state construction projects or acting as intermediaries between foreign companies and the state. Through directly setting wages and prices, the Iraqi government cultivated a broader level of economic dependency among labor and consumers, who were protected from inflation during the 1970s and then through eight years of war with Iran.

Thus, while weak legitimacy fostered economic policies designed to create a loyal base of support in both societies, the composition of this base of support differed radically. When the market reforms were introduced in Saudi Arabia, they were opposed by the private sector and their patrons in the bureaucracy. In Iraq, where the more radical reforms cut at the stability of prices and wages enjoyed by labor, consumers, and state employees, the privatization and liberalization policies were preceded by the abolition of the labor unions and the dismissal of an entire tier of the bureaucracy. The Iraqi regime, so adept at testing the fragilities of the human body, encountered no resistance to its policies, as the only groups that could have effectively organized against the policies were neutralized at the onset. Through the sale of government factories and services at highly preferential rates to individuals with links to the top leadership of the government, however, and up until its invasion of Kuwait, the Iraqi regime was on its way to creating precisely the kind of parasitic entrepreneurial class that exists in Saudi Arabia. Yet, the resentment of labor and consumers against the new private-sector elite in Iraq had grown to a feverish pitch by the turn of the decade. Distancing itself from the shortages and inflation that had accompanied the privatization measures, the regime would certainly have wide support if it decided to renationalize. If this were to happen, the pattern of profiteering, failed regulation, and nationalization would mirror exactly the events of 1958–64 in Iraq.

These two cases illustrate the severity and depth of the difficulties that regimes encounter when trying to liberalize the market and foster competition. While the immediate cause of the failure of the Saudi attempts and the initial success of the Iraqi government is to be found in the organizational strength of social groups opposed to economic restructuring, both governments failed in achieving even a partial transition to a market economy. To the extent that their experiences reflect the diverse sources of opposition and resistance to "market forces," these cases might be instructive to the proponents of the new economic liberalism. If nothing else, the Saudi case shows that the private sector is not always in favor of "markets." Indeed, the absence of a large and pampered entrepreneurial elite was critical in Iraq's initial successes. The issue of whether the initial process of market reform might be easier in completely state-dominated economies where a protected entrepreneurial class does not exist might be one focus of future inquiry.

On the other hand, the barriers to sustained investment necessary for competitive, functioning markets are likely to be high in cases where potential investors fail to gain confidence in the regime's commitment to free enterprise. Certainly, the Iraqi case demonstrates the importance of confidence and clearly defined property rights in enabling initial successes to be transformed into lasting changes.

While major oil exporters are unique in a variety of ways, the entrepreneurial elite in all countries with import substitution regimes are accustomed to a level of protection and privilege that eschews market reform. It would not be a surprise to find that resistance to economic liberalization is located precisely in the upper echelons of the private sector in developing countries.

Like oil exporters, many less developed countries have relied heavily on external capital inflows over the past fifteen years to meet their foreign-exchange commitments, with many of the same distorted outcomes as those found in the two countries discussed here. Although in some countries, such as Algeria and Jordan, economic reform has been accompanied by political liberalization, the two are unlikely to coexist for a simple reason: while in the short term, political liberalization appears to be qualifying such countries for some portion of a shrinking pool of development aid, long-term economic growth can only be achieved with the help of foreign investors who are likely to demand low domestic wages, repatriation of profits, tax holidays, and so on. Providing these will require holding down local wages and squeezing nationals for tax revenues through arrangements well documented by students of bureaucratic authoritarianism in Latin America. Because of the broad-based protection offered to entrepreneurs in mixed economies as well as the wage policies made possible by import-substitution policies (which, unlike export-led strategies, do not necessitate holding down domestic wages) the political constituencies of liberalizing regimes are likely to shrink suddenly in the very near future. The contours of these changes are unlikely to be understood within the neoliberal framework but, rather, through comparative historical research which revives themes common to the old orthodoxy in development economics.

Notes

1. I thank Rem Kinne, Steve Solnick, and David Laitin for comments on an earlier draft of this chapter. Field research was funded by the Social Science Research Council and the American Council of Learned Societies. Writing was supported by the Kukin Fellowship from the Harvard Academy of International and Area Studies. Neither organization is responsible for the content of this essay. While the case material presented here draws heavily on material collected in Iraq and on interviews of businessmen, bureaucrats, policy makers, and labor leaders in Baghdad, no references to these interviews will appear in the text. The author apologizes for this necessary breach of professional norms.

2. For an excellent review of these difficulties and a critique of some of the assumptions made by the neoliberals, see Tony Killick and Simon Commander, "State Divestiture as a Policy Instrument in Developing Countries," *World Development* 16, no. 12 (1988): 1465–79.

3. When compared with the results of Egypt's much advertised *infitah* policies, which resulted in the privatization of exactly one state-owned enterprise between 1975 to 1989, the Iraqi success is truly striking. See Said El-Naggar, ed., *Privatization and Structural Adjustment in the Arab Countries* (Washington, D.C.: International Monetary Fund, 1989).

4. The massive destruction of Iraq by coalition forces in the Gulf War of 1990–91 and by civil insurrections after Iraq's defeat further calls into question the direction of economic liberalization and reform.

5. Kiren Aziz Chaudhry, "The Price of Wealth: Business and State in Labor Remittance and Oil Economies" (Ph.D. diss., Harvard University, 1990).

6. For an account of this process that is based partly on first-hand experience, see Samir al-Khalil, *Republic of Fear: The Politics of Modern Iraq* (Berkeley and Los Angeles: University of California Press, 1989).

7. Building on the work of Karl Polanyi and Douglas North, the excellent essays in Victor Nee and David Stark's edited volume *Remaking the Economic Institutions of Socialism: China and Eastern Europe* (Stanford: Stanford University Press, 1989) discuss this issue in detail.

8. This argument is developed in detail in Kiren Chaudhry, "The Price of Wealth: Business and State in Labor Remittance and Oil Economies," *International Organization* (Winter 1989).

9. Only in Kuwait, where returns on foreign investment cushioned the recession, did the government reinvigorate its parliament.

10. Consider the following excerpts from speeches of the leadership. The first was made by Saddam Hussain upon dissolving the labor unions, the second by King Fahad when queried about the role of the private sector in the economy.

> . . . (There will be no need for workers' federations or trade unions), . . . now that all are becoming state officials. If there had been no private sector in Iraq, it would have been the duty of the leadership to create it, simply because the coun-

try needs this sector: our brand of socialism cannot live without the private sector either now or after the war. (Saddam Hussain, Chairman, Revolutionary Command Council of the Arab Socialist Republic of Iraq. Excerpts from speeches made in March and February 1987, quoted in *Middle East Economic Digest,* 28 March 1987)

Observers of the progress of Saudi industries believe the philosophy of the Saudi system is superior to other systems. But the private sector in some industries believes that the participation of the state as a partner in industrial projects is a factor which creates confidence. It is from this that the state's participation in industrial projects arises. . . . . The Saudi worker assumes ownership at no cost to himself, since his payments come from the profits. The producer, that is the worker, becomes the owner. This is a system which is not found in any other country. It is one of the facilities offered by the state. (Fahad ibn 'Abd al Aziz Al Saud, Khadim al Haramain. Interview, *Al Siyasah,* 19 May, 1987, as quoted in *Middle East Executive Survey* 30, no. 33 [25 May 1987])

The ambiguities embodied in these statements reflect the overriding fact that regardless of ideological proclivities, the role of the state in both economies has been large enough that creating classes and distributing wealth on a wide scale was viewed as a part of the normal range of policy options.

11. Agricultural policy and production trends are summarized in Robert Springborg, "Infitah, Agrarian Transformation and Elite Consolidation in Contemporary Iraq," *Middle East Journal* 50, no. 1 (1986).

12. Of these, 66 factories were sold by auction and 4 were transferred to the "mixed sector," in which the Industrial Bank, individuals, and other mixed-sector companies hold shares.

13. Licenses granted for private factories to be set up with the use of foreign exchange held abroad went from 7 in 1987 to 63 in 1988 to 117 in 1989. Total investments in these factories was, however, small, comprising only ID 17 m in 1988 and ID 33 m in 1989. At the official exchange rate, the 1989 figure comes to about $99 million. Most of the planned private investment is in plastics (60%), the rest in textiles and construction (15%), food processing (15%), and metal industries (10%).

14. In 1988 total private-sector imports were ID 1.1 billion for 80,843 licenses, while in 1989 only 30,000 licenses were issued for ID 1 billion.

15. An example might clear up this otherwise confusing assessment. The Dialah Tomato Canning Factory, sold to an experienced industrial family, used to produce 7,350 tons of canned tomatoes from concentrate imported from Czechoslovakia. When it was government-owned, the factory worked all year and employed 286 workers. Concentrate imports were cut completely in 1989, forcing the factory to use only domestic fresh tomatoes. Working for only 3 months and employing only 200 workers, under private ownership the factory produced 3,000 tons of canned tomatoes in 1989. While retail prices were ID 2.56/kg in 1988, in 1989 the retail price was 3.66/kg (a price hike of 43%), but as shortages drove the product into the black market, consumers generally paid much more.

16. These activities appear in official statistics under the euphemistic title of "small industries" and employ over 220,000 workers, roughly twice the number of workers in state-owned industries, but cover only a minuscule proportion of total economic activity. Official Statistical Yearbook, 1988.

17. The resulting violence against foreign workers, mainly Egyptians, prompted the government to lower the limit on legal remittances to ID 10 per month, precipitating an exodus of foreign labor. This policy served the purpose of lowering the government's foreign-exchange commitments in the form of remitted earnings of foreign workers. Amid rather naive attempts to cloak the recent changes in labor laws in terms of enhancing the status of public-sector workers and "freeing" private labor to form their own unions, the government has clearly abrogated its longstanding commitment to protect Iraqi labor.

18. For a general and optimistic view of the possibilities for foreign investors and contractors in Saudi Arabia, see Joe Saba, "The Investment Climate: Its Risks and Returns," *Middle East Executive Report,* October 1985, p. 9.

19. Laws protecting local industry and contractors were issued in 1979 with *Royal Decree* M/14, dated 7/4/1397 (1979).

20. *The Present Condition of the Private Sector and Its Role in the Saudi Economy,* Saudi Consulting Center for Finance and Investment. Study commissioned by the Riyadh Chamber of Commerce and Industry, March 1986 (in Arabic), p. 183.

21. *The Present Condition . . . ,* CCFI report, pp. 173–74 and 176.

22. Interview, Muhammad Al Muammar, Chairman, Committee on Industry, Riyadh Chamber of Commerce, 20 December 1985.

23. *Annual Supplement: Saudi Arabia,* Economist Intelligence Unit, 1985. An earlier ruling, issued on August 6, 1984 had required foreign contractors to include the names of local contractors which would receive 30% of the contract work. *Country Report: Saudi Arabia,* Economist Intelligence Unit, no. 4, 1984.

24. Rules on standard forms for public-sector contracting, consulting, and supplies were issued in *Al Riyadh,* 6 November 1984, p. 7. The implementing rules for revised "buy Saudi" regulations and subcontracting were issued in *Ministry of Finance Circular,* no. 5767/404, 6 August 1984 and supplemented the *Council of Ministers Decree* 124, dated 29/5/1403 (1983).

25. *Arab News,* 10 December 1985. The Export Promotion Committee was to work in conjunction with a newly created Exporter's Association created in 1985 in the Riyadh Chamber of Commerce. (Interview, Abdulrehman al Jeraisy, Chairman, Committee for Trade, Riyadh Chamber of Commerce, 16 December 1985.)

26. *Saudi Gazette,* 22 February 1986, p. 3.

27. See statement of Turki al Sudairi, President, Bureau of the Civil Service, in *Saudi Gazette,* 14 March 1986, p. 3.

28. *Middle East Executive Report,* January 1988.

CHAPTER

9

ECONOMIC AND POLITICAL LIBERALIZATION IN A RENTIER ECONOMY: THE CASE OF THE HASHEMITE KINGDOM OF JORDAN

Laurie A. Brand

The riots that broke out in Maʿan, Jordan on 18 April 1989 following the announcement of a Jordanian government–IMF agreement that was to raise prices of certain basic commodities served as a watershed in the political history of the Hashemite Kingdom. Not since the November 1966 Israeli raid on the West Bank town of al-Samu had widespread rioting occurred, not since the 1955 controversy over joining the Baghdad Pact had large-scale popular discontent been manifested on the East Bank, and never before in the kingdom's history had rioting had its origins in the economic concerns of average Jordanians.

There is little doubt that the downward economic spiral in which Jordan found itself, particularly in the wake of King Husayn's announced disengagement from the West Bank, combined with years of political repression, is the immediate backdrop against which the April riots and the subsequent November 1989 elections should be understood. However, these developments must also be placed in the broader context of the nature of the Jordanian state and economy, the region-wide economic recession that has plagued the area since the early 1980s caused by the drop in oil prices and the Iran-Iraq war, and the attempts by the regime in the mid-1980s to address the growing economic crisis by implementing policies generally placed under the rubric of economic liberalization. Concomitantly, the government indicated an inclination to deal with the longstanding problem of the absence of political participation and political freedoms in the kingdom.

This chapter explores the economic liberalization policies of the Jordanian government from late 1984 until the April 1989 riots against the background of the regime's record in addressing the issue of political reform. On the economic front, the desire to liberalize was clear, although the successes were few. On the political front, the early expressions of good intentions gradually faded into increasing repression.

THE NATURE OF THE ECONOMY: JORDAN AS AN EXAMPLE OF A RENTIER

Work done by Hossein Mahdavy on Iran first suggested that states dependent or based upon *external* sources of income should be understood as qualitatively different from those that rely on domestic extraction (taxation).[1] The fact that the income has little or no basis in indigenous productive forces, that it is in effect unearned, is critical to the analysis. Such states are referred to as rentiers, with rent broadly defined as "any income not originating from the productive activity of the concerned unit, the flows and dimensions of which are not directly linked to the beneficiary's activity."[2] In the Middle East, the examples par excellence of rentiers are the oil states: rent (the oil revenues) make up more than 90 percent of state budgets, and no more than 2 to 3 percent of the workforce is engaged in the production and distribution of the oil wealth.[3]

However, rent need not be understood as comprising only income accruing from oil. Of particular importance for the case of Jordan, for example, are rents in the form of expatriate remittances: the salaries of expatriates abroad are higher than they would be had they remained at home and the differential constitutes a form of quasi-rent.[4] Large numbers of Jordanians[5] have, since the early 1950s, sought employment in the emerging oil states of the Gulf. In addition to remittances, locational rents—payments received for pipeline crossage, transit fees, and the like—have been particularly critical for Jordan. In broader strategic terms, the locational rent that Jordan has collected over the years should also be understood to include payments for foreign military bases and facilities for foreign troops (such as Britain provided from 1921 to 1956). Along these same lines, locational rent may also be understood to comprise foreign-aid payments intended for strategic or economic reasons to assist a country's military or economy in order to support the regime or to encourage it to carry out policies in keeping with the interests of the rent-payer. Such rent payments have been critical to the regime's consolidation and survival (whether provided by Britain, the United States, or shifting coalitions of Arab states).

However, just as the nature of rent varies from one state to another, so the concept of rentier as an undifferentiated category fails to account for distinctions critical to understanding the nature of the state, state finances, and potential development and crisis-management strategies. One useful distinction is that between rentier *states* and rentier *economies* (also referred to as semi-rentier states).[6] In the case of the former—countries such as Saudi Arabia, Kuwait, Qatar, and the like—revenues from oil extraction are quite substantial and accrue directly to the state. In a rentier economy, on the other hand, the rent does not accrue directly to the central government. Moreover, the absolute and relative percentage of rent is lower (vis-à-vis GNP), and expatriate remittances constitute a large proportion of the rent. In other words, in a rentier economy the role of the state as recipient and dispenser of rent income is far smaller than in a rentier state.[7]

The characteristics of Jordan's economy place it in the category of a rentier economy. It is heavily dependent upon unrequited transfers in the form of expatriate worker remittances and economic aid,[8] the vast majority of which come as a direct or indirect result of the area's oil wealth. A second characteristic of a rentier present in Jordan is that of a major disequilibrium in the trade balance: in the case of oil producers, it is a trade surplus, in the case of semi-rentiers like Jordan, it is a chronic trade deficit. The third characteristic that places Jordan in this category is its large budget deficit: in 1988, for example, the figure exceeded JD 128 million, with the deficit for 1986–88 nearly JD 300 million.[9] Fourth, the rent income has for years permitted a level of consumption and investment well above what the country's GDP could sustain. Finally, there is the obvious weakness of indigenous economic productive forces. For example, in 1987, agriculture's share in GDP was only 8.8 percent, manufacturing's was 12.9 percent, and mining and quarrying's only 4.5 percent.[10]

Hazem Beblawi and Giacomo Luciani[11] argue that the Middle Eastern states' continuing heavy reliance on external rents and their failure to adopt effective industrialization policies to strengthen the indigenous productive base of their economies has rendered them highly vulnerable to their external political and economic environment.

Jordan currently has a workforce of about 885,000, of whom about 330,000 work abroad, about 85 percent of them in the Gulf.[12] Further exacerbating the situation, Gulf economic retrenchment has meant the gradual return of longtime expatriates as a result of nonrenewal of work contracts: the economic "safety valve" that employment in the Gulf had constituted since the late 1940s for Jordan, Lebanon, Syria, and Egypt had gradually closed.

According to Beblawi and Luciani's argument, in rentier states the government provides numerous services (which citizens come to expect) while making few if any economic demands on them (i.e., taxes).[13] The consequent assumption is that the state is held less accountable by the citizenry for its policies because it does not use the people's money.

Even limited external revenues can markedly improve a regime's ability to buy legitimacy through distribution, thus increasing stability.[14] However, under the conditions of economic recession and necessary retrenchment that developed in the mid-1980s, the equation began to change as the state struggled to balance available resources with distributed income.[15] The state increasingly found itself in dire need of both cutting expenditures and expanding its revenue base. It is to this end that privatization schemes have sometimes been introduced. In order to accomplish the short-term goal, the regime has two choices: either to liberalize politically, that is, provide for greater popular participation as a means of making the financial extraction more palatable and legitimate; or to resort to coercive or repressive measures to implement its austerity and extraction programs. While Luciani admits that there may be no immediate link between taxation and representative democracy, nevertheless, whenever the state relies on taxation, the issue of democracy may arise.[16] As a result, one may find a correlation between the imperative to increase revenue and cut domestic spending on the one hand and the development of greater political coercion or liberalization in rentier states on the other.

It is the possible existence of such a correlation in the case of Jordan that this chapter seeks to explore. In that regard, two critical questions arise: First, how has Jordan responded on an economic level to the challenges of the post-1981 region-wide recession? Second, have attempts to broaden political participation been made in order to make palatable the expected austerity policies that lay ahead, or was coercion the preferred path?

THE BACKDROP TO
THE LIBERALIZATION DRIVE

Unlike the other countries discussed in this volume, Jordan has traditionally been viewed as a free-market economy, never having joined in the Arab-socialist or state-capitalist experiments of the 1950s and 1960s of a number of its neighbors. Nevertheless, to conclude from the apparently small size of the public sector that the state plays only a minor role would be inaccurate, for, as is the case in many countries, drawing a neat line between the public and private sectors is not an easy task.

The role of the state in a rentier economy is greater precisely because it is "the inevitable intermediary in the collection and redistribution of foreign revenue of public origin."[17] In the case of Jordan, official statistics do not differentiate between pure private-sector concerns and publicly owned enterprises. For example, according to government statistics, the Jordan Phosphate Mines Company is listed as being part of the private sector because it takes the form of a shareholding company; however, the public sector in fact owns 90 percent of its paid up capital and is responsible for management and decision making.[18]

The extent of the state's role in the economy is demonstrated by the following figures from the 1981–85 development plan: 27 percent of development funds were to be spent by the central government, 34 percent by autonomous public institutions,[19] and 39 percent by the private and mixed public-private sector.[20] In mid-1986 it was estimated that the public sector employed 45 percent of the country's workforce, produced 40 percent of GNP, contributed 50 percent of capital formation, and was responsible for 30 percent of exports.[21]

The beginning of Jordan's current economic woes may be traced to 1980, with the launching of the Iran-Iraq war which, combined subsequently with falling oil prices, led to a shrinkage of regional markets and a drop in oil-state liquidity. That same year, aid from the United States stopped altogether because of Jordan's failure to join the Camp David process.

As early as 1982, Jordan reformed its tax laws, setting rates lower in hopes of greater compliance in payment, but it was the government budget for 1984 that first seemed to herald a period of austerity, to be characterized by a real decline in government spending. Then, further exacerbating the situation, by 1984 only Saudi Arabia continued to pay its pledge, but its contribution represented only 28.6 percent of the original inter-Arab package.[22] Jordan was forced to resort to eurodollar loans in both 1983 and 1984 to address the problem of the budget deficit. Other troubling developments, in part traceable to the factors mentioned above or to the boom of the earlier years also began to unfold by 1983–84.

The country began to witness the demise of a number of private companies that had either been established initially with insufficient capital or which were redundant given the needs of the Jordanian market.

In other cases, profit levels dropped precipitously. Industrial firms were hardest hit. For example, in 1985, twenty of ninety public shareholding companies suffered losses: thirteen of these were in industry or mining; six were in services; and one was in insurance. Some of the large companies in which the government was the largest shareholder were also hard hit, leading to liquidations or mergers. Exacerbating the problem was a crisis of domestic liquidity and revelations of scandals of poor management and corruption in both public- and private-sector firms. The exposure of a number of companies which existed only on paper and reports of falsified financial statements from others undermined public confidence in the stock market. Trading fell off markedly and the value of market shares plummeted.[23]

Ahmad ʿUbaydat, who was named prime minister in January 1984, resorted to various financial and fiscal instruments to adapt to the changing economic conditions. He kept spending at the levels of the previous government, preferring to compensate for shortfalls through external aid, increased domestic taxes, and external borrowing. Customs duties were altered for a number of items in order to limit imports and support domestic production of similar goods. In addition, the government attempted to finesse some of the losses of both private and mixed companies in two different ways: by guaranteeing loans (generally, very burdensome commercial loans) aimed at raising productive capabilities; and by raising prices or by artificially supporting production.[24]

One example of government intervention to protect local industry was that of the Jordan Glass Industry Company (JGIC), based in Maan, which received government assistance in the form of a ban on foreign competition and a reduction of the burden of interest payments on outstanding loans. The JGIC had had trouble marketing in Jordan, since imported glass was able to undercut its prices by 20 percent. The government therefore approved a JGIC request for a JD 2 million capital injection to raise the company's capital base to JD 7 million. The increase was expected to come from its major shareholders: the Pension Fund, the SSC, the Housing Bank, and the Arab Investment Company of Riyadh. In 1986, thanks to cost cutting and government bans on imports of white glass, the company was able to cut its losses by a third.[25]

At the same time, however, the government instituted more stringent policies on licensing new companies, to protect against future failures. As an anticorruption step, the government legislated the separation of the positions of president of the board and general director in public institutions and large companies in which the state had the majority of shares.[26]

Some of the new fiscal policies intended to stimulate the local economy were not without partially offsetting negative effects. For example, the government was dedicated to keeping imports down, but that in turn limited customs duties, traditionally a major source of state revenue. Moreover, the government was intent upon stimulating the private sector through tax exemptions and incentives, but such a policy, at least in the short term, deprived the state of potential revenue.

None of the ʿUbaydat program involved far-reaching changes, but the government, nonetheless, encountered the opposition of various elements in the private sector, especially the larger financial and commercial bourgeoisie, who believed the policies exacerbated the tendencies toward stagnation. Furthermore, the government's announced intention to review the priorities of public and private spending, to confront the problem of failing companies, and to guide (*tarshid*) economic decisions were even more distasteful from the point of view of some elements of the private sector. Such proposals implied the strengthening of the state, an expansion of the role of the bureaucratic bourgeoisie, at a time when the financial and commercial bourgeoisie were complaining about what they called competition from the government. If anything, these sectors wanted a retreat of government from the economy. Thus, the ʿUbaydat government was in effect rowing against the current of most sectors of the power elite in the country. Nor did its policies conform to the prescriptions of the United States, the IMF, or the World Bank, which argued that the way out of economic stagnation was to unleash market forces, encourage the private sector, disassemble and sell off the public sector, reduce the role of government in the economy, float the local currency, and lift price supports from basic commodities.[27]

The most significant step—both practically and symbolically—toward liberalization came in April 1985, when Husayn's longtime friend and former prime minister Zayd al-Rifaʿi was appointed to replace the politically and economically unpopular ʿUbaydat. Rifaʿi more than any member of the Jordanian political elite was associated with economic liberalization (if also with corruption). The king made a plea to the new cabinet upon its installation to stimulate and invigorate the economy. Husayn also asked for another revamping of the investment law, a law that had been reworked only the previous year.

The prevailing belief in the new government appeared to be that the only way to revive the country's economy was through providing privileges to capital, particularly big capital. Shortly after coming to office, Rifaʿi announced the government's intention to reduce its rigid price-fixing policy in the near future and to remove restrictions on private-sector business hours. The government also committed itself to regular meetings with the chambers of commerce and industry as well as with large financial and business concerns in order to increase communication and coordination between the government and the business communities.

In August 1986, the cabinet approved a five-point program on public-private-sector relations comprising the following elements: a number of public enterprises were to be transformed into public companies operating on a commercial basis (although they would continue to be owned by the public sector); the private sector was to be encouraged to share in the ownership and management of such public enterprises; the views and suggestions of relevant ministries and public enterprise directors on the first two points were to be submitted to the prime minister's office; and a permanent ministerial committee was to be established to study and determine the principles and timetables for transforming the public enterprises.[28]

Only a few months later, in early November, a "Paper on Privatization" was presented along with the 1986–90 development plan to the Jordan Development Conference. The paper had two major thrusts:

First, the private sector was to be promoted in its traditional areas of activity through minimizing market distortions, increasing support for research to enhance efficiency, devising incentives to attract private investment, applying government policies in a uniform fashion in order to treat domestic and foreign firms more equitably, and developing a more supportive legal environment in the fields of property rights and commercial law.

The second thrust concerned the transformation of the role of public enterprises: government shares in mixed enterprises were to be offered to the private sector for purchase; autonomous public enterprises were to be transferred to the private sector; the establishment of private universities was to be authorized; and agricultural land was to be leased to the private sector.[29]

In late 1986, the government established an economic consultative council composed of leading representatives from the public and private sectors intended to coordinate and diffuse tension between the two. However, Jordan was embarking on its program of encouraging the private sector and attracting foreign investment at a time when attracting foreign capital to the country was likely to be difficult. Whatever the philosophy of the government, the contraction of regional markets meant neither Western nor Arab money was likely to be terribly interested in investing in the country.[30]

REVIEW OF LIBERALIZATION EFFORTS

Jordan's record in the 1985–89 period is mixed, as will be demonstrated below through a brief review of its liberalization moves. Government policy combined attempts to stimulate greater domestic private investment, attract foreign investment, cut inefficiencies through mergers, provide capital to certain industries to enable them to compete more effectively, cut certain subsidies (not including the

IMF-triggered explosion), privatize certain public-sector companies, and ease banking regulations, with efforts aimed at protecting developing industries with tariffs and regulations and at easing the unemployment situation through greater regulation of the employment of foreign nationals.

Agriculture. In mid-1985, in an attempt to avert another annual glut of tomatoes, the government introduced a cropping pattern system for the first time. According to this system, farmers who exceeded their allocation of tomatoes (production stimulated by government-guaranteed prices) were to be subject to fines. The policy was aimed not only at making Jordan more food self-sufficient but also at saving the Ministry of Agriculture JD 1.25 million per year in grower support. This was the government's first attempt to intervene in crop choice and it was not clear how successful it would be: the policy had been proposed by Rifaʿi's predecessor, Rifaʿi himself was a large farmer, and the policy was blatantly interventionist.[31] However, by late 1986, government efforts appeared to have met with some success. Tomato cultivation in particular was cut and subsidies offered by the Agricultural Marketing and Processing Company (AMPCO) were encouraging farmers to grow such badly needed crops as potatoes, onions, and wheat.[32]

In early 1986, the eight-year-old system by which retail prices of agricultural produce were rigidly fixed was scrapped in the hopes of stimulating production and increasing returns. To encourage further agricultural development, in the spring of 1986, the government leased parcels of state land in the southern part of the country at very low rents. Having constructed the necessary infrastructure, including electricity transmission lines and having already demonstrated that agricultural production in the area was possible, the government hoped that the administration of the project would then be taken over by the private sector.[33]

In late spring 1987, the government created the Jordan Marketing Organization (JMO) to undertake research and advise the government on marketing and pricing policies.

Banking. In 1982, there were sixteen commercial banks registered in Jordan, in addition to three Islamic banking institutions, five investment banks, two real-estate savings and loan associations, and six specialized credit institutions. Early in the Rifaʿi administration the government cancelled a then recently instituted requirement that 51 percent of the ownership of branches of foreign banks operating in the kingdom be in the hands of Jordanian nationals. The change in the law came as the local financial community as well as branches of foreign banks were beginning to step up their opposition to the 51 percent ownership requirement, with criticism stemming most notably from the local stock exchange and the powerful Arab Bank. The banking community continued to oppose the increase in the minimum capital level on the grounds that it would result in the diversion of already scarce liquidity from industrial ventures to the stock market to help build up bank capital (although the law did require that 15 percent of the banks' capital be in equity). The banks also complained that they were already underlent, without an increase in the minimum capital requirement.[34]

In addition, the Central Bank raised its lending rate by 0.5 percent to 10.5 percent to increase the banks' maneuverability. During the previous two years, competition between commercial banks had become so fierce that most depositors—regardless of term of deposit—were paid the then upper limit of 8.75 percent. Some were even paid 9 or 9.5 percent in defiance of regulations, as banks sought to attract additional customers and capital.[35] In turn, the maximum lending rate of 10 percent prevented banks from differentiating between good and high-risk borrowers. The banks ended up favoring firms, such as large public-sector companies, which enjoyed a government guarantee and for which they received higher yields owing to the tax-free status of the companies. In this way many private-sector companies were squeezed out of the credit market, thus aggravating the recession. To address the problem, beginning in November 1986, the Central Bank exempted deposits of JD 200,000 or more from the existing rigid interest-rate system. It was not until September 1988 that the Central Bank removed all outstanding restrictions on interest rates. The following month, the government finally decided to let the dinar float.

In a further move to encourage private-sector initiative, the Industrial Development Bank began offering in December 1988 risk capital loans to entrepreneurs to encourage local participation in industrial and tourism development projects. The loans were to be given to any beneficiary who had a sound project but had insufficient capital to begin. The bank was offering to grant money at its own risk (after completion of careful study of the proposed project) and without recourse to the borrower for repayment in case of losses.[36]

Development Planning. Unlike previous plans, the formulation of the development plan for 1986–90 involved a lengthy and conspicuous process of consultation. A 500-member general assembly representing most major economic and social constituencies and twenty-four sectoral committees was involved in order to increase people's identification with the plan and their participation in it, presumably because of the economic troubles that were expected in the near future. Particular attention was given to the level and quality of private and public services, and according to it, the private sector was expected to play a higher profile role than it had in the past.

In a related move, in late January 1989, the cabinet set up a higher planning committee to determine and review development objectives. It was intended to take overall charge of the activity of corporations directing and executing economic and development policies in the private and public sectors and to make recommendations concerning measures to guarantee integration and efficiency.

Investment. In order to attract more foreign capital and promote inter-Arab economic cooperation, in early 1986, a cabinet decision lifted most major restrictions on investment in the country by non-Jordanian Arabs. Arabs were thereby allowed to invest freely in agriculture, industry, and various services. They also became eligible for the same tax concessions as locals, were accorded protection from nationalization, and were permitted to buy and sell real estate. However, they were not permitted to hold more than 49 percent interest in single projects unless their home countries offered reciprocal agreements to Jordanians.[37]

The government was particularly keen to promote the establishment of joint ventures and in the development of high-tech light industries for export. In September 1988 the Jordan Technology Group, a private company to promote high-tech joint ventures, was set up as part of the drive to establish Jordan as a regional center for technology transfer and maintenance services. In December 1988, a new Law on Companies was amended, among other reasons, in order to facilitate opening new avenues for investment. It contained provisions related to holding companies, joint-stock and limited companies, and companies that had been exempted under the old law, and it reduced government intervention in these firms.[38]

In what has become an organized and ongoing process of recruiting expatriate interest in investing in Jordan, the government began, in 1985, to hold annual "expatriate conferences," gatherings intended to draw Jordanians living abroad (especially in the Gulf) to Jordan to discuss investment opportunities in the kingdom. It should also be noted that these conferences were conceived of in an atmosphere not only of economic recession but of increasing political competition with the PLO, and they were thus also intended to assert Jordan's claim to sovereignty over the large Palestinian/Jordanian population in the Gulf.[39]

One of the outcomes of the first expatriate conference was that an amendment was made to the Social Security Corporation (SSC) law to allow Jordanians working abroad to be covered by its provisions. This move followed government concern with declining levels of state income and fears that remittance levels might be ready to fall. Since its inception in 1978, the SSC had proved an effective way of mobilizing private income for investment in productive enterprises. More than 317,000 Jordanians contribute 5 percent of their monthly salaries to the SSC, and over JD 70 million of SSC capital has been invested in development and social projects in Jordan, most in hotels and rest houses.[40] In the second meeting of the expatriate conference, in July 1986, two holding companies with paid capital of JD 25 million and JD 10 million respectively were founded. Funds for the two were to be generated by selling shares to expatriates. The income from the companies was planned for investment in a variety of local projects in the fields of tourism, trade, agriculture, industry, transportation and housing.[41]

Public versus Private. In the fall of 1985, the government announced its intention to privatize the Telecommunications Corporation (TCC), which, established in 1973, had a monopoly of telephone and telex service in the country and was known for its top-heavy management structure. A feasibility study regarding privatization was then carried out in an atmosphere in which the principle of selling off state assets was gaining ground. In September 1988, it was announced that part of a World Bank loan was to be used to cover the costs of consultancy services needed to help the TCC be transformed into a public shareholding company. The shares were first to be owned by the government and then gradually turned over to the public. The main objective of the loan was to assist in financing the corporation's five-year development, which included expanding network capacity, improving the quality of service, and increasing the TCC's coverage in the kingdom,[42] all presumably to make the company more attractive to outside investors. However, by late 1988, due to the economic downturn, it was announced that the scale of the project would be cut back and that it would be carried out over a longer period of time.[43]

In 1983, after ten years of profitability, Royal Jordanian Airlines (Alia) had announced a loss of JD 2 million.[44] In early 1986 it was announced that the airlines, an important part of Jordan's attempt to market itself as a regional center, intended to privatize. USAID conducted the privatization feasibility study, and by early 1987 Royal Jordanian was ready to offer 10 percent of its shares to its employees, while offering another 35 percent of its equity to Jordanian and institutional investors. However, problems of complexity of implementation and low investor demand slowed progress in the privatization process.[45]

In the field of relations between the public sector and the private sector, at least one attempt to expand countertrading of Jordanian minerals and agricultural produce was thwarted. A public-sector company intended to coordinate barter deals was dissolved under pressure from the private sector. The merchants, accustomed to handling the profitable trade in imports for the private sector, blocked the new company because they stood to lose their cut, estimated at JD 12.5 to 20 million.[46]

Mergers. As noted above, part of the government's drive to increase efficiency involved promoting mergers of weak companies and tightening up on licensing requirements for new companies. In late 1985, two large cement companies were amalgamated. In spring 1986, the Jordan Phosphate Mining Company was given cabinet permission to take over the Jordan Fertilizer Industries Company in a move intended to facilitate marketing and promote an integrated approach to countertrade. In late 1986, two major public shareholding companies with sizable holdings in a number of industrial and service companies and retail outlets merged to consolidate their financial position: Jordan Industrial Investments Corporation and the Jordan Management Consultancy Corporation. Additional mergers in the insurance industry, forced by government legislation that imposed a minimum capital base for companies, followed. In some cases, the deteriorating position of a number of major firms, often the result of marketing problems, gave the government some leeway to impose mergers without having to resort to legislation.[47]

Labor. To address the issue of rising unemployment in the kingdom, a law was enacted, in early March 1986, to penalize employers illegally using foreign labor. The law also limited the jobs in which foreigners could be employed, excluding such areas as office administration, accountancy, marketing, education, and any other fields in which qualified Jordanians were available. The Ministry of Labor also moved to increase the cost of employment permits for non-Arab workers by as much as 300 percent. In late 1987, the number of categories from which foreigners were to be excluded was further increased, and stiff penalties were imposed for those hiring foreign workers illegally. Then, in early 1988, ministries and public-sector institutions as well as one hundred municipalities and 347 village councils were ordered to hire engineers. At the same time community colleges, private schools, and major industrial establishments were directed to hire one full-time doctor and two medical assistants. These directives were issued in order to cut unemployment among an influential professional class. At the same time, however, they created jobs for which there was no rationale and which students had been increasingly dissuaded from entering through a public information campaign.[48] By 1988, with unemployment an increasingly serious problem, the government began to provide incentives to Jordanians working abroad: a fund for "salary topping," perhaps as high as JD 500,000, was created to supplement the salaries of Jordanians working in countries in which salaries are low.[49]

Trade. The government has maintained its overall commitment to free trade but holds that protectionism is essential if home industries are to develop. In sum, the government has sought to be protectionist enough to allow indigenous industry to develop but not so protectionist as to stifle customs duties revenues. The right to import is restricted to resident Jordanians possessing a trade license, registered companies (with at least 51 percent local ownership), organizations covered by the Encouragement of Investment Law, and foreign contractors working on government contracts.[50] In mid-1985, the Ministry of Supply, Industry, and Trade announced its intention to ease some of the tight restrictions on the import of foodstuffs, an inevitable move given the economic philosophy of the government. However, whatever reform did take place was incremental in nature and did not depart from the existing rigid system of retail price setting. Moreover, the ministry retained control over the import of such staples as rice, flour, sugar, and meat; and a ban on the import of chicken, olive oil, and red lentils continued to protect local suppliers.[51] In the fall of 1985, certain protectionist measures were introduced to protect and encourage domestic industries. Import of beer, iron nails, bottled water, milk, ice cream, and olive oil was proscribed.[52]

However, in late 1985, the ministry was ready to unveil a new supply law limiting the role of the government in importing commodities and regulating the retail sector. The law also established a Higher Supply Council, thus giving the private sector an institutionalized role and channel for voicing its preferences regarding supply policy. The law further provided for a "supply court" so that those charged with price-level violations would not be taken to the inevitably rather unfriendly military courts.[53]

In early 1986, the ministry introduced new regulations to stimulate the export economy, in particular the manufacturing base in Jordan. All Jordanian companies marketing their products abroad were exempted from paying income tax, and the ministry urged the Department of Customs to remove all routine and administrative obstacles that had discouraged importing with a view to reexporting. At the same time the ministry was working to encourage merchants to use barter as a method of paying regional and international suppliers in order to conserve declining foreign currency reserves.[54]

In August 1988, in a reversal of its 1985 policy, the government began to move from an emphasis on banning the import of certain items to the use of high tariffs. Bans on all but a few goods—tomato paste, tobacco, cigarettes, milk, yogurt, some cheese, mineral water, and table salt—were lifted. Perhaps not coincidentally, the minister, Hamdi Tabbaʿ, had close connections with Jordan's merchant community and had been unhappy with the total ban on some imports. At the same time, the series of policies included a provision for the establishment of an investment unit at the ministry intended to compile and disseminate information on investment procedures and to process applications for industrial licenses. Additional measures, such as customs and fees exemptions on imports for use in projects already set up, were also included. The thrust appeared to be aimed at encouraging producers to export, for it was further announced that several specialized companies designed solely to export Jordanian products were to be established to pool marketing skills. The number of trade centers in Arab and foreign countries was to be increased and commercial attachés were to be appointed to Jordanian embassies in the Arab world, the United States, and Japan.[55] However, the lift on the import ban was short-lived, for as the dinar began to decline in value in the fall of 1988, new action had to be taken. On 5 November 1988, a ban on the following items was imposed on both the public and private sectors: goods and passenger transport vehicles, television sets and antennae, video sets and cameras, refrigerators and freezers, air conditioners, furniture (except that used in medical fields), chandeliers, microwaves, marble tiles, roof tiles, granite, statues, and works of art. In addition, customs fees on a number of nonbasic items were raised.[56]

INTO THE ABYSS

Some local commentators complained that the Rifaʿi liberalization program, far from stimulating the economy, had in fact done no more than increase the profits made by a few large concerns. Indeed, some made the case that the additional freedom and incentives given to the private sector were deliberately biased in favor of large firms and that the state's major policy divergence from liberalization—protectionist measures—helped to subsidize industries that would never be competitive, but the presence of which, for varying reasons, served the interests of large private capital. To what extent the policies promoted the interest of large capital for its own sake rather than out of a genuine belief that only large private-sector firms had the capability to revive the economy remains open to debate.

Nevertheless, the record shows that what had kept the Jordanian economy going over the years was not a lively and productive private sector but, rather, the state sector, most notably through the expansion of government services. Rifaʿi himself admitted, in October, that the role of the private sector in tackling economic stagnation is not as we had hoped. Figures and statistics show that the public sector's expenditure has activated the national economy. The public sector's expenditure is also the direct reason for achieving a 3 percent growth rate.[57]

In late 1988 the inflation rate began to rise as a result of austerity measures implemented to address the crisis of the plummeting dinar. Attempt was made to blame the country's money-changing industry for the speculation that supposedly led to the dinar's demise. However, whatever their faults, the moneychangers appeared to be scapegoats, their currency trading and speculation more an effect than a cause of decreased confidence in the dinar. The government also moved to tighten its exchange-rate policy, setting the price of the dinar at 540 fils to the dollar in March 1989, a 48 percent devaluation compared with June 1988.[58] Some argued that the devaluation was good, that it reduced the demand for imports and would therefore improve Jordan's trade balance. However, in the case of Jordan, which imports virtually all its basic needs, the scope for import reduction is limited.

As indicated earlier, a major cause of Jordan's budgetary problems was the drop in rent. Foreign-grant support for the Jordanian budget, which had peaked in 1981 and 1982 when it exceeded $1.2 billion, had declined to $660 million in 1988 and dropped further to $420 million in 1989.[59] In January, for the first time in its history, the kingdom was unable to meet its scheduled debt payment, leading to a further plunge of the dinar. As of late February 1989, Jordan's total civil and military foreign debt was hovering just under $6 billion, with debt servicing running at about $900 million. Jordan's participation in the 15 February 1989 founding of the Arab Cooperation Council (ACC)—a regional political, economic, and military cooperation and integration grouping that also comprised Egypt, Iraq, and North Yemen in addition to the kingdom—should be understood in part as an attempt to seek additional ways of dealing with its declining economic fortunes.

But there was no easy or fast way out of the downward spiral, and on 9 March, a meeting of the Higher Planning Committee officially decided to hold consultations with the IMF and the World Bank on rescheduling the kingdom's debt. Initially, it was felt that the recovery program would not be painful, since many of the policies prescribed by the international financial community under adjustment programs—privatization, austerity measures, and a free-market economy—were, to some degree, already in place in Jordan. But the announcement of the agreement (which included increases in the prices of butane, gasoline, diesel and kerosene, alcoholic drinks, and cigarettes) sparked demonstrations in Maʿan that gradually spread as far north as Salt.

The unrest was triggered by the new economic measures, but its roots were to be found in the kingdom's near decade-long economic malaise and decline. In recognition of the serious nature of the outbreak of violence, Husayn, then in the United States, cut his trip short and headed home.

POLITICAL LIBERALIZATION

The economic measures and developments detailed above must be placed in the context of political developments in the kingdom for two reasons: The first is in order to gain an appreciation of the full range of factors that shaped the Jordanian economic policy-making process during the period. The second is to provide additional material to serve as a basis for evaluating the applicability to Jordan of Luciani's hypothesis (discussed in the opening section) regarding the possible link between economic decline in a rentier society and the push for democratization. How did the ongoing Arab-Israeli conflict and, in particular after December 1987, the *intifadah,* affect Jordan and its economy?

In general, an examination of the period reveals that until the riots of 1989, the government's commitment to political liberalization lagged far behind its commitment to economic liberalization. General elections had not been held since 1967, the parliament had been suspended in 1974, and since then a National Consultative Council (NCC) had operated in its place. The population, under martial law since 1957, was deprived of the right to form political parties or to engage in any other of the most basic forms of free political expression. The only opportunities for open political expression came during elections for leadership posts in Jordan's various professional unions—associations of doctors, lawyers, engineers, journalists, and the like—in which candidates were generally elected on the basis of their known political leanings.[60]

To the outside observer, the kingdom appeared to be benevolently authoritarian. For most citizens of the kingdom, however, the pervasive sense of *mukhabarat* presence, the confiscation of passports for alleged illegal political activities, and the regime's closure of most avenues of political expression created a sense of political frustration, intimidation, and entrapment. The feelings increased during the 1980s as economic woes increased while, effectively, only lip service was paid to the need for economic and political reform. Some broader, democratic forum would have to be allowed to underwrite what the government believed would be harsh economic decision making,[61] in keeping with Luciani's hypothesis, discussed earlier.

However, in addition to the more generalized dissatisfaction with the lack of institutionalized forums for political expression, some members of the Jordanian political elite had been pushing for the reconvening of parliament which, unlike the NCC, would be seen as more responsible or accountable to the country. As a result, in January 1984, the parliament was indeed recalled and the seven vacant seats (belonging to those West Bank deputies who had died since the 1967 elections) were filled with lesser-known, but pro-Hashemite deputies. Not surprisingly, various West Bank institutions condemned the move as did Syria. On 16 January, a new cabinet was formed headed by former security chief Ahmad ʿUbaydat, and elections were held on 12 March for the vacant East Bank seats.

The record of political liberalization during the next few years, however, is one of fits and starts, demonstrating that the commitment to political liberalization was more apparent than real, aimed at little more than cosmetic changes intended to give the illusion of greater popular participation. Following the recall of parliament, lobbying began for a general election and for permission to organize coherent groups (since political parties were banned). The first real clash with the government came during the last session before the 1984 summer recess. The parliament condemned the continuation of martial law, the activities of the *mukhabarat,* the harassment of students returning from abroad, and travel restrictions on West Bank Palestinians, and it called for the release of political prisoners. As a former *mukhabarat* chief, Prime Minister ʿUbaydat in particular was implicated in the debate, but he insisted that subversive activities in the country were extensive and that security, far from perhaps being relaxed might in fact be stepped up.[62] Calls for change, for freedom to form political parties, and for an increase in the number of East Bank seats (to take account of the influx of Palestinians that had occurred in 1967 as a result of the war) all continued.

By early fall 1985, a recognizable opposition bloc composed of leftists in a loose alliance with Islamic fundamentalists had emerged in the Lower House. The alliance included a quarter of all deputies and focused on such issues as freedom of speech, human rights, and corruption.

In early 1986, a new election law increased the number of seats in the parliament—a common demand—but it also set aside eleven separate districts on the East Bank that were to be considered West Bank seats. The measure created a furor. In all but one case the districts were Palestinian refugee camps, and therefore, the provision was criticized on the grounds that the regime was not only acquiescing in the status quo (of the occupation of the West Bank) but was, in fact, institutionalizing the difference between Jordanians of East and West Bank origin, always a sensitive issue in the kingdom. A further objection to the new law stemmed from the fact that it prohibited anyone with a "political past" from standing for elections. In practice this would have meant that the vast majority of skilled leaders representative of opposition opinion in the kingdom would have been denied the right to run for election because of past association with or membership in one of the illegal political parties.

The building political and economic tensions finally exploded, if in an unlikely venue: Yarmuk University. There, students who had expressed grievances on such diverse issues as tuition hikes, lack of progress in implementing Arabization policies, the United States raid on Libya, and the dismissal from school of a number of their colleagues (for political activity) just prior to the examination period, joined together in a sit-down strike which was eventually broken up by the king's Bedouin guard. The assault left at least three students dead and tens of others wounded or in hiding. Of greatest concern to the security forces at the time, however, was that the demonstrations brought together students from across the political spectrum and from both Banks: it was a coalition of forces that government political and economic policies had effectively thwarted the formation of since the nationalist surge of the mid-1950s.

A further indication of domestic political tension came in mid-June, when the government ordered the closure of the Jordanian Writers Association on the grounds that it was a front for fringe political activity. The JWA's membership was not large, but it had been one of the few remaining avenues of political expression. Therefore, its closure represented for many yet another in a long series of government attempts to deprive the population of any legitimate channels of free speech. Less than a month later, a new organization, the Jordanian Writers Federation, was established in the JWA's place. Not surprisingly, senior posts in the JWF were filled by people closely identified with the regime.

Because of the large Palestinian component in the Jordanian population, Palestinian-Jordanian relations have had periods of domestic political unease in the kingdom. The PLO reunification in April 1987 did nothing to improve PLO-Jordanian relations. The summit's preoccupation with the Iran-Iraq war and the consequent downgrading of the Palestinian issue appeared to be another success for Husayn in his political battle with Arafat. It therefore came as a major blow when scattered but intense resistance to the Israeli occupation in the West Bank and Gaza developed in December 1987 into a more systematic popular uprising.

The challenge to Jordan came not just as a result of the uprising itself but because by February 1988 it had become obvious that the leadership of the uprising was in the PLO camp. Before the political sympathies of the Unified National Command of the Uprising were clearly manifested, there had been some hope on the part of the regime that the movement might assert its independence of the PLO.

Even when the association between the leadership of the uprising and the PLO became clear, the regime could not simply repress all forms of popular sympathy with and support for the intifadah. Hence, while permission for demonstrations and the like were not forthcoming and the regime reportedly encouraged factionalism within Palestinian ranks and between Palestinians and East Bankers,[63] it nevertheless had to allow—again for the sake of domestic stability—some limited channels for popular expression.

The king proclaimed Jordan's legal and administrative disengagement from the West Bank on 31 July 1988. Husayn certainly solved no short-term problems by the move. Cutting the West Bank free did not limit the political influence or appeal of the intifadah on the East Bank. What it did succeed in doing was to create tremendous anxiety among East Bank Palestinians regarding the security of their presence and their property as *Palestinian* citizens of Jordan. And, if anything, the move may have exacerbated the kingdom's financial situation. It is true that the termination of salaries to West Bank employees may have saved a bit of money. It is also true, however, that the consequent termination of the West Bank development plan in fact saved the kingdom nothing: the expected contributions from the West and from international donor agencies had never materialized, and thus the plan was essentially already dead. More important, however, the anxiety created among Palestinians by the disengagement decision reportedly led to the withdrawal of substantial Palestinian financial reserves from Jordanian banks, thereby further weakening the already ailing dinar and setting the stage for the final plunge to half of its former value.[64] Rifaʿi claimed such reports were "nonsense" and that "the PLO had no funds in Jordan."[65] Crown Prince Hassan took a more moderate line, admitting that part of the pressure on the dinar was uncertainty regarding the disengagement combined with the fact that West Bankers had begun to convert their savings to cope with the financial hardship imposed by the uprising.[66] Political reform or opening up of the political system was not just put on hold; there was a sense that the political screws were being tightened even further as the economy deteriorated rapidly.

The regime's election stalling tactics eventually lost their magic, and when regime survival required that elections be called and held, they in fact finally were. The impetus came in April 1989 with the riots that were referred to in the Arabic press as *habbat Nisan* (the squalls of April). Rifaʿi, who had come to symbolize the corruption and unresponsiveness of the regime, served as the sacrificial lamb, offering his resignation in order to avoid being dismissed as prime minister. The king's cousin, Zayd bin Shakir, was brought in to take Rifaʿi's place.

The various economic and political developments discussed above should be seen as the necessary backdrop to the riots and to the government's swift reaction to them: the economic decline culminating in the plunge of the dinar; the nearly thirty-year absence of meaningful political participatory structures and the intifadah across the river. However, this time the severity of the crisis and the chronic nature of its causes led to regime promises, subsequently fulfilled, of an opening up of the political system in the most striking way to date in the Arab Middle East. The election law was redrafted and elections were called for and held in early November 1989.

CONCLUSIONS

This juxtaposition of accounts of economic liberalization policies and political developments in the Hashemite Kingdom between 1984 and 1989 suggests that Luciani's hypothesis regarding the possible correlation between economic retrenchment in rentier states and increasing pressures for political representation finds support in the Jordanian case.

The review of regime-promoted economic liberalization policies demonstrates that while certain policies aimed at broadening the economy's productive base and encouraging investment were taken, they were insufficient—too little and too late— to avert the growing economic crisis. At the same time, the regime's historic annual bailout (subsidies from Arab states along with remittances from its nationals abroad) had dropped too far too fast to allow Jordan's rent-based economy to develop effective alternatives. Moreover, the development plans of the period appear to have been drawn up based on the assumption that oil prices and unrequited transfers, although declining, would soon return to their previous levels. Year after year budget targets were not met, the deficit increased, and development-plan targets appeared increasingly unrealistic.

Considering the budget deficits the kingdom continued to run in the mid-1980s, which required annual borrowing from international financial markets beginning in 1983, one may legitimately question the depth of the regime's commitment to economic reform. The evidence suggests that Jordanian policy makers failed to understand that much of what had been billed as Jordan's economic success stories were in fact houses built on sand. The economic crisis was triggered by the regional recession, but it was rooted in chronic structural problems that outside financial infusions had enabled the regime to ignore for years. Jordanian policy makers instead viewed the crisis as only temporary, believing that the country could ride out a short period of austerity through a two-pronged strategy of: (1) providing all forms of incentives and support to private capital, especially the large financial and commercial bourgeoisie; and (2) borrowing abroad until Arab money began to flow in again to avoid a painful, more thoroughgoing economic restructuring.

On the political front, it is clear that while the recall of parliament in early 1984 boded well, few additional concrete steps were taken toward liberalization. Issues of free speech, martial law, establishment of political parties, harassment at borders, and the like were raised by the parliament, but no meaningful action was taken. At this point, the economy had not yet deteriorated to the point where the "political contract" between the regime and the political elite—the foregoing of political rights in exchange for economic freedom—that had been successful for so long was voided by its constituency. Nor had the economic crisis so strapped the regime that the degree of coercive force available was called into question.

The extent to which Jordan's economic situation has historically been influenced by regional political constraints has been discussed in detail elsewhere.[67] The evidence from the period covered in this discussion suggests that had it not been for the additional political strains imposed upon the system by the uprising, the regime might have been able to continue to pursue its course of economic liberalization combined with increasing austerity measures in the context of continued repression, occasionally sweetened by halting or superficial attempts at political liberalization, for at least a while longer. But the intifadah did add an extra, if unquantifiable, burden to the system. When the April 1989 economic riots demonstrated that the traditional response, repression, could no longer work, the king took what he probably viewed as the only step possible if the monarchy was to survive. He began to move toward genuine liberalization which, rather than simply culminating in free elections, has in fact spurred a further opening up of the system. While the elections and the subsequent reforms (freezing of martial law, the easing of certain security restrictions, and greater media freedom) have given Jordanians a greater sense that the government is accountable to them, the country is by no means "out of the woods." Jordanians, members of parliament, and average citizens, appear to expect that the new parliament will be able to solve the economic crisis. At the same time, fears are expressed that the economic crisis is the greatest threat to Jordan's new democratic experiment. The record would suggest that as long as Jordan's budget continues to be deprived of its former, high levels of foreign grants and aid, the austerity measures will have to continue, and the government will be unlikely to take the chance of retreating from the recent political reforms. Again, according to Luciani's formulation, the perception among the citizenry of government accountability will be critical to continuing attempts to implement such measures.

Notes

1. Hossein Mahdavi, "The Pattern and Problems of Economic Development in Rentier States: The Case of Iran," in M. Cook, ed., *Studies in the Economic History of the Middle East* (London: Oxford University Press, 1970), pp. 428–67.

2. Michel Chatelus and Y. Schmeil, "Towards a New Political Economy of State Industrialization in the Middle East," *IJMES,* no. 2 (1984), as cited in Hazem Beblawi and Giacomo Luciani, eds. *The Rentier State* (London: Croom Helm, 1987), p. 12.

3. Hazem Beblawi, "The Rentier State in the Arab World," in Beblawi and Luciani, *Rentier State,* p. 53.

4. Thomas Stauffer, "Income Measurement in Arab States," in Beblawi and Luciani, *Rentier State,* p. 27.

5. An estimated 95 percent of whom were Palestinians, Bilal al-Hasan, *Al-Filastiniyyun f-il-Kuwayt* (Beirut: PLO Research Center, 1974), p. 11 n.

6. Beblawi uses the rentier–semi-rentier distinction. Luciani uses the rentier state–rentier economy distinction as well as a distinction between what he terms allocation and production states. According to this division, all the oil producers as well as Jordan and Syria are classified as allocation states because of the distributive role of the state as well as the percentage of state expenditure in relation to GDP.

7. Giacomo Luciani, "Allocation vs. Production States: A Theoretical Framework," in Beblawi and Luciani, *Rentier State,* pp. 69–70.

8. The ratio of foreign grants and loans to domestic revenues was 57.7 percent in 1984, 65.6 percent in 1985, and 78 percent in 1986; calculated from figures taken from Philip Robins, "Jordan to 1990," *Economist Intelligence Unit,* 1986).

9. *Economist Intelligence Unit Quarterly* (London), (hereafter *EIU*), no. 2 (1989): 11.

10. *EIU,* no. 3 (1989): 2.

11. Beblawi and Luciani, "Introduction," in Beblawi and Luciani, *Rentier State,* p. 2; and Luciani, "Allocation vs. Production States."

12. *Middle East Times* (hereafter, *MET*), 17–23 December 1988.

13. Beblawi, "The Rentier State in the Arab World," p. 53.

14. Luciani, "Allocation vs. Production States," p. 76.

15. Michel Chatelus, "Policies for Development: Attitudes toward Industry and Services," in Beblawi and Luciani, *Rentier State,* p. 114.

16. Luciani, "Allocation vs. Production States," p. 73.

17. Michel Chatelus, "Rentier or Producer Economy in the Middle East? The Jordanian Response," in Bichara Khader and Adnan Badran, eds., *The Economic Development of Jordan* (London: Croom Helm, 1987), p. 208.

18. Fahed al-Fanek, "Is Jordan Ready for Privatization?" *Jordan Times,* 31 August 1986.

19. *EIU,* "Jordan," no. 1 (1985): 10. Autonomous government projects include the Telecommunications Corporation (TCC), Royal Jordanian Airlines, the Ports Corporation, the Jordan Valley Authority (JVA), the Industrial Estates Corporation, Amman Municipality, Aqaba Railway, Free Zones Authority, public transportation, housing and vocational training authorities, municipal and village councils, and universities.

20. *EIU,* "Jordan and Syria," Annual Supplement (1983): 31.

21. Fanek, "Is Jordan Ready for Privatization?"

22. *EIU,* Annual Supplement (1984): p. 41.

23. Hani Hourani, "Azmat al-Urdun al-Iqtisadiyyah" (Jordan's economic crisis), part 1, *Al-Urdun al-Jadid* (Cyprus) (Fall-Winter 1986): 35–36.

24. Idem, "Azmat al-Urdun al-Iqtisadiyyah," part 2, *Al-Urdun al-Jadid* (Spring 1988): 37.

25. *EIU,* no. 2 (1985): 16; no. 1 (1988): 16.

26. Hourani, "Azmat al-Urdun al-Iqtisadiyyah," part 2, p. 37.

27. Ibid., p. 38.

28. Mohammad Qasem Ahmad Al-Quaryoty, "Reconciling Development Planning with Privatization: The Case of Jordan" (paper presented at the 1988 Midwest Political Science Association annual meeting, 14–16 April, Chicago, Illinois), pp. 42–43.

29. Ibid., pp. 43–44.

30. *EIU,* no. 2 (1985): 4 and 11.

31. *EIU,* no. 3 (1985): 13.

32. *EIU,* no. 1 (1987): 15.

33. *EIU,* no. 2 (1986): 14.

34. *Middle East Economic Digest* (hereafter *MEED*), 24 May 1985.

35. *EIU,* no. 3 (1985): 15.

36. *Jordan Times* (hereafter *JT*), 8–9 December 1988, from *FBIS,* 8 December 1988.

37. *EIU,* no. 1 (1986): 13.

38. *Sawt al-Sha'b,* 12 December 1988, from *FBIS,* 20 December 1988.

39. While PLO chief Yasir Arafat encouraged Palestinian Jordanians to attend the first expatriate conference, by the time the second conference was held in the summer of 1986, PLO-Jordanian political coordination had broken down, and Palestinian offices in the country had largely been closed. *Al-Qabas,* 10 October 1986.

40. *EIU,* no. 4 (1985): 15.

41. *EIU,* no. 4 (1986): 13.

42. *JT,* 21 September 1988, from *FBIS,* 23 September 1988.

43. *MET,* 17–23 December 1988.

44. *EIU,* Annual Supplement (1984): 40.

45. *MET,* 24–30 December 1988.

46. *EIU,* no. 1 (1987): 16.

47. *EIU,* no. 1 (1987): 11.

48. *EIU,* no. 1 (1988): 12.

49. *EIU,* no. 4 (1988): 12.

50. *EIU,* Annual Supplement (1983): 42.

51. *EIU,* no. 3 (1985): 13.

52. *EIU,* no. 4 (1985): 11.

53. *Ibid.*

54. *EIU,* no. 1 (1986): 16.

55. *EIU,* no. 4 (1988): 10–11.

56. Amman TV Service, 5 November 1988, from *FBIS,* 7 November 1988.

57. Amman TV Service, 16 October 1988, from *FBIS,* 18 October 1988.

58. *MET,* 28 February 1989–6 March 1989.

59. *MET,* 7–13 March 1989; and Chatelus, "Policies for Development," p. 207.

60. For a discussion of the role of these organizations, see Laurie A. Brand, *Palestinians in the Arab World: Institution Building and the Search for State* (New York: Columbia University Press, 1988), pp. 177–79.

61. *MEED,* 14 December 1984.

62. Statement by Ahmad ʿUbaydat at the House of Representatives, 15 May 1984, as carried by Amman Domestic Service and translated in *FBIS,* 16 May 1984.

63. Asad Abd al-Rahman and Riad al-Khouri, "The Meaning of the Intifada for the Arab World, and the Case of Jordan" (paper presented at the 1989 annual symposium of the Center for Contemporary Arab Studies, Georgetown University, "The Palestinians: New Directions," 3–5 May 1989, Washington, D.C.), p. 10.

64. Said K. Aburish, "The Mideast's War of Money," *Washington Post,* 30 October 1988.

65. *Al-Sharq al-Awsat,* 3 March 1989, from *FBIS,* 7 March 1989.

66. *MET,* 17–23 December 1988.

67. Chatelus, "Policies for Development," p. 204.

CHAPTER

10

BREAKING WITH SOCIALISM: ECONOMIC LIBERALIZATION AND PRIVATIZATION IN ALGERIA

Dirk Vandewalle

"It doesn't matter whether the cat is black or white. What matters is that it catches mice." With those words Messaoudi Zitouni, Minister of Light Energy, in 1985 summarized the attitude prevailing among Algeria's economic reformers, the supporters of President Chadli Benjedid's *infitah* that started in 1980.[1] Coming barely six years after the death of the former president, Houari Boumedienne, who had guided Algeria through an intense nationalist/socialist economic experiment, Zitouni's statement hinted at the pragmatism and determination with which Algeria is now grappling with the effects of that earlier strategy. But it masks at the same time the brinksmanship—and some inside Algeria would argue the political naïveté—among the country's technocrats that are spearheading the current reforms. Perhaps nowhere in the Arab world, with the possible exception of Egypt under Nasser, had a government so clearly flaunted its *tiers mondiste* credentials and so firmly committed itself to a fully articulated socialist development as Algeria in the wake of its independence from France in 1962.[2] As in other centrally planned economies, the story of Algerian socialism since then was one of massive state intervention in all sectors and aspects of its economy. The country's legal system, its fiscal and monetary policy instruments, its regulatory systems to insulate the country's state companies from competition—and, as it turned out, from concerns about efficiency and profitability—formed a tightly integrated set of mechanisms meant to protect its internal market from undue interference.

Following the virtual collapse of the nation's economy as the French withdrew, Algerian planners argued that only the state could assume the burden of providing the massive investments necessary to market the hydrocarbons that would finance the country's industrialization plans. At the same time, close state control would guarantee that Algeria mastered the technological complexity necessary to deepen that industrialization strategy from primary to intermediary and consumer goods. Under Houari Boumedienne, the country's austere president from 1965 until 1978, this tightly integrated vertical "bureaucratic dictatorship" was part and parcel of a deliberate policy to prevent international capital and potential local *compradors* from influencing economic decisions. To further avoid any dissipation of economic and political decision-making power that could introduce friction and slow down the original strategy, Algeria's leaders created a single-party system that traced its credentials back to the War of Independence. The Front de Libération Nationale (FLN) thus not only symbolized Algerian nationalism but, more importantly, it also provided the link through which central decision makers obtained social and political control and provided patronage to a far-reaching network of clients throughout the country. One of the most important aspects of this system, according to the country's leadership, was that only this close symbiosis between party and state could guarantee equity for all Algerians—an equity demanded under Boumedienne's egalitarianism for an entire generation that had lived through the war and that would now endure austerity for the sake of the country's economic reconstruction.

When the socialist strategy was gradually abandoned almost two decades later, Boumedienne's successor, Chadli Benjedid, demanded a renewed austerity to give his market-oriented economic strategy a chance to succeed. Shortly after Boumedienne's death in 1978, Algeria embarked upon the current president's ambitious economic restructuring program. Its central tenet has been the replacement of the vertically integrated bureaucracy associated with the socialist experiment with the horizontal structures implicit in a more market-oriented approach. No matter how difficult the country's economic situation was in 1979, however, Benjedid's real conundrum consisted of a much larger and more powerful combination of socio-economic and political factors that challenged the role of the state as it had been fashioned after 1962. The main ideological underpinning of Algeria's *dirigisme* and *étatisme* after 1962 had been a nationalist ideology rooted in the 1954–62 revolution. To preserve the achievements of that revolution, the government cast both its economic development strategy that emerged after 1965 and the calls for internal austerity to make it succeed in a strong nationalist light. A generation later the ability of the Algerian government to use this nationalist myth as a mobilizational tool had dissipated. By the time of the 1988 riots, nearly 70 percent of the country's citizens no longer had any direct knowledge of the war. More than half of this younger generation was unemployed. Equally worrisome was the fact that the FLN, the instrument to guide and implement *étatisme,* had lost much of its appeal and credibility by the time of Boumedienne's death. This process accelerated in the 1980s, particularly after the self-imposed austerity measures of 1983, when severe economic difficulties decreased the Party's ability to further provide its traditional patronage.

By 1980, the value of the FLN as propagator of Algerian nationalism and as a provider of goods and services through its patronage system had already been severely circumscribed: it had become valued by most Algerians for what it could deliver, not for what it stood for politically or ideologically. Almost a decade later, which coincided with Benjedid's attempt to create a more market-oriented economy, the October 1988 riots demonstrated that the credibility of the FLN had diminished even further as its functionaries were targeted by a younger generation both for mismanagement and incompetence and for being apparatchiks who had profited handsomely in the past from the socialist experiment while chronic shortages of goods existed in the street.[3]

It is against this more general socioeconomic background that Benjedid's efforts at structural liberalization, and their potential for further economic change, must be measured. The reform of the Algerian economy has taken place in a period of dramatic economic, political, and cultural upheaval, a period François Burgat has characterized as "the third stage of de-colonization."[4] Will the move toward privatization in Algeria—and the rapid removal of the socialist orientation—lead to the same kind of harrowing debate and crisis of the state as it did in Tunisia after Bourguiba's renunciation of Ahmed Ben Bella's socialist strategy in 1969? The Algerian strategy is still too new to draw definitive conclusions. But it has already demonstrated—as in the Egyptian, Turkish or Tunisian case—how extraordinarily difficult it is to move from economic and political *dirigisme* toward a laissez-faire approach.

The shift in economic orientation raises a number of important questions concerning state control over the direction and the speed of the proposed changes. In Algeria, as in other centrally planned economies, these questions have provoked considerable and prolonged debate. Several of the reform measures proposed by Benjedid have been delayed for months, in some cases years, before they are implemented. The debate over the new strategy and the infighting continue: when Benjedid dismissed Prime Minister Kasdi Merbah in September 1989, he refused to leave in the hope that the opponents of *infitah* would come to his rescue. There is little hope that such further challenges can be avoided in a political system where crises have almost always led and been exacerbated by a "show of force . . . between different clans in the political and military arenas."[5] In addition, Benjedid's move away from *dirigisme* has been caught up in a powerful and multidimensional movement toward greater autonomy for groups within Algerian society. The reemergence of Kabyle demands for greater autonomy and the rapid growth and political organization of Islamic movements are but two examples of a cultural reawakening among several groups inside Algeria that clamor for greater recognition of their own claims from the state.

Because of the country's historical legacy and the more recent sociopolitical contestation, the path toward structural reform and privatization has been deliberately slow. Compared to its Maghrebi neighbors, Morocco and Tunisia, Algeria still lags somewhat in encouraging market-based activities. It has been reluctant to remove many of the obstacles that would establish a truly functioning commercial climate. Suspicion of freely conducted economic activity remains very high; private entrepreneurs still face enormous bureaucratic hurdles even where legal impediments have been amended to facilitate investment. In some instances bureaucratic controls have increased, or have been more strictly enforced, as legal hurdles have been removed by the central government. In general, many of the low- and mid-level functionaries of the country's ministries and highly articulated bureaucracy remain opposed to Benjedid's strategy. And although direct foreign investment has been allowed since March 1990, multinational corporations still face numerous hurdles and remain skeptical of the overall economic climate.

Despite these remaining drawbacks, however, it is instructive to note the changes in the Algerian economy since 1980. After almost two decades of centralized pricing for all commodities, several of those earlier restrictions have now been lifted. State intervention in the agricultural sector has fallen to a level below that now found in any other Maghrebi country. The banking sector, until recently lagging substantially behind in the restructuring effort, has been dramatically reformed and reinvigorated after the 1988 riots. The country's monetary policy is now determined by an independent central bank, and most public companies are legally, if perhaps not financially, autonomous.

POLITICAL ECONOMY OF REFORM

From the beginning of the new strategy's implementation in 1980, Algeria's planners have identified two basic problems at the heart of the country's structural reforms. The first is foremost political: how does the government retain some measure of control in a rapidly changing climate when political *dirigisme* gives way to a greater autonomy for different groups in society? The second is economic and concerns the timing and speed of the reforms: will Benjedid's deliberately slow pace of reform yield enough momentum to achieve real reform (and tangible results for the population) or will it falter somewhere between the old bureaucratic approach and the market-oriented strategy? Liberalization and privatization is in essence a race against time. On one side is the necessity to design and implement an integrated set of macroeconomic policies that promise long-lasting reforms and the much heralded trickle-down economic effects. The change from a centrally planned economy toward a market-oriented economy hinges critically on the ability of the government to move toward a system that provides economic information and incentives to individuals and institutions and to grant them the responsibility to put this information to efficient use. In practical terms, only the liberalization of interest rates, wages, prices, and, ultimately, exchange rates can provide both this economic information and the incentive structure necessary—a road Algeria has only partially traveled. On the other side are the realities these reforms are already engendering in Algeria: greater numbers of unemployed and dramatic increases in food and other subsidized items, which were causes of the 1988 riots.

As several planners in Algeria reiterate, not moving fast and far enough in designing and implementing the broad macroeconomic reforms necessary to turn the economy around invites the risk that the government will yield to political and economic difficulties and muddle through, or simply change the principle of allocating goods and services within the economy while retaining public ownership. As C. H. Moore has noted,

Changing patterns of allocation rather than ownership may produce the kind of political economies that will give an exhausted statist regime a new lease of life. Instead of managing economic exchanges directly, such a regime may manage them indirectly, while still continuing in principle to own the means of production. Supporting client groups then becomes less expensive because some of the costs are farmed out. . . . But how long can a regime have it both ways, conserving its power and autonomy while selectively unloading economic decision-making onto a protected marketplace?[6]

Can the Algerian government, traditionally distrustful of a broad macroeconomic approach, now implement such a strategy that promises long-term reforms without yielding, for a number of sociopolitical reasons, to an incrementalism that destroys both the sequencing and the rapid implementation necessary to give that strategy its chance to succeed? Again, it is perhaps too early to answer that question in the case of Algeria. But there is little doubt that the country has often moved forward in implementing its *infitah* at a snail's pace, despite the mistaken appearance of speed and enthusiasm hinted at by the flurry of decrees, directives, and laws that have appeared in support of the strategy since 1980. And this plethora of laws notwithstanding, the government's overwhelming concern has been with liberalization for the sake of efficiency and higher productivity: only in the agricultural sector has state property actually been handed over to individuals, and there is little evidence to suggest that the government will move beyond this. Whether the Algerian strategy will end at simply "changing the patterns of allocation" is the principal question of this chapter.

ALGERIA'S *INFITAH* AND AUSTERITY

For analytical purposes Algeria's *infitah* strategy can be subdivided into four distinct periods: 1980–82, characterized by a number of still isolated liberalization measures; 1982–85, when the first wave of integrated directives took place; 1986–88, an intensification of the earlier efforts that was concluded by the riots; and the last period, which started in the aftermath of the riots when most of the remaining political opposition to *infitah* was removed and the government rushed forward with further reforms. Even though the tools at its disposal and the political climate inside the country changed dramatically during the decade, the overall goals of the Benjedid government remained the same. The strategy put forward by Benjedid was not so much a step-by-step as an ambitious overall three-legged reform plan that would quickly move the country toward a more market-oriented economy. Algeria's planners realized that the sequencing and smooth implementation of the reform measures was a sine qua non for its success. Taking a long-term view of Algeria's developmental needs and after identifying the major existing bottlenecks in the economy, the strategy that emerged focused on three interlinked sets of concerns considered vital in the move toward a more liberal economy that would be marked by a greater allocative efficiency and improved productive capabilities:

(1) The pursuit of greater efficiency, including (a) decentralization of the economy, (b) curtailing the power of the country's bureaucracy, (c) rewriting the commercial and investment codes, and (d) reforming the banking sector, the state companies, the pricing system, and the state monopoly on imports. By 1987 many of the decrees, laws, and recommendations that resulted had been bundled into a five-part guideline, the *Cahiers de la Réforme* (Reform Notebooks).[7]

(2) Minimize the impact of a projected loss of income in the 1980s while preserving and extending the overall impetus toward a more liberal economy. The uncertainty and setbacks in the sale of natural gas necessitated some form of stabilization. The Benjedid government, in 1983, adopted an austerity plan that was partly an attempt to avoid the opprobrium of rescheduling international debt or of seeking help from international financial institutions.[8]

(3) Create supplementary sources of income and minimize foreign-exchange outlays, focusing in particular on attempts to increase non-hydrocarbon exports and to make agriculture more profitable.[9]

Launched by presidential decree on 4 October 1980, the restructuring of the country's public companies was the outcome of a detailed study by a special FLN subcommittee that had met for the first time in November 1979 and whose recommendations were subsequently discussed by all social partners at a national colloquium in March 1980.[10] At the meeting some of the participants had described the position of the public companies as that of a Trojan horse, a state within a state, ruled by overprotective bureaucracies and riddled by inefficiency. New regulations restricted their workforce to a maximum of 30,000—SONATRACH at the time employed almost 100,000—and limited each smaller company's responsibilities to specific aspects of the production process. Company managers were given limited authority over production and pricing decisions.[11] Many of the new rules had little immediate effect, however, since the highly politicized system of financing was left unchanged and the stultifying bureaucracy remained in place; four years after the reforms, *El Moudjahid* complained that their impact had been minimal.[12] Nevertheless, by the end of 1983, one hundred of Algeria's largest public-sector companies that accounted for three-quarters of all economic activity were, at least in theory, broken up into five hundred new enterprises, and some restrictions had been put on public hiring.

In January 1983, the modalities under which the private sector could engage in economic activities were outlined in even greater detail.[13] At the sixth session of the FLN Central Committee in December 1981, the private sector was described as being "complementary" to the public sector. Private enterprises were given new fiscal and financial incentives. The new Investment Code of 1982 decreased tax rates and offered some credit to export-oriented enterprises. Provided private-sector projects met the Code's new guidelines, they were eligible for state investment grants, certain tax benefits, and easier access to credit. Particular awards were available for those private-sector companies that invested in labor-intensive projects located in the interior of the country. In a significant departure from its previous policy on multinational corporations, the 1982 Code made minority foreign participation in joint ventures with state companies possible.[14] A number of long-standing problems, however, were left unresolved. Algeria's private industrial sector consists overwhelmingly of companies involved in light industry and some manufacturing. Since it enjoyed no real juridical status under the 1966 Investment Code, private industrialists have not shown great evidence of real market-oriented behavior in this uncertain climate: in general they have opted for risk-free enterprises from which they could withdraw their capital quickly, or have built up companies that could handily reap profits at the margins of the public sector.[15]

The austerity measures that were announced at the end of 1983—implemented according to the Algerian government to prevent a rescheduling of the country's foreign debt—in reality dovetailed with the overall liberalization strategy and were meant in part to reinforce it. Several of the stipulations included in the plan—a further dismantling of the public sector, diversification of non-hydrocarbon exports, encouragement of the private sector, and decontrolling interest rates and prices—simply repeated some of the measures the government had already attempted to implement since 1980, or would soon seek. Under the often repeated battle cry of keeping the International Monetary Fund and the World Bank at bay, Algeria adopted a self-imposed "stabilization program" that in essence called for all the adjustments normally sought by the international agencies: a further deregulation of domestic prices, adjusting investment codes laws to encourage foreign direct investment, greater efficiency for the state companies, export-oriented growth, a severe restriction of the money supply, and a halt to guaranteed employment. For reasons of nationalist sentiment or because of political sensibilities, the government did not include three standard measures in the plan: a call for the deregulating of domestic interest rates, the devaluation of the Algerian dinar, and the immediate removal of subsidies.

The austerity program, however, was also to some extent an indication of the government's political weakness in pursuing a coherent macroeconomic framework after 1980. The set of liberalization measures after 1980 had largely been disjointed, despite the seemingly coherent strategy Benjedid had outlined. The country still lacked a clear monetary policy, and the government remained unwilling to delink the state companies from the public Treasury. The first three years of the austerity plan did not substantially alter the country's economic plight: Treasury deficits increased rapidly as central government expenditures continued to rise; internal production was slashed in half between 1982 and 1985; non-hydrocarbon exports stagnated; and the trade and current accounts were balanced only by increased natural gas exports, after the completion of the Trans-Med pipeline to Italy, and because of the decrease in imports. Several measures not yet adopted at the time of the austerity plan's implementation at the end of 1983 soon became part of the liberalization strategy. By 1984, a new statute abolished most of the collective farms, some of which were sold to private individuals. In addition to reducing the role of the central agricultural marketing organizations, private individuals were allowed to market farm machinery and other needed goods. In a radical departure from previous practice, private individuals also received permission to engage in trade between the different provinces, a monopoly until then held by the Office National de Commerce (ONECO).

A RENEWED CALL FOR REFORMS, 1986–89

For all the new directives, laws, and regulations adopted after 1980 and the austerity measures after 1983, the real Achilles heel of Algeria's economic strategy remained its incomplete, often lackluster implementation—a failure linked not only to political opposition or to the government's need to avoid a popular backlash but also to the lack of a coherent macroeconomic program. The lack of implementation was particularly worrisome since the government after 1980 had viewed institutional reform—decentralization and public enterprise reorganization—as crucial to the future of *infitah* in Algeria. It had spent half a decade trying to design an administrative and legal framework to support liberalization. Despite this effort, many of the new rules and regulations had only a marginal impact. The presence and intensification of a number of economic problems (inflation, unemployment, and the massive size of the black market in particular) persisted. Although the need for further fiscal and monetary reform obviously existed and would need to be addressed, the government perceived part of its challenge as an attempt to move beyond the institutional reforms it had pursued since 1980 and to actively restructure the country's incentive system—primarily prices and interest rates and, at a future time, the country's currency exchange rate.

This call for a shift of emphasis in the *infitah* strategy was in part based on the realization that the sluggish performance of the Algerian economy since 1980 had created intense resentment among the population. But it was above all fueled by the vicissitudes of the international energy market. The drop in the country's hydrocarbon earnings (plummeting from almost $13 billion in 1985 to $7 billion in 1986), in addition to the fall in the value of the dollar and the ensuing recession, jolted many of the country's planners into demanding even more intense austerity measures and a more rapid extension of the liberalization strategy which they considered hobbled by weak political will and a number of more technical macroeconomic deficiencies.[16] They pointed out that notwithstanding the substantial reductions of government expenditures during the first two years of the austerity plan, the fiscal deficit as a percentage of GDP had climbed rapidly and that the country's debt service in the spring of 1986 consumed almost 60 percent of all exports of goods and services.

Benjedid embraced both demands made by the country's planners, closely intertwined at any rate. The severity of the self-imposed austerity plan can be gauged by the fact that Algeria found itself in the "remarkable position of having experienced three years of economic recession from 1986 to 1989, while still managing to produce a surplus in its international trade balance and keeping up its debt-service payments."[17] The second—the adoption of a stringent macroeconomic stabilization policy that included a reduction in real domestic demand and led to the dramatic merchandise import cutbacks Pfeifer noted—allowed local planners to stick to their determination not to use payments arrears to finance its balance of payments and to forgo debt rescheduling.

The decision to pay closer attention to the use of incentives rather than to concentrate further on institutional reform characterized Algerian *infitah* after 1985. The country's economic performance, even after two years of the austerity plan, raised some doubts about the possible effectiveness of the shift. But, according to the government, there were few alternatives: the need to drastically reduce government spending and to compress domestic demand even further under the austerity plan meant that a new system of incentives rather than further regulation was, for political as well as economic reasons, one of the few options available.

Many of these new orientations were contained and explained in the 1986 National Charter (an update of the 1976 version) and in the 1986 Investment Code.[18] A number of important decrees followed their publication. In light of Algeria's traditional insistence on centralized management, one of the most telling changes of the new orientation consisted of Benjedid's decision to hand over even greater autonomy directly to managers of public companies by abolishing, in 1987, the Ministry of Planning that had guided the country's socialist strategy since the early 1960s. The ministry was replaced by a Conseil National de Planification. The CNP, in contrast to its predecessor, is no longer in charge of setting prices or foreign-exchange allocations and, with very few exceptions, no longer determines investment levels for companies. This process was extended in 1988, when the government started to grant actual legal autonomy to the state companies; by the end of 1989, one third were operating fully independently. The only control over them belongs to eight newly created *fonds de participation* who hold equity shares to the companies. As holding companies, the *fonds* are managed along market principles and are expected to operate independently and to maximize profit from their portfolios. Their legal statute as autonomous organizations in principle protects them from direct intervention by government ministries; in reality, Algerian planners argue, many holding companies' directors are actual or former ministry employees, and some interference in the management of companies through them does take place. In addition to these holding companies that watch over profitability and efficiency, the government, in May 1989, halted the traditional and once virtually automatic subsidizing of investment and operational needs of companies by the national Treasury through the "home" banks.

SECTORAL REFORMS

Despite the rapid and often spectacular changes in the status of the public companies and their management, the most visible reforms after 1986 took place in the agricultural sector. Extending the earlier decisions to liberalize pricing mechanisms inside the country, the state started to break up the self-management units (DAS) in 1987 by signing usufruct rights over to private groups and individuals who can transfer their shares of property through inheritance or exchange. Although there remains some uncertainty, Algeria's agricultural sector is now, for all practical purposes, completely in private hands. At the same time, credit to the sector was tightened up while most product prices have been freed and the marketing of agricultural products is privately regulated. Subsidies on agricultural inputs (with the exception of water and seeds) and minimum guaranteed wages for farm workers were abolished. Not all impediments have been removed, however; the Algerian state retains a monopoly on processing facilities and large-scale storage. Although the limited data available until now allow for only impressionistic evaluations, observers have noted that more agricultural goods are being marketed and that rural incomes are rising for the first time since the 1971 Agrarian Revolution.[19]

If the autonomy of enterprises and the liberalization of the agricultural sector had been important achievements, the reforms in the country's banking sector were clearly perceived by the Benjedid government as the most crucial, for they would provide many of the financial incentives and disincentives it had sought to put into place. The reform of the country's banks and their operations started in the fall of 1986 and was extended in 1988, 1989, and 1990. The August 1986 banking law broke the umbilical link that had existed between the Banque Centrale d'Algérie and the national Treasury, in effect allowing the BCA to chart a truly independent course. Aided by a number of new instruments, the BCA started to draw up yearly National Credit Plans that put limits on the actual amount of credit created. In an effort to further increase the role of the bank in the planning process and to mobilize local savings, it also started to revise interest and rediscount rates.[20] So far, however, this interbank market has been restricted to the seven domestic commercial and development banks; it has not included the foreign banks established after March 1990. Although the BCA would clearly like to see its new role as a policy-making and supervising institution extended, so far it has been forced to attempt to deal almost exclusively with the legacy of *domiciliation* that left among at least four of the country's banks a deficit of hundreds of billions of dinars.

Despite this, the future role of the BCA, however, was strengthened by another stipulation of the 1986 law, extended further in June 1989, that allowed domestic interest rates to increase. Since real interest rates (actual rates discounted by inflation) in Algeria had remained negative since they were fixed in 1972, this practice had long provided a source of "unofficial" subsidies to the public sector. Although most observers agree that the real rate on commercial bank deposits remains negative even today, the BCA has reiterated on several occasions that it is committed to real positive interest rates by the end of the current Five Year Plan, thus ending the domestic industry's traditionally high consumption of inexpensive credit.

The January 1988 banking law ended what had been one of the cornerstones of the country's banking system, *domiciliation bancaire unique,* establishing a money market for interbank transactions. As in neighboring Tunisia, the abolishing of *domiciliation* has been a mixed blessing so far. For a number of essentially political reasons, public companies are reluctant to leave the bank they had earlier been assigned to. In addition, there has been some speculation that, as in neighboring Tunisia and Morocco, an informal system of interest rates has been set in oligopolistic fashion by the banks. Further, banks still suffer from a continued distrust among depositors, resulting in mostly short-term deposits. In order to increase the level of competition and to introduce more expertise into the local banking system, the new banking and investment law in March 1990 finally granted foreign banks the right to operate branches in Algeria and to retain full ownership of operations and profits.

The new banking laws also included a number of provisions regarding foreign-exchange allocations, once one of the prime instruments socialist Algeria used in controlling economic growth and investment. Still unwilling to move toward a freely convertible dinar, the Benjedid government in 1989 introduced new measures to allow public companies greater control over the acquisition and spending of foreign currency. Under the new regulations, the so-called *budgets devises,* they can now keep earnings from exports in their own accounts. Control by one of the ministries over allocations has been abolished, with the banks now directly in charge of foreign currency operations. To offset the continuing restrictions on the dinar's inconvertibility, the BCA has quietly allowed its value to decline—an estimated 42 percent since 1986—and has pledged itself to bringing the official and black-market rate in line with each other by the end of 1992.[21] Algerians can now deposit directly into foreign-currency accounts and earn competitive international deposit rates on them. Planners hope that this will attract a sizable amount of the hard currency expatriates earn overseas.

Finally, and despite the October 1988 riots, a number of sensitive reforms in prices and wages were introduced in 1989. While staples such as bread, semolina, and sugar are still subject to controlled pricing—and to guaranteed produce prices—most other goods have lost that protection. Electricity and transportation remain heavily subsidized, with Algerian planners seemingly hesitant to move further on this front, at least for now. One of the more visible results of the price liberalization has been a rapid increase in inflation. This, in addition to the flourishing black market and the continuing unemployment, clearly worries the Benjedid government; but so far, it seems to gamble that its overall monetary and fiscal policies and its limited political liberalization in the wake of the riots will outpace discontent. Whether the gamble can work is uncertain: unemployment has grown rapidly since the austerity plan, underemployment is rampant, and real income and private consumption continue to decline—ideal conditions for simmering dissatisfaction. Perhaps in an attempt to vent some of this anger, the government under the new constitution of February 1989 now allows workers to strike and to belong to independent unions. But at the same time, individual companies are now allowed to set their own wages and employment levels, tailoring in effect their size to efficiency concerns. The former system of automatic hiring by state companies has been put on hold.

In light of the self-imposed austerity plan and the reforms since 1980, the absence of conditionality clauses in the agreement with the International Monetary Fund concluded in July 1989 should come as no surprise. Except for a suggestion to devalue the Algerian dinar officially to speed up the reforms, the agreement reiterated most of the measures the Algerian government itself had stressed since embarking on its *infitah*.[22] What Algeria needed in July 1989 was not a full-fledged stabilization program but, rather, a short-term arrangement to solve a current deficit problem expediently.

THE OCTOBER 1988 RIOTS[23]

Although the October 1988 riots had no immediate or direct impact on Algeria's economic strategy, they had important political consequence that allowed the Benjedid government to recommit itself to the *infitah* policy and to return to and speed up the implementation of a broad macroeconomic policy in September 1989. Less than a month before the riots, Chadli gave a speech for an audience of provincial officials about the state of the Algerian economy.[24] He savagely attacked virtually all social groups in the country for laxity, mismanagement, and downright indifference to economic progress. He called for an extension of the decentralization of the economy, further administrative reform, and an even greater management autonomy for state companies. Although he stressed that the country's economic situation was "difficult, but [has] not reached a critical stage," his condemnation of the nonimplementation of the plethora of new, more liberal laws and regulations since 1986 was widely interpreted in Algeria as a sign of his own frustration with the "Iron Triangle" of Algerian politics: those within the FLN, the army, and the bureaucracy that continued to oppose his reforms.

The riots led to long and acrimonious debates in the National Assembly on the meaning and future of Algerian *infitah*. The new Prime Minister Kasdi Merbah and his team, appointed soon after the riots, were seen as a caretaker government, a temporary link between Algeria's old generation with their nationalist credentials and solid power structure within the National Assembly and the new technocrats Benjedid favored. As soon as the political infighting—Algeria's old *guerre des clans*—was settled to Benjedid's advantage, he appointed a new government under Prime Minister Mouloud Hamrouche closely in tune with his own ideas about *infitah*. Despite the prolonged debate they provoked, the riots have been, at least from Benjedid's point of view, a catalyst: in their aftermath several of the most vocal political opponents within the National Assembly, the FLN, and the army departed or were ranged out.

The orientation of the Hamrouche government that came to power in September 1989 is abundantly clear. Of its twenty-three new ministers, fifteen had never held office and were practically unknown technocrats. Only Hamrouche himself had a direct link to the War of Independence, having been an officer in the ALN. Seven of the new ministers at one point headed one of the country's main public enterprises, and all were known for their support of the reform measures and their technical expertise. Ghazi Hidouci, now Minister of Economic Affairs, is the principal theoretician of the country's *infitah* strategy and was responsible for the drawing up of one of the country's most important *infitah* laws, the law on the autonomy of the public enterprises. In addition, Sid Ahmed Ghozali, the economic *enfant terrible* who was sacked in the 1970s as Minister of Energy for promoting market-oriented policies and who once headed SONATRACH, was appointed as the country's Foreign Minister. He is known for his close links to European and international financial institutions.

With his new team in place, Hamrouche moved quickly to tighten up further the fiscal and monetary policies of his predecessors. Indicative of the new stringent climate is the fact that the 1990 budget adopted by the National Assembly projects a Treasury deficit of 2.3% of GDP, in contrast to deficits in excess of 10 percent since 1980. Further restrictions were imposed on the BCA to prevent advances to the Treasury not commensurate with the overall goal of keeping monetary expansion within limits. With price and exchange controls partly liberalized, the Hamrouche government now hopes to stem the hyperinflation that several other countries implementing the same strategy have experienced—and which almost invariably leads to large-scale popular dissent.

THE FUTURE OF THE ALGERIAN *INFITAH*

Ten years after the start of its *infitah,* the Algerian government is now poised at an important and historically unique juncture. After a decade of plodding along, due to a mixture of political and economic structural problems and a lack of consensus over the nature of national objectives, many of the existing bottlenecks have, at least for now, been removed. Despite occasional setbacks and lingering popular resentment and distrust, the Benjedid government has managed to overcome enormous bureaucratic and political resistance, to reform a weak macroeconomic policy environment to its advantage, and to tone down a political legacy that made private investment and private initiative for the collective good unattractive, and it has weathered the consequences of both underdeveloped capital markets and political upheaval. Symbolic perhaps of the government's determination to irrevocably continue with its current economic direction is that the word "socialism" is not mentioned a single time in the new constitution of February 1989.

It is important to gauge both the strengths and weaknesses of the current political and economic environment before moving on to more general issues that will determine the future of Algeria's reforms. With a president and a team of top advisors dedicated to the strategy, with the legal and financial system stabilized, and with a commitment from bilateral and international lenders, the Algerian *infitah* has the potential of becoming one of the most far-reaching reform efforts in the Arab world. In addition, the removal of old-guard adherents to the country's socialism (like former FLN deputy leader Mohamed Cherif Messaadia) should give Benjedid, at least temporarily, more breathing room. In some ways, Benjedid's position as a strong president enjoying the support of the military, and his new role that followed from the political reforms in the wake of the riots and puts him "above" politics, adds to this stability.

Even if several obstacles to the implementation of *infitah* have been removed, a large number of social, political, and economic uncertainties remain. Perhaps not surprising in light of the country's historical legacy, the *infitah* strategy in Algeria retains a good measure of tutelage and *dirigisme*: for almost every concession that is made, a matching restriction is imposed. Liberalization and closure continue to go hand in hand.[25] The sense of closure and the loss of momentum these setbacks potentially entail, however, could dramatically alter the direction and the outcome of the country's *infitah* strategy. The change from a centrally planned economy to a liberal, market-based system demands a coordination and sequencing of economic reforms that the country's leaders have already found very difficult to achieve. A number of major microeconomic and macroeconomic difficulties to efficient resource allocation remain in Algeria. At the microeconomic level, the *Cahiers de la Réforme* still have not clearly identified the correct labor, asset, capital, and product markets for each sector. One aspect of the problem is that information available to planners and managers often remains incomplete, compartmentalized, and distorted by the layers of bureaucracy through which it is filtered. In this regard, Algeria faces another serious obstacle: many of the second level of managers and administrators have relatively little knowledge of market economics, its strategy, and its objectives. In addition, a large number of company managers and public administrators and mid-level bureaucrats responsible for their implementation remain opposed and could easily derail that sequencing by seeking out supporters within the National Assembly. Already the voting on the joint-ventures legislation, for example, was repeatedly vetoed and ultimately delayed for several months. Other legislation has been so severely amended as to make it virtually meaningless. To add to these difficulties is the fact that under a more liberal system, the cooperation of these mid-level managers and administrators is crucial since their role is no longer limited to meeting centrally planned production targets but now includes the responsibility to efficiently allocate resources.

From a macroeconomic point of view, the challenges are equally daunting, and the possible solutions strongly pit basic political and economic requirements against each other. On the one hand, the country's long-lasting domestic deficits indicate that real absorption must taper off while increases in overall productivity must continue to increase sharply. A greater flow of supplies to the Algerian market, particularly consumer goods, is needed to offset the continuing decline of real income since the late 1970s. But, as one observer has noted, the problem is "how to impose a significant decline in real living standards on an entire nation, how to instigate a rapid supply response while retaining the popular will to reform, and how to bridge liquidity crises prudently during a turbulent period."[26] What Barrett hints at remains one of the crucial dilemmas of the Algerian *infitah*: the political imperative of gradual reform and the economic exigency of rapid change. Liberalization and privatization is a race against time, but in light of the 1988 riots,

Algeria's leaders may be even more cautious in attempting to solve its economic dilemmas in a precipitous fashion, and the new political liberties announced at that time may take a further bite out of the proposed reform program.

Indeed, Benjedid's gradualist approach toward structural economic reform has provided ample evidence of the Algerian leadership's often willy-nilly attention to a number of nationalist and other local concerns that could derail it. Calling the new strategy a "democratization of the economy," imposing one's own adjustment plan rather than suffer the opprobrium of calling in the IMF prior to July 1989, refusing to reschedule the country's debt, producing the *Cahiers de la Réforme* locally rather than asking an outside agency to design a liberal economic blueprint: all hint at the lingering nationalist and more concrete political concerns Benjedid must placate. At the same time, the government remains determined to move forward. Despite the riots and the hardships induced by the austerity plan, Prime Minister Hamrouche and his team remain candidly committed to demanding from the Algerian population the necessary sacrifices: ". . . reform in Algeria necessitates austerity. There will be no more blood, I hope [referring to the riots]; but tears, yes."[27]

Here the government faces further difficulties. Implementing a new development strategy extends beyond a consideration of costs and benefits and the technical problems associated with them. It also demands a consensus, a vision of the future shared between those who design and implement the strategy and those it will affect. Faced with scarce economic resources and limited time, the government has tried to avoid delays by moving forward in a typically tutelary fashion, without consultation with what they often decry as an undisciplined society. Although Algeria's government realized how extraordinarily difficult it would be to implement *infitah,* they seriously underestimated and ignored political challenges to it and felt no need to prepare those who will carry its heaviest burden until the strategy pays off. If there is one feature that distinguishes the Algerian *infitah* from its Turkish counterpart, for example, it is that the government, despite its referendums, has not received the public support the Turkish Prime Minister Ozal received in 1983 when he moved forward with that country's own *infitah*. There have not been in Algeria as in Turkey "increasing segments of the electorate [who] believed that the poor financial performance of state-owned enterprises was one of the fundamental structural problems impeding the country's growth and development, and that it was the government's responsibility to address the problem."[28] Above all, the feeling in Algeria is one of political apathy and a feeling of helplessness.

This constitutes, above all, the terrible legacy of Algeria's one-party system and the abuses to which it was put. There is still a tinge of surrealism to a leadership that now sharply criticizes "the old regime" to which it once belonged! or to a president who once boldly proclaimed a few years ago that "we must distinguish between those who are for or against the revolution."[29] The perception still lingers in popular opinion that the problem with socialism was that of corruption and nepotism, perpetuated by the FLN. The rapidly growing bifurcation between rich and poor, mixed with the fraudulent rhetoric of egalitarianism, was one of the main elements that fueled the riots. But will public reaction differ if that economic and social cleavage is maintained or exacerbated through the magic of the market, a market few Algerians can enter as active economic actors? A new economic direction alone seems unlikely to alter the basic feelings among Algeria's *muha-dhafeen* (dispossessed) that the cards are stacked against them. And it seems likely to erode even further the solidarity demanded by the government: the apparent ease with which that government abandoned the economic philosophy of the Bou-medienne regime, no matter how unavoidable, added to the cynicism and further widened the credibility gap between those governing and the governed. For some Algerians, neither the solidarity the government demands nor *infitah* itself is at issue any longer; a growing number fall outside the country's formal economy. By the government's own admission, a large percentage of those now unemployed (one quarter of the active population) will never find regular employment during their lives. The result is a flourishing parallel market of unregulated labor and a growing importance of alternative economic networks, such as the Islamist volun-tary organizations that have taken over several of the services once provided by the state.[30]

What the Algerian government is now—belatedly, under pressure, and only after several hundred of its young citizens were killed in the riots—trying to ac-complish is to match the economic liberalization and privatization with what the government calls a greater *espace de liberté* for Algerian society. To that extent, the *infitah* is only a part of a much larger debate: the place of the individual and his rights and liberties within that society. The first form of state-building in postin-dependence Algeria was characterized by a strong new state that anchored its le-gitimacy in the anticolonial struggle. It was marked by an internal modernization movement that contained a number of specific political, economic, and ideological forms of expression. That form of state-building has now come to an end. Neither the economic strategy nor the official ideology nor the unique position of the FLN have been able to halt the emerging social, political, religious and in some cases ethnic protest against the former *étatisme*. And despite the obligatory references to the national unity this first period of state-building provided, in this second phase, the state wants to take a step back from involving itself so intimately from eco-nomic management or from dominating so completely political and cultural expression. This attempt at a new legitimacy, marked by economic liberalization and privatization, and at democratization is, however, a long and uncertain process that Algeria has embarked upon.

Whether this new legitimacy can persuade opponents of the new economic strategy to join its advocates remains uncertain. After almost twenty years of main-taining that Algeria's socialism was ideologically, socially, and scientifically the best form of development, its sudden and irrevocable demise as an anachronism and an aberration raises a number of disturbing questions that have never been an-swered adequately by Benjedid and his top supporters: if indeed Algerian socialism is now deemed backward, why did it represent the country's unquestioned and unquestionable strategy for two decades? And is there still a viable role to play for the single party that for so long identified itself with that strategy? All of this points out the possibility of a continued lack of control over the new economic strategy if political contestation continues. The riots and the political indecision in their immediate aftermath confirmed the inability of the country's leadership system to manage a society that had become totally transformed in the years since the War of Independence ended. It also put into stark view a political leadership that demoralized not only potential opponents but also those directly at the service of the state. And it finally demonstrated the effects of a failing patrimonialism that brought part of the country to open defiance.

Ironically, one of the most profound paradoxes Algeria now faces in its pursuit of a liberal, market-oriented economy is that the state has the ability to democratize faster than to improve the economic situation of its citizens and that this improvement will come at the expense of a clientelist system that, until recently, guaranteed a high level of political acquiescence. In pursuit of a future state committed to intrude less, the current government has no other choice in the short term than to intrude more, and more forcefully, to bring about the long-term success of its desire to reduce *étatisme*. This unsolved, and in essence unsolvable, contradiction explains both the gradualist economic reforms in Algeria and demonstrates once more how economic liberalization and privatization and political reform infringe upon each other.

CONCLUSION

What direction does the Algerian *infitah* seem likely to take? The country's current economic strategy is clearly still perceived by the top leadership as the most important national objective; the reshuffle in September 1989 reinforced the team dedicated to its implementation. At the same time, the publication of the *Cahiers de la Réforme* is a clear sign of the determination of the government to move forward and, like the earlier Morgan Guaranty master plan in Turkey, seems destined to focus the debate about liberalization and privatization further. But the *Cahiers* show how heavy the legacy of the socialist strategy remains: many of its guidelines remain confusing and mired in layers of bureaucracy, with myriad opportunities for groups and individuals to intervene in the pursuance of their own interests. What Algeria will ultimately need if it wants to keep its *infitah* on track is a politically neutral, national commission that can impose central directives without any interference from the ministries, the FLN, or the National Assembly. Undoubtedly, this will be an extremely difficult task in a country where clientelism formed a way of life for almost two decades.

Clearly, Algeria has opted for a gradual and mid-level *infitah* approach. From a legal and managerial point of view, the country's public companies are becoming what Europeans call parastatal enterprises that are strictly speaking neither public nor private but in which the government retains complete or substantial ownership while management, profit considerations, and efficiency are delegated to individuals at the company level. These enterprises then "could conceivably combine the putative managerial advantages of the private sector with the social responsiveness and accountability expected of the public sector."[31] So far, there are no indications that the Algerian leadership intends to actually sell state companies, and in light of lingering nationalist sentiment and its own concerns with legitimacy, it seems unlikely to do so for now. But the ultimate goal of these reformed and decentralized parastatals must be efficiency and productivity. Otherwise the new arrangement under which they now operate only changes the pattern of allocation—and leaves the underlying problems unattended. It is too early yet in the Algerian case to ascertain whether the broken-up national enterprises under this new form of management have not simply transferred the high-cost and low-accountability methods of the socialist experiment onto the reformed companies: only since the riots have many of the earlier rules and regulations been actively applied.

In private conversations, however, several managers express a guarded optimism that their companies will operate more efficiently and produce a profit. They also point out that no matter how fast the government wants to move forward, a lag time between the implementation of further liberalization and its effects is unavoidable—at the company and at the national level. During that time, Algeria will need substantial financing from the West. So far, both the International Monetary Fund and the World Bank (in addition to the French and Spanish governments that extended more than a billion dollars each in bilateral aid in 1989) have been very receptive to the country's plight and to the political complications its aid engenders. Despite the remaining weaknesses in both the design and implementation of the economic directives of Algeria's *infitah* and the unavoidable socio-political complications and setbacks, the momentum generated so far makes it likely that Algeria can pass this critical gestation period—and that the memories of the dislocations caused by the inefficiencies of the former public sector and the government's ability to free up economic resources for the benefit of its citizens will eventually combine into stronger popular support for the current economic strategy.

The field research on which this chapter was partly based was made possible by grants from the Institute of Current World Affairs and the European Economic Community. The author would like to thank in particular some of the researchers at CREAD (formerly CREA) and CENEAP as well as a number of managers and officials in the Algerian government for interviews conducted on three visits to Algeria in 1987 and 1988. A special thanks to the staff of the IREMAM library in Aix-en-Provence for assistance during visits in the summer and winter of 1988, and to Dr. Christopher Barrett of the International Institute of Finance and Prof. Karen Pfeifer for sharing drafts of their own work.

Notes

1. Zitouni's interview can be found in *El Moudjahid,* 14 October 1985.
2. As Bruno Etienne succinctly summarized in regard to the origin and content of socialism in Algeria: ". . . Algeria rejects marxism-leninism as being an ideology foreign to Africa; if it is inspired [by socialism] it is to blend it with other legacies such as Islam, arabism and nationalism . . ." in *L'Algérie, cultures et révolution* (Paris: Editions Seuil, 1977), p. 32.
3. A more detailed account of the October 1988 riots and the challenges and opportunities it provided can be found in Dirk Vandewalle, "The Prospect for Algeria," *UFSI Field Staff Reports,* Africa/Middle East 1988–89, no. 17.
4. Consult Vandewalle, *L'Islamisme au Maghreb: La voix du sud* (Paris: Editions Karthala, 1988).
5. For the Merbah incident, consult *Le Monde,* 12 September 1989.
6. C. H. Moore, "Money and Power: The Dilemma of the Egyptian Infitah," *The Middle East Journal* 40 (1986): 637.
7. Although the *Cahiers* cannot strictly be called a master plan, they include both a summary of changes already implemented and a number of general suggestions for each sector and area of reform. See Abderrahmane Roustoumi Hadj Nacer, *Les Cahiers de la Réforme* (Alger: ENAG Editions, 1989). Cahier #1 deals with the planning system, autonomy of companies, and labor statutes; Cahier #2 with the agricultural sector; Cahier #3 with the central administration in Algeria; Cahier #4 with financial institutions; Cahier #5 with monetary aspects of the country's economy.
8. As a result of Algeria's self-imposed austerity plan, the International Monetary Fund standby arrangement that was eventually extended in 1989 carried very light conditionality. Many of the necessary reforms had already been undertaken by the Algerians themselves, making Algeria one of the few countries where bread riots happened *before* the IMF came in. For a more detailed description of policies and events leading up to the IMF agreement, consult Karen Pfeifer, "Algeria's Implicit Stabilization Program" (paper prepared for the Middle East Studies Association annual meeting, 15–18 November 1989, Toronto).
9. For a comprehensive look at what Algerian planners in 1980 saw as the most important challenges for the decade ahead—and a slightly different description of the three issue areas here outlined—consult Zoubir Souissi and Kamal Zemouri, "Le nouveau triptyque: production, assainissement, decentralisation," *Révolution africaine,* no. 831 (1980): 19–35.
10. Among a plethora of sources on the restructuring debate, consult in particular "Restructuration des entreprises: idées forces," *El Moudjahid,* 8–9 January 1982, and FLN, Commission juridique et de l'organisation générale, *Rapport de la commission ad hoc chargée de la restructuration des entreprises* (April 1980, Algiers, mimeo, 2 vols.), which includes a number of reports dealing with other aspects of the liberalization strategy as well. See also *El Moudjahid,* 11 January 1982, which provides a list of the enterprises that had been restructured; and *El Moudjahid,* 21 September 1983 and 20 October 1983, for further details and criticisms.
11. SONATRACH was eventually broken up into twelve smaller companies, each of which was involved in a specific aspect of the oil and natural gas industry.
12. In a number of interviews in Algiers, Oran, and Annaba in 1987 and 1988, company managers still made the same complaint to the author, and they cited instances of almost complete paralysis in decision making: the new responsibilities had not been clearly defined and the risk of antagonizing ministry officials—and jeopardizing careers—was felt by several

to be too high to take personal initiative. Presidential Directive 80–242 of 4 October 1980 contained the guidelines for the dismantling of the public industrial sector. A good synopsis of these earlier measures is provided by Marc Ollivier, "Industrie et stratégie de développement en Algérie," *Annuaire de l'Afrique du Nord* 21 (1981).

13. The most comprehensive review of the role, the development and the legal statutes pertaining to the private sector in Algeria can be found in a special issue of *La Revue du CENEAP*, no. 2 (1985). Consult in particular the articles by Abdelhamid Amirouche and Mohamed Kamel Chelgham, "Le secteur privé dans la doctrine économique nationale," pp. 27–46, and Walid Laggoume, "Dossier: secteur privé," pp. 139–48.

14. Mohand Issad, "La loi du 28 août 1982 sur les sociétés d'économie mixte," *Revue algérienne des sciences juridiques, économiques et politiques,* no. 2 (1984): 263–78. A number of clarifications on 17 January and 17 December 1983 followed the initial law, specifying the remuneration of both parties. Until 1986, when an effort was made under the new National Charter to guarantee foreign partners a more flexible application of the laws, foreign investment remained disappointingly low. One reason that still applies today is that European governments, for a number of reasons, have preferred to extend aid to Algeria rather than to entice their companies actually to invest there.

15. A comprehensive overview, now somewhat dated, of Algeria's private entrepreneurs is provided by Jean Peneff, *Industriels algériens* (Paris: CNRS, 1981). See also Djillali Liabes, "Entreprises, entrepreneurs et bourgeoisies d'industries en Algérie. Quelques éléments pour une sociologie de 'l'entreprendre,' " *Cahiers du C.R.E.A.,* no. 1 (1984) and his more comprehensive treatment in *Capital privé et patrons d'industrie en Algérie, 1962–1982* (Alger: Centre de Recherche et Economie Appliquée, 1984). Detailed information on the private sector within the different provinces is provided in "L'Industrie dans les entreprises communales et de wilaya et dans le secteur privé en 1981," *Statistiques,* no. 1 (1983): 44–50.

16. As one Planning Ministry official told the author in 1988, "Our choice was to worry now about an immediate political backlash or wait for one a few years into the future. Either way we had no choice, so it was better to proceed immediately with unpopular measures." Other Algerians, as well as outside observers like Pfeifer, saw the recession partly as a result of the reform strategy rather than the reverse.

17. Pfeifer, "Algeria's . . . Program," p. 19. Important in light of the riots of 1988 is that Pfeifer also stresses that "cutting imports . . . is a more important factor than export expansion in explaining the positive trade balance" (p. 21).

18. An excellent summary of the new National Charter, complete with references to the appropriate legislation, can be found in Jean Leca and Nicole Grimaud, "Dossiers et documents: le secteur privé en Algérie," *Maghreb-Machrek,* no. 113 (1986): 102–19.

19. For some earlier information on changes in the agricultural sector, consult Ahmed Sadoudi, "Présentation de la loi de finances algérienne pour 1985," *Annales des Sciences Financières, Juridiques et Economiques,* no. 1 (1985): 96–115. More recent figures can be found in the article by Francis Ghiles in the *Financial Times,* 1 February 1990, p. 26.

20. According to Barrett the ratio of M1/M2 dropped from 91 percent in the 1982–86 period to 82 percent at the end of 1989, indicating that some of the money supply once put into demand deposits or simply kept in circulation had been transferred to time deposits. See Christopher Barrett, "Saharan Perestroika: Economic Revolution in Algeria" (Washington, D.C., mimeo, Institute of Financial Studies, n.d.), pp. 10–11. For recent developments in the banking sector, consult *Cahiers de la Réforme,* parts 4 and 5.

21. Barrett, "Saharan Perestroika," p. 15; see also the interview with Prime Minister Mouloud Hamrouche in *L'Express,* 13 October 1989, for his views on the parallel market.

22. As noted below, an official devaluation of the dinar remains politically impossible for the Algerian government. But the BCA has unofficially allowed the value of the currency to slip by almost 50 percent since 1986.

23. For more information on the riots and their meaning for Algerian political life and

the dynamics of the country's economic strategy, consult Vandewalle, "The Prospect for Algeria," *UFSI Field Staff Reports,* no. 17 (1988–89).

24. Reproduced in *El Moudjahid,* 21 September 1988.

25. The closure has primarily taken place in regard to the private sector where there is now a distinction between the "good" private sector, those enterprises that will contribute to increased savings and improved living standards, and a "bad" private sector, one that is speculative and mercantilist. In everyday situations, local bureaucrats must make the differentiation, and bureaucratic obstruction has become almost legendary. In a recent case the author researched, a major private cheese manufacturer in the Algiers region—who had managed to survive financially during the socialist period despite the restrictive pricing system—finally closed his factory after local bureaucrats restricted his output by insisting on the application of obscure regulations that had never been applied before. For another flavor of more general difficulties on a daily basis, consult "Secteur privé en Algérie: La société ERIC," *Maghreb développement,* no. 89 (June 1986): 2–10.

26. Barrett, "Saharan Perestroika," p. 3.

27. Interview with Mouloud Hamrouche in *L'Express,* 13 October 1989, p. 28.

28. Roger Leeds, "Turkey: Rhetoric and Reality," in Raymond Vernon, ed., *The Promise of Privatization* (New York: Council on Foreign Relations, 1988), p. 158.

29. Speech by Chadli Benjedid to a meeting of the country's workers' union, in *Révolution africaine,* 8–14 May 1981.

30. They are particularly prevalent in the poorer, urban areas, such as the casbah in Algiers. One of the Islamist leaders has put the number of members subscribing to the services provided by the voluntary organizations at three million. Although undoubtedly exaggerated, even the casual observer notes the dramatically increased economic activities of the Islamists in contemporary Algeria.

31. Vernon, *The Promise of Privatization,* p. 18.

CHAPTER
11

PRIVATIZATION AND DEVELOPMENT IN TUNISIA [1]

Iliya Harik

The tendency on the part of the state to shed off some of its major responsibilities as a business entrepreneur in Tunisia is only a few years old, although the change in attitude and policies toward the private sector goes back to the beginning of the 1970s. The continuing progress toward liberalization points up to policy flexibility in the system, but not without international nudging and compelling economic pressures. The fact that such a change in economic policy reflects adversely on the official socialist ideology makes the switch in policy even more impressive. Yet, socialist ideological commitment in Tunisia cannot be compared with the dramatic ascendancy of ideology in such Less Developed Countries (LDCs) as China, Tanzania, or Egypt.

The turn to privatization is an unequivocal and an official admission by the state of its failure to play the role of an entrepreneur whose objective is the acceleration of economic growth through central planning and direct management of business. In the words of the governor of the Central Bank and a former Minister of Planning, Ismail Khelil,[2] "experience has shown that it [the state] is a bad manager."[3] This is as true of Tunisia as of most other countries on the privatization lane. The state's shortcomings as a business manager do not mean, however, that it is imperative to have the state stripped from all economic functions.

In this chapter, we shall identify efforts made by the Tunisian government to liberalize the economy and to privatize state-owned enterprises. The view taken in this study is that modern states, advanced industrial as well as developing ones, play an important role in the national economy; hence, privatization is not synonymous with state withdrawal and a laissez-faire system. The transition to liberalization marks a change from a controlled to a regulated economy. The degrees of freedom in a regulated market may vary with the political orientation of the elite, social pressures, and the particulars of national economies.

The national government has avowed in principle to denationalize, yet in practice it has moved at a slow pace. This is partly because of immobilism and indecision on the part of the government during the last few years and partly because of the difficulty of the task itself. A major reason for the slow pace is the fact that privatization has no coherent constituency to speak of, whereas the old order of state enterprises and welfare is based on a tacit and mutual support system between the national leadership on the one hand and the labor unions on the other. Even though labor opposition to privatization in Tunisia does not seem intense, the government remains wary of general public unrest if it lets all former controls on wages and prices loose.

It will also be maintained here that the economic *policy change* comes above and before structural transformation in the reform process, for it is quite possible for the state to denationalize public-sector firms and still pursue policies which adversely affect the private sector and economic growth in general. On the other hand, the state has a great potential to enhance the transition to a market economy. However, the state has not yet fully appreciated the dynamic role it could play as a promoter of economic growth, in contrast to being a business entrepreneur.

STATE INVOLVEMENT IN THE ECONOMY

The Tunisia of Bourguiba was a patron state.[4] The role of the Tunisian state as an economic manager and/or entrepreneur created considerable political tension when in the early 1960s Ben Salah, then the czar of the Tunisian economy, sought to expand state control over trade and small agricultural plots into commercial olive and fruit groves. His excesses were limited to such things as gaining state control of traditional crafts, monopolizing external trade and retail shops, and getting into other small businesses such as restaurants, some of which had only recently been privatized. Many of these measures were rescinded after his ouster in 1969.

The Bourguiba regime was heavily involved in the economy: it started industries and other businesses, with state monopoly of trade in certain commodities such as milk and wheat, including control of foreign trade and of prices and crops. Stepping in as the major industrial investor in the early years after independence, the state contributed in a significant way toward growth and diversification of the economy at a time when very few alternative investors were available. Government enterprises served as a model for private entrepreneurs to emulate, especially in tourism and in the textile industries. Many entrepreneurs who entered these two fields were previously employees of state public enterprises. Moreover, public enterprises stimulated the small private sector in what is often called backward linkages and later on with forward linkages as well. To this day, the state is the major client of many small businesses, especially in construction.

Another feature of Destourian socialism is that of welfare. The state entered as a provider of such services as free education, subsidized transportation, housing, and health and of basic consumer goods. For instance, the *Caisse de Compensation* spent in 1987 about 220 million dinars (MD) (1 dollar = 0.82 dinar) in subsidies for wheat and flour, milk, cooking oil, sugar, and other basics. The sum spent in previous years was much higher. Because of the 1988 severe drought, the government allotted 285 MD for food subsidies, and most of that increase was for importing cereals.[5] The cost of subsidies continued to escalate in 1989 as the state had spent 377 MD to bridge the gap between the cost of buying on the international market and the receipts from local sales.[6] It is no surprise, therefore, to see that the *Caisse de Compensation* was 108 MD in arrears in 1989. The subsidy was consuming 4 percent of the Gross Domestic Product (GDP), and the government declared its intention, in November 1989, to reduce the ratio to 1.5 percent.[7]

LIBERALIZATION

Liberalization, which can be traced back to 1970 in Tunisia, took a variety of forms: (1) encouragement of the private sector; (2) reducing the range of various controls; and (3) denationalization, which included selling some of the State Economic Enterprise (SEEs), dismantling the cooperatives of the sixties, and restoring titles to previous owners. Also, in the realm of agriculture, some 270,000 hectares of nationalized colonial farms were sold to private farmers, and some were given in rent to large farmers.[8] Later, in the 1980s, state-monopoly trade in agricultural inputs was terminated, and farmers, especially of wheat, received better prices from the state marketing agency.

The stepped-up economic activities of the state generated new businesses for private entrepreneurs, especially for builders and contractors, a phenomenon witnessed in most Middle Eastern and North African countries. The 1960s thus contributed to the emergence of indigenous Tunisian entrepreneurs, a trend that continued throughout the 1970s.

Just as it is not true that the 1960s stymied private entrepreneurs across the board, so also it is not true that the 1970s brought about the efflorescence of private enterprise or the withdrawal of the state from the business sphere. On the contrary, the public sector continued to expand;[9] and in 1989, it accounted for 60 percent of manufacturing value added.[10] Official controls continued in most areas to which they had applied previously. Price controls remained practically unchanged until 1982, when a decree[11] was issued reducing the range of price controls and limiting them to what was called basic and strategic goods. The list of goods still under controls today remains, however, quite impressive. It includes: bread, flour, *couscous,* edible oils, sugar, tea, coffee, cement, fuel oils, fertilizers, transport services, school books and supplies, pepper, pharmaceutical products, pasteurized milk, and, provisionally, chicken and meat. Distribution and requisition of some of these items remained a government monopoly. Dozens of other commodities were to be priced with the consent of the government. While price controls of agricultural products have been relaxed, 55 percent of industrial products are still under official price controls, according to the governor of the Central Bank.[12] The state-owned business sector has remained dominant, with some 400 enterprises employing about 10 percent of the active work force and responsible for 33 percent of wages, 20 percent of GDP, and 80 percent of exports. Curiously enough, wages of workers, which remained depressed during the socialist period of the 1960s, were ameliorated during the relative liberalization period of the seventies.

Denationalization, in the sense of state disengagement from an economic activity, took place first in the early 1970s with the dismantling of cooperatives created by Ben Salah. After the dissolution of the cooperatives and the sale of some nationalized colonial farms, no further denationalization occurred until the mid-1980s.

By 1986, the state came to the firm conclusion that a measure of privatization had become necessary. The objective of the new policy was to have the state disengage from as many as possible of the "non-strategic" industries and businesses and turn them over to private citizens or institutions. The very idea of a patron state was challenged by this new official outlook. In the words of the governor of the Central Bank of Tunisia, Ismail Khelil:

> En fait, toute notre politique tend à responsabiliser le Tunisien et à dégager l'Etat. Ce dernier ne peut plus s'occuper de tout. La notion de l'Etat-providence est dépassée. C'est un grand luxe que de continuer à l'être. D'ailleurs, la Tunisie n'a plus les moyens pour continuer dans cette voie.[13]

In short, the resort to privatization is an explicit recognition by the political elite of the limitations of state ability to interfere successfully in every aspect of life and in particular to play the roles of entrepreneur and provider. Briefly stated, it is a renunciation of the patron-state idea by the political elite. In practice, however, the disengagement of the state does not seem to be commensurate with its official protestation, as we shall see.

How does the state perceive itself now that it has adopted the disengagement stance? Again, Khelil explains:

> L'Etat doit être là pour aider, encourager, orienter et tracer les grandes lignes. C'est pour cela que toute notre politique—actuelle—consiste essentiellement à créer l'environnment nécessaire pour que l'entreprise tunisienne puisse s'activer et surtout assumer pleinement sa responsabilité.[14]

If that is the ideal self-image of the new liberal state in Tunisia, it could be confidently stated that it has not yet been realized, though it is moving ever so slowly in that direction.

According to the laws which define a public-sector enterprise, the effects and range of official management and state-imposed constraints are greater than state material participation would suggest. Prior to 1985, an enterprise in which the state owned at least 10 percent was administratively considered a public-sector enterprise subject to state management. In 1985, however, a new law (no. 85–720) raised that limit to 34 percent, thus relatively reducing the number of enterprises subject to state intervention.

Public-sector enterprises have been posing an accelerating financial burden on the state since 1970, the year economic liberalization and reform started. State support for the troubled public sector has risen from 13.5 MD in 1971 to 248.3 MD in 1982, disbursed as loans, as maintenance subsidies (*subventions d'équipement*), and for new investments.[15] In addition, subsidies paid by the state to public-sector industrial firms (*subventions d'exploitation*) to keep prices low rose from 3.9 MD to 169.2 MD in 1982.[16] Tidying up financially (*opération d'assainissement*) state-owned enterprises rose to 172 MD.[17] The cost of maintaining the public enterprise in business kept accelerating and reached a critical stage in 1986.[18] Despite the specificity of these figures, the total expense to the government is usually very difficult to make out accurately. On the whole, as a round figure, the cost to the government of maintaining the public sector is estimated at 2,039 MD during the Sixth Plan (1982–86).[19]

The reasons for the failure of public-sector enterprises in Tunisia are much the same as everywhere else, with one exception—Tunisian officials have not made as many poor investment choices as leaders in other states. They have, however, fallen victim to underestimation of investment needs in many projects, giving rise to an unbalanced ratio of capital to debt, a kind of economic behavior which was later repeated in the activities of the private sector. Aside from that, the source of trouble lies in state-imposed constraints on enterprises in terms of pricing, overstaffing, and interference in management. Directors of enterprises (PDG) were often selected for political loyalty more than for their expertise. Associated with this is the traditional attitude of Tunisians toward public property, which they refer to as *rizq al beylik,* a phrase synonymous with an attitude of indifference, negligence, and license for personal profiteering.

Heavily committed to expenditures of various kinds, the patron state tends to cover the shortfall in its revenues by extracting from the productive elements in agriculture, industry, and services. As a result of this tendency, state policy undermines its own developmental objectives and obstructs growth. As in Egypt and other Arab countries, the state partly finances consumer needs by extracting revenue from the productive system, both state-owned and private enterprises. In Tunisia, especially during the socialist period in the 1960s, farmers were paid extremely low prices for their products, a condition which contributed to their impoverishment.[20]

Underpricing of the products of state industrial firms in the domestic market are meant to reduce the financial burden on the consumer. Of all the distribution schemes, this type is the most detrimental to growth and development. Still, one finds supporters for it in both Tunisia and Egypt who claim that because the public sector is made to serve social objectives, assessment of its performance should not be made purely on the basis of financial accounts. When industrial firms are not able to improve their financial position, their ability to reinvest and grow is severely limited. Indeed, they may not be able to operate at capacity, as was the case for the past few years in Tunisia when the performance of some firms was reputed to have fallen to about 30 percent of operational capacity.[21]

DENATIONALIZATION

The decision by the government of Tunisia to structurally reform the economy and to sell all but strategic enterprises[22] goes back to 1981, five years before the famous agreement with the IMF and World Bank on structural adjustment was made.[23] The first law (no. 85–72) was promulgated in July 1985, followed by law (no. 85–47) of August 1987. What has been defined as strategic, however, leaves a sizable proportion of the 400 public-sector enterprises out of harm's way.

Before undertaking any divestment measures, legislation was passed in 1985 and 1987 to regulate the process. These laws, however, were found to be complicated and cumbersome in implementation, primarily because they created additional bureaucratic agencies and rules. In February 1989, a new law was passed which superseded the previous ones and created a single governmental agency in charge of privatization: La Commission d'Assainissement de la Restructuration des Entreprises et de la Participation Publique (CAREPP).

Among the practical problems that face denationalization of SEEs is the limited capital available in private hands due to weak propensity to save. Second is the unattractiveness of SEEs that have been put up for sale. Serious financial problems and redundant labor, with its hard to dispose of privileges,discourage potential buyers. Aggravating this situation is government indecision as to which enterprises to denationalize and the impression among observers that it wants to get rid of only those firms that are financially ailing. As usual, the debate on this issue is in the form of a paradox: should the state decide to sell losing enterprises, it would find no buyers; should it decide to sell profit-making enterprises, then it would unjustifiably be giving away sources of revenue. Specialists usually advise and have advised Tunisia to tidy up its losing firms first in order to make them attractive to potential purchasers.

Tunisia has a very small stock market, one of the smallest in developing countries.[24] Like most countries of the Middle East and North Africa, business firms tend to be family enterprises, the disadvantage of which is the limitation such a mode of entrepreneurship has in raising capital for investment. Aside from the difficulty associated with raising capital, however, family enterprises are usually successful and should not be disparaged, as they usually are in the Western-oriented literature. Under prevailing social conditions, the family plays an economically dynamic role.

The Tunisian government has been trying in the last few years to invigorate and encourage the stock market, la Bourse de Valeurs Mobilières de Tunis. So far there has been little progress shown in that direction. Hardly any denationalized public firms have gone through the Bourse.[25]

The idea of selling state-owned firms to employees has been in the air for as long as the debate on the mode of privatization has been going on. The experience of Tunisian employees in self-management remains an unknown variable, and banks are not likely to risk going to the aid of a labor managed firm should it run into financial trouble. A paper on employee participation in the ownership of their firm in Tunisia, given by Hassine Trad, secretary general of the Bourse, is quite instructive on Tunisian economic behavior. The Société Tunisienne de Banque (STB), a major public-sector firm, introduced a plan in 1971 offering its employees stock shares financed by regular paycheck discounts and STB contribution in the amount of the difference between worker contribution and the current share price in the stock market. The shares transferred were to be blocked for three or five years. Only 11 percent of employees joined in the plan, and the number declined to 6 percent in 1988. The experiment naturally was terminated.

PRIVATIZATION OF STATE-OWNED HOTELS

Transferring state-owned hotels to the private sector in Tunisia has been one of the earliest and most successful privatization operations. The state administration of hotels, Société Hôtelière et Touristique de Tunisie (SHTT), started out with two hotels in 1962 and ended up with fifteen in the 1980s, before sales to private businesses began. The SHTT had been operating below capacity and running a heavy debt to the state and to commercial banks. Some of its losses were due to poor management and/or bad investment decisions, as was the case in Mabrouk Hotel of Sfax, Jugurtha of Gabes, and Corniche Bizerte, which were built to host government guests and for nationalistic reasons. Other losses were due both to high interest rates (1.6 million dinars in 1986) charged on loans borrowed originally to build the hotels and to redundant labor caused by the political patronage system. Not to be underestimated in this regard is corruption and embezzlement by some hotel managers, who enriched themselves before they moved to private business in tourism.

The SHTT losses were big; the government had to spend 27.5 MD in 1984 to tidy the corporation up financially, according to a high-ranking official in the Ministry of Finance.[26] The losses of Mabrouk Hotel alone in the year 1984 came to 69 thousand dinars. Losses in some other hotels were moderate, amounting to a few thousand dinars a year.

With the money earned from the sale of hotels, the SHTT paid off its short-term loans, which amounted to 16 MD.[27] The remaining debt consisted of 8 MD to banks and 3 MD in government loans. This according to the PGD of the SHTT is manageable, and his corporation, he maintained, could survive from here on.[28] The corporation did show in 1987 and 1988 a slight improvement in its returns, although it should be remembered that tourism in those two years was at its best in Tunisia,[29] and it would be difficult to attribute the results to a turning point in the SHTT, as its supporters maintain.

Overstaffing in the hotel business is estimated by some government officials as varying from worst case of nearly 40 percent to lowest case of about 20 percent. According to one PDG of a major tourist hotel of the public sector, most of the overstaffing was in the administrative offices of the SHTT, especially at its head-quarters in Monastir. The SHTT was not any different in that respect from other public-sector organizations. To cope with its financial problems, the SHTT relied on government assistance, took loans from banks, and, in some instances, failed to honor its financial commitments to its clients. According to an official source in the Ministry of Finance, failure of the SHTT to pay rent cost the government a loss of nearly twenty-five thousand dinars annually.

Another method by which the SHTT copes financially is to divert profits made by the successful hotel units to keep the financial status of the losing units in order. This has deleterious business effects because it denies the successful units the opportunity to improve their services and/or expand their business operations. It is a practice reminiscent of the distribution of income among extended rural families in traditional societies of the Middle East, which exerts downward pressure on incomes across the board.

Some of the fifteen state-owned hotels have already been sold while the others are in the process of being privatized. Six have been sold in the last three years. These are: Hannibal Palace at Port al Kantaoui (Sousse), Miramaar (Hammamet), Skanes Palace (Skanes/Monastir), Ulysse of Djerba, Oasis of Gabes, and Mabrouk of Sfax. Five other hotels had their title transferred from the SHTT directly to the government in 1970 and then rented out to the SHTT. One of these (al Ribat Hotel) has been demolished, and the land on which it was built sold; the rest are slated to be sold when and if the legal complications regarding their status are solved. The other three are Corniche Bizerte, Aghlabites of Kairouan, and Jugurtha of Gabes. Basically, the SHTT was left, by 1988, with the management of nearly 45 percent of its original capacity, 2,370 rooms out of an original capacity of 5,300.

At the end of 1989, the SHTT had sold the three Tanits of Monastir, Hammamet, and Djerba and had invited bids for two major three-star hotels, the Hotel du Lac in Tunis, and the Esplanade in Monastir.[30]

The six large hotels sold by the government went as direct-sale deals to other parties rather than through the stock market as shares to the public. This is a subject of considerable debate in Tunisia. The Ministry of Finance leans toward private deals, which bring in more money and are less risky. On the other hand, the governor of the Central Bank and the president of the Tunis Stock Market (la Bourse des Valeurs Mobilières de Tunis) are very much in favor of a key role for the stock market in the privatization process, because they see a future for economic development in the expansion of the stock market operations.

Among buyers, one finds a couple of wealthy Tunisian businessmen, the STB, and the Banque Tuniso-Koweïtienne de Développement. In part, the government has been shuffling ownership titles among its various organizations, for the STB is a public-sector bank (government share 45 percent). Government banks, it should be pointed out, are slated to play a central role in the privatization process. Officials maintain that the public-sector banks can mobilize capital for privatization purposes where the public cannot. They are viewed as first buyers who would then facilitate the sale to privates. This has already occurred in the case of hotels and, as we shall see, in the other major privatization case, that of Société Industrielle des Textiles (SITEX), a very large producer of denim jeans.

It is still too early to say how well the private sector will run the privatized hotels and how it will affect labor. So far, hotel workers have not been dismissed, and at least one acquired hotel, Ulysse of Djerba, has plans to expand, and its employees have overcome their concerns about privatization, according to its PGD.

PRIVATIZATION OF STATE-OWNED INDUSTRIAL FIRMS

Progress in privatizing industrial firms has been slower than in the hotel industry. A leading example of a successfully privatized industrial firm in Tunisia is SITEX, a textile and garment conglomerate of the public sector and a subsidiary of SO-GITEX, which had played a pioneering role in Tunisian industrialization. A holding company, SOGITEX was 100 percent government-owned and consisted of the following firms: Sitex, Somotex, Tissmok, Sovel, Pantaloisire, and others. The dossier for Tissmok and Somotex is in the process of privatization. As for Sovel, it was sold for its assets value, as was the case with Confort Electroménager. Pantaloisire was sold through the Bourse. In all these operations, the development banks in Tunisia acted as intermediaries. SOGITEX and its other subsidiaries had been experiencing financial problems, as the case of SITEX will demonstrate.

Overstaffing, poor management, and financial deficits characterized the operations of SITEX until 1979, when reform efforts were introduced and it started to turn in a profit and distribute dividends. It has also succeeded in raising its capital from 50 thousand dinars to 10 MD in 1985–86.

SITEX may eventually serve as a model for the privatization of industrial firms in Tunisia. The firm was subjected first to a process of financial tidying up, which took a number of years starting in 1979. Financial reform was made with expert help from abroad, including the World Bank and the Canadian firm, SWIFT, which eventually acquired a major share in SITEX. Its marketing management, especially for export, was modernized, a process which led to improvement of performance. By the time it was sold out, all the reforms had been completed and SITEX was quite solvent.

Critics of the government protest that SITEX was sold without public disclosure, for SITEX was sold directly through negotiations with interested parties: the International Finance Corporation (affiliate of the World Bank), the Canadian company SWIFT, and the Banque de Tunisie. The shares were as follows: 22.5 percent for the Banque de Tunisie; 19.1 percent for SWIFT; 15.0 percent for the IFC; and 43.4 percent remained as the property of SOGITEX. More recently, SOGITEX sold 17.0 percent of its holdings to SWIFT, thus giving the latter the largest single share, 36.1 percent, while SOGITEX's holdings dropped to 26.4 percent. With the new distribution of shares, SWIFT assumes a central management responsibility for the company.

It should be noted here that unlike the privatization of hotels, state and foreign parties played the major role in title transfers in the case of SITEX. No private Tunisian businessmen were involved. Both the capital and the necessary technology seems to tip the balance in favor of foreign business. The IFC in this case has been playing a facilitating role and may well soon get out in favor of another party.

A more interesting and recent case of privatization is that of financially troubled CONFORT. CONFORT produces refrigerators, kitchen stoves, refrigeration cases, and insulation materials. CONFORT in particular was a very difficult case for privatization. The company was heavily in debt, its losses constituted several times the value of its assets. Unlike SITEX, tidying it up financially was not a viable proposition. Its debt to the state alone rose from 4.5 MD in 1983 to 15.6 MD in 1988. Total debt for the same period rose from 14.4 MD to 38.6 MD. In effect, the company's assets in 1988 were far less than its debt: 13.9 MD to 38.6 MD. It was, moreover, a hotbed of labor militancy against privatization. Very few observers thought that it could attract buyers or that the government was in a position to tidy it up financially and make it attractive for sale.

The sale of CONFORT should thus be considered as an indicator of the strength of official will and seriousness of purpose. It was clear that to stop the financial drain resulting from continued functioning of CONFORT, the state had to accept the fact that the company is too costly to tidy up financially, and a loss on past investments must be accepted. By agreement with the creditor banks, the firm was sold. The creditor banks had the right to first returns from the sale, while the government had forgone its priority. CONFORT was eventually sold in 1990 to a private Tunisian entrepreneur for its asset values only, out of which debts were paid off.

The government of Tunisia insists that prospective buyers should not dismiss any workers and that all social benefits be maintained. In the CONFORT case, the company employed 1,200 in 1983, which were reduced to 830; some were dismissed as casual labor, others through disciplinary action, and others left voluntarily. In 1989, when a private entrepreneur bought CONFORT, he agreed to accept 600 workers only. The government compensated some of the rejected workers, while others retired. At present he has only 500 workers.

In less publicized cases, the public sector reduced its shares in the interest of private buyers. In textiles, for instance, the buyers of Société des Industries Textiles Réunies (SITER) included the Bank of Qatar, IFC, and DMC of France, accumulating in all 51 percent of the company's shares. A third case is TISSMOK, the textile firm of Moknine, which was bought by United Arab Emirates and Saoudi banks.

Another industrial firm that has been denationalized is SOTUVER, the glass firm of Megrine. The government owned 25 percent share in SOTUVER until the year 1980, which meant then that it was a public-sector firm under official management. When it went into financial difficulties in 1978, the Banque de Tunisie (private bank, partly French-owned) expressed willingness to take SOTUVER over provided the government assumed the responsibility for the firm's debt. The government agreed, and it withstood a 3 MD loss as a partial disengagement price. Thus, in 1980, the Banque de Tunisie played the broker's role by selling part of the government's share to private entrepreneurs, including a joint state-private bank, the Banque de Développement Economique de Tunisie (BDET), and Banque de Sud. The new owners and managers increased the working capital of the company and by 1988 had managed to make a profit. A plan in 1989 to put all SOTUVER's share on the stock market with the BDET as the transaction agent was postponed by the government in response to protest from employees, who were concerned about their benefits and future employment under the new plan.[31]

Other small state-owned businesses or real estate which have been sold include the Contoir Sfaxiene, Tunisie Bois (wood) and Marbrairie de Thala (marble). Those were bought by some private banks such as Banque Internationale Arabe de Tunisie (BIAT) and other entrepreneurs. In December 1989, almost the entire stock shares of STUMETAL (Société Tunisienne d'Emballages Métalliques) were sold to one agent, the STB, for 8.8 MD.[32]

As far as the question of liquidation of industrial firms is concerned, we find only one case where a company's doors have been shut. In January 1988, the automobile assembly plant of the Société Tunisienne d'Industrie Automobile (STIA) of Sousse was closed due to the huge deficit it experienced and the large sums that were necessary to tidy it up. The company's losses came to 40 MD, and its debt reached 90 MD.[33] The government pledged to continue to pay the 2,200 workers until they find new employment. The company is still running its bus assembly line.

In all, the number of public-sector firms in which the state's share has actually been sold in full or in part is officially given as thirty-eight enterprises, worth some 92 MD. This figure includes state-owned hotels, all of which were sold except two, the Esplanade of Monastir and Hotel du Lac of Tunis, which are in the process of being sold. In other respects, some state monopolies such as transportation are being opened up for competition.

In conclusion, the denationalization process in Tunisia is in progress and will continue, slow as it may be. To this date, however, it has not made a dent in the large and costly public-sector enterprises such as phosphates, chemicals, cement, telecommunications, and transport, not to mention oil, gas, electricity, and other infrastructure projects which are not envisaged for sale. Almost all those enterprises are officially considered strategic and therefore not subject to denationalization. In short, the government's explicit commitment to denationalization remains very limited, some 30 firms out of 400.

MODE OF TRANSFER

The privatization of state-owned firms in Tunisia reveals some interesting facts about property transfers. The roster of buyers shows diverse groups involved: international agencies, substate units, and private individuals. One of the most interesting is the role of public sector banks in the privatization process. Banks were slated by the government to play, first, a middleman role (warehousing) in transaction—that is, purchasing a state economic enterprise and then managing it until a private buyer could be found. In the second place, public sector banks played the role of bona fide buyers of SEEs, which they manage alone, or with partners, for profit.

The transfer of enterprises from the central government to an autonomous government agency is an important development in the privatization process, not only because private buyers of public enterprises are hard to come by but also because it has the effect of producing results which are generally expected from decentralization of the management of state-owned firms. It is the closest thing to separating ownership from management. Although this approach is promising, it is of limited application since it could not be extended to enterprises which affect the livelihood of the mass population. The reason is that it would have the same effect of genuine decentralization of enterprises—namely, market prices and removal of surplus labor. Governments have difficulty living with such conditions.

Other buyers of SEEs in Tunisia have been transnational corporations such as SWIFT, IFC (World Bank), and Arab banks and businessmen, mainly from oil-producing countries of the Gulf. Tunisian entrepreneurs were drawn to hotels but not to state-owned industries. Hotels do not involve too much capital or labor and promise quick returns. What had not yet been done as of 1989 was to sell to the public through the stock market. While there are advocates for this course of action, the Tunisian public does not seem drawn into it, though it is true that it has not yet been tried in that country. Tunisia has one of the smallest stock markets even in the developing countries, and Tunisian leaders are trying now to correct this situation.

PROGRESS OF THE PRIVATE SECTOR

By far the more significant aspect of the privatization process in Tunisia has been the economic liberalization trend as of 1970. The specter of socialism, which had intimidated and constrained businessmen, was removed. Trade, for instance, was no longer considered a dirty word in the political lexicon of the time. On the contrary, the Nouira government (1970–80) moved to relax its monopoly hold on banking and foreign trade and allowed the private sector a share in the import and export business. In the 1980s, the government was no longer asking but practically pushing entrepreneurs to do more trade, especially in exports. In the mid-1980s, banks were given greater freedom of action by the Central Bank under Khelil's leadership. However, the idea of economic liberalization in the 1970s did not include denationalization of industrial firms or withdrawing from further governmental investment in industry, although there was a slowdown in investment by the government until the year 1978. Only in agriculture were collectivized lands returned to their original owners and some nationalized colonial farms sold to private individuals.

The liberalization drive of the seventies is associated with the appointment of a business-minded Prime Minister, Hedi Nouira, who dominated the new drive to reshape Tunisia's economy for the rest of the decade. A series of legislative acts aimed at relaxing the official hold on the economy were introduced in 1972, 1974, and 1981. Like most LDCs who opted for an economic liberalization course, Tunisian officials sought, in the first place, to attract foreign investment capital for industry, export promotion, and employment generation. Those areas, it was felt by the regime, were the most pressing economically and politically. The package offered foreign investors was the usual: tax concessions, duty free imports of equipment, raw materials and intermediate goods, and freedom to repatriate profits. In 1974, benefits received by foreign investors were extended to Tunisian citizens, and in 1981, incentives were extended to foreign businessmen who invested in the service sector such as banking, warehousing, and distribution.

In the mid-1980s, new legislation associated with the structural adjustment plan of the IMF provided for denationalization and further encouragement for business by relaxing rules on foreign exchange, imports, and investment. In 1985, a new law (no. 85–72) was aimed at reforming the public sector and reducing the government role by redefining a public establishment as one in which the state has 34 percent ownership participation, compared to 10 percent previously. The reforms produced results, and the net direct private investment rose from $16 million in 1970 to $159 million in 1986.[34]

Although foreign investors responded to the Tunisian initiative in the 1970s, their investment contribution remained relatively small, only about 7 percent of the projects operating directly under the scheme.[35] The major response came from Tunisian investors who, by 1978, had committed some 614 MD to industrial projects compared to 57 MD by foreigners.[36] This raised the investment share of the private sector in the national economy to 41 percent at the end of the 1970s compared to 28 percent at the end of the 1960s.[37] There was, however, a slump affecting the private sector that started in 1982 and reached its worst in 1985 and 1986. The low levels of private investment continued, however, until 1988, which caused considerable concern in official circles that had expected the new spirit brought with the November 7 regime of President Ben 'Ali to increase confidence and give impetus to new investments and growth. A number of problems of economic rather than political nature, however, were holding back businessmen from increasing their investments, as we shall see.

By 1989, the regime of President Ben 'Ali had started to show a firmer commitment to liberalization, and it launched an impressive campaign to attract new foreign investments in Tunisia, made more attractive by the renewed Maghrebian cooperation. At present, some 650 partnerships have been formed by Tunisian nationals and foreign investors, mostly Italian and French with growing British interest. The French government has stepped in to encourage such joint ventures with low interest loans.

PRIVATE BUSINESS RESPONSE

From the beginning, the private sector responded to the incentives of the liberalization drive in a selective way. First, it tended to be attracted strongly to textiles and garments (178 firms out of 276) for practical reasons having to do with quick returns, inexpensive labor made up heavily of female workers, simple technological levels, and, until 1977, easy access to the EEC market. Second, its response was in direct relation to the degree of freedom allowed by the government; businessmen invested in areas where there was the least government interference. For instance, investors avoided commodities whose prices were controlled by the government. In food processing, disproportionate investments went into the production of soft drinks and jam, while dairy products and sugar were avoided. In much the same order, we find that private investment in the production of bricks and tiles was very high and innovative,[38] while investment in cement was avoided. Thus, investment changes occurred in a direct relation to the extent of freedom from official controls. In other areas, such as trade, we find that the private sector stayed out completely from import of a number of basic food commodities such as coffee, tea, sugar, and milk, for the simple reason that these have remained a state monopoly not affected by the liberalization process. Similarly, the export and distribution of a major crop such as olive oil remained a state monopoly.

The three main targets of the liberalization policy—greater investment by the private sector, increased employment opportunities and export—registered significant progress, and the official strategy must be considered a relative success. The government, however, discovered before the 1970s were over that the economy was ill-served by the low level of official investments in infrastructure vital for industry and agriculture alike. Similarly, it realized that its participation in investment in certain areas of industry was necessary for the healthy growth of the national economy. Thus, in the Fifth Plan (1977–81), the government expanded its investment in oil refining, cement production, food processing, and iron and steel. At the same time, it reduced its levels of investment in textiles, electrical engineering, and metals.[39]

The private sector, however, was not immune from the adverse factors which had caused a national economic crisis. Moreover, a considerable segment of it was dependent on the government as a client and on the business generated by the public sector. The fact that the government was on an austerity drive, in addition to being in arrears in payments to what it owed to private businessmen, did not help. The construction sector in particular suffered in this respect. Palliatives extended by the government in 1987 did not prove very effective. Some of the palliatives consisted of the following: forgiveness of tax delinquents, amnesty for those who had smuggled currency abroad, relaxing the foreign-exchange controls on recipients of remittances from expatriate workers, and the allowance extended to exporters to retain a small amount (10 percent) of their returns in foreign exchange.

Liberalization remains, moreover, circumscribed within officially defined limits due to the difficulties of transforming a patron state in a short time without sufficiently strong determination. The government is unable or unwilling to give up what it calls strategic industries. Those are linked to national prestige. Moreover, private entrepreneurs who could purchase them are hard to find. One could safely say, for instance, that there are no Tunisians able to undertake a project such as oil refining, while in the case of another large industry, cement, deliberate official restrictions kept the private sector out.

Then, there are the consumer industries of basic foods and other essentials. The government is reluctant, for political reasons, to lift price controls on such commodities, a measure which would bring with it inflation and popular discontent. The Tunisian government now spends about 220 MD on subsidies of essential consumer goods.[40] Private entrepreneurs, for the most part, avoid investment in industries the price of whose products are controlled. The government finds itself neither free nor able to give the private sector full freedom of action in those areas.

WEAKNESSES OF THE PRIVATE SECTOR

It should be remembered that in a developing society such as Tunisia, the private sector has weaknesses of its own and cannot suddenly be made to play the savior's role. The small number of entrepreneurs is one such constraint, and in countries which had been socialist or *dirigiste,* as Tunisia was in the 1960s and 1970s respectively, this category of people so vital for the economic-development process was mostly repressed and is just emerging now in a very slow and cautious manner. Its weaknesses are legion. One such weakness witnessed in Tunisia is the reluctance of entrepreneurs to submit their projects to private or public agencies for feasibility study. The result is recurrence of businesses whose investments have not taken account of, or misread, the market for their products and have grossly underestimated the capital necessary to complete the project.

In effect, a very large number of projects, especially of medium and small nature, have an unsound balance in the ratio of capital to debt. In a recent study of Tunisian industry, it was shown that the debt to capital ratio in 1983 was 71/29, risen from 67/33 in 1977.[41] Moreover, more than 90 percent of the debt is short-term. With unsound financial arrangements such as these, it is not surprising that over 600 medium and small businesses were in serious financial difficulties in 1988. Some of those had already closed their firms, and others were searching for a solution, mostly at the front steps of the government. The crisis started in 1984, and by 1987, 389 small- and medium-size projects had failed and closed their doors at a cost of 65.8 MD.[42] Of the 630 ailing enterprises in 1988, nearly 400 had fiscal problems. One encouraging sign is the readiness of large numbers of people to undertake new business projects. However, inexperience and low capitalization undermined the spirit of preparedness to respond to official encouragement. In addition, observers in Tunisia assign a high proportion of the blame for failing businesses to poor managerial skills.

Easy access to credit, a policy followed by the government to encourage the private sector, has been counterproductive. Since the 1970s, the Tunisian government has been leaning on the banks to act generously in extending loans to business entrepreneurs. Although bank managers felt that government directives were financially ill-advised and risky, they felt constrained to make the loans. They made them, however, on a short-term basis, which added to the aggravation. Not only did the easy-money policy encourage high levels of indebtedness, but it also gave rise to a type of "entrepreneur" skilled in extracting huge sums of money from government banks and unconscionably wasting them. Another type of "entrepreneur" specialized in borrowing money for projects which the government encouraged and spending the capital in more profitable projects which give faster returns.

THE SOCIAL COST OF STRUCTURAL ADJUSTMENT

Structural adjustment invariably brings with it hardship to many social groups including the private sector. For instance, depreciation of the local currency in Tunisia in 1986 raised the cost of imported equipments, intermediate goods, and raw materials to local businesses. This hurts businessmen mostly at the initial stage; then they pass on the extra expense to customers, hence contributing to inflation. Improvement of export performance, which devaluation brings with it, fails to make up for the difference because most developing countries export raw materials through state monopolies. Tunisia, however, has registered a marked growth in its exports of manufactured goods in the last two years. Relaxation of import restrictions also hurts local business at the initial stage, since most are set up for survival under a protected, not a competitive, market. Fear of import liberalization leads many businessmen to hold back on new investments. However, this initial stage should be possible to surpass given sound national policies. In Tunisia, official hesitation regarding the ultimate range of import liberalization and effective lobbying by the business association, UTICA, have kept tariff barriers high.

Privatization hurts people on fixed incomes, which is to say the majority of the labor force, including government officials. Denationalization of state firms, while reducing the deficit and eventually inflation, increases unemployment. Moreover, wages tend to lag behind price increases, a fact which further binds the hands of officials in their efforts to reduce subsidies, a measure strongly recommended by international creditors. Elimination of subsidies of basic foods in countries with widespread poverty is not a realistic option; their rationalization, however, is that governments talk rationalization with respect to subsidies, especially in Egypt and to a lesser extent in Tunisia, but in practice ignore it, or just apply cosmetic changes. Whether in Tunisia or Egypt, subsidies of basics are there to stay for the foreseeable future.

An alternative to the elimination of basic-needs subsidies is for the state to dispose of inefficient public-sector firms and end state monopolies. Redundant employment, which is endemic in the public sector, is not an improvement on unemployment. For one thing it contributes to a reduced capacity of the state to make new investments and renovations, and it exerts downward pressure on labor wages. The cost to the economy of maintaining financially ailing firms is much greater than basic subsidies and more detrimental to the national economy. Indeed, subsidies may go down in volume should the serious distortions in the public sector be ended. Economic adjustment has become an international convention, yet its effects have been to squeeze the middle- and low-income population while leaving the rich hardly affected, which is politically damaging, especially in populist regimes. Greater emphasis in the readjustment program should be made on official divestment of wasteful public-sector enterprises. Servicing the poor is humane and economically functional; wasting national resources on unprofitable business enterprises has no justification. The state's role in the national economy, for those who are concerned about the eminence of the state, will not be eliminated by divestment.

In another respect, liberalization leads in the short run to inequality, and the fact that it creates some economic improvements does not seem to make up for the conspicuous differences in life styles and injustice as seen by the ordinary citizen, especially by intellectuals. The wealthy flaunt their wealth through conspicuous consumption, and those who do not share in the new wealth experience social resentment and jealousy. Such a situation contributes considerably to the popular sentiment in favor of state intervention and state controls. Socialism thus enjoys a considerable reservoir of good will and support among the population, while resentment is reserved for the free-market economy.

CONCLUSION

The state in the LDCs cannot and would not fully disengage from direct involvement in economic activities. An entrepreneurial role is thrust upon it. The question is where to draw the line to minimize the damage that will inevitably arise given the horde of debilitating factors which surround public enterprises. Further, the state's impact on the economy is not easily removed by denationalization; the state can do just as much damage to private enterprise without having any economic enterprises of its own. The question in both cases is how to set government conduct of public affairs in order, limit its capacity for capricious action, reduce its fears, and guarantee it a decent revenue sufficient to keep its hands out of the pockets of others.

The record of the Tunisian state shows that its main problems as a business entrepreneur did not stem so much from economically irrational choices of business projects as from inability to successfully manage the enterprise. Not that the problem is bureaucratic but, rather, that political considerations lead the state to impose detrimental policies on the public-sector enterprises as well as on private ones. The blame, which in the literature on Third World countries is placed on the bureaucracy as an inefficient and poor agent of implementation, falls actually on political leaders who are responsible for decision making. It is the economic policies made by national political leaders that lack rationality and defy implementation, let alone successful implementation.

The temptation by the state, because of its perceived special role, to go into heavy industry—such as iron and steel, aluminum, shipbuilding, and auto assemblies—tends to be irrepressible. In most cases, though, such undertakings have been ill-conceived and motivated by national visions of grandeur rather than by sound economic considerations. Ideologically, the state should be first cured from the idea that it is the best candidate to play the entrepreneur's role, an idea grounded in the central-planning approach.

Welfare policies are without question expensive, but they are not the albatross that holds down the economy. Rationalization of welfare policy and administration could cut down on waste but the issue of economic growth lies elsewhere. The main financial drains on the budget are the inefficient state-owned enterprises, and that is where the deficit should be treated, not at the bread shop of the poor. Consider, for instance, the financial drain on the budget caused by one state-owned firm, CONFORT. Its debt had reached almost three times its assets, and yet the government injected another sum of money in 1988 to keep it running. How much did the government spend that year and in previous years on one firm? No one can really tell. What is certain is that CONFORT has cost every Tunisian untold amounts of money over the years, has contributed to the national deficit, and has handicapped the government's ability to offer the needed services for the poor. It also made investment capital less available for productive enterprises.

Second, the state has an obsession with legalistic controls, which cripple business initiative and bloat the bureaucracy. Fair public conduct and reducing cheating of the state by individuals and organizations are matters that cannot be achieved by means of legislation and police action alone. When the bureaucracy grows, such controls develop a life of their own that has nothing to do with the original purpose for which they had been devised. In Tunisia, for instance, the number of official documents necessary for the sale of foreign assets to a Tunisian citizen was sixty-seven, reduced in the administrative reforms of 1988 to thirty-one![43]

A financially pressed state which is committed to distributive policies often resorts to extraction from those who have—that is, from those who mostly tend to be the productive elements in society. The number of people who are rentiers or who enjoy hereditary wealth in LDCs is quite negligible, and distribution by itself does not solve the problems of poverty or social injustice. Reform governments such as we see in Tunisia tend to extract from the producers, both private and public, because they are the only available candidates. This is not done necessarily through direct taxation, which in most LDCs is poorly implemented, but by means of price and revenue controls. Such measures discourage producers and business initiative more than direct taxation.

The point here is that it is not enough for the government to divest itself or denationalize; it should follow positive economic policies which are fair and conducive to the functioning of business and government as well. It is possible for the state to hurt by its policies both the economy generally and private entrepreneurs in particular without having any business enterprises of its own. It could do that through irresponsible spending, printing money, borrowing, and a variety of business disincentives such as price controls.

What should be remembered is that regardless of the ownership nature of enterprises, the state is a regulator by definition and a rentier-type partner in every business project; no one can reasonably recommend divesting it from these roles. The issue is how and toward what goal should interventions be made. In addition to these two roles, the state is ultimately an "insurance company" of last resort. Failing private enterprises could well leave destructive impact on the national economy, and the state finds itself compelled to come to their rescue. Business operations such as the stock market, banks, imports, and exports could not possibly function without the state playing the role of an insurance company of last resort and promoter as well, especially in LDCs.

The Tunisian government has been trying to assist the 600 failing private enterprises in the hope that they would, with financial assistance, be able to reverse the trend and make a profit. We have seen this happen in a number of countries such as the Intra-Bank in Lebanon, the official takeover of ailing private businesses in the Philippines and Mexico, and, last but not least, the S&L case in the United States. The cost of the rescue operation to the government of Tunisia, needless to say, is nowhere as near as that which it commits to the ailing state-owned enterprises. It is nevertheless a major burden and responsibility.

The state has a much more vital role to play as a promoter of business, *animateur,* than as a business entrepreneur. Though the idea of official promotion is a central one in the development drive, it has only recently been considered seriously but not sufficiently. Its potential has not been fully explored. Promotion of production by the state, whether private or public, in LDCs is an idea which receives lip service by states that are chronically in financial deficit and are grasping for revenue. With pressures of deficits hanging over them, governments are more interested in extraction than promotion. Hence, market and price controls.

Promotion is not easy nor problem free, as it first seemed to governments well disposed to encourage the private sector. Making credit available to entrepreneurs on easy terms, for instance, proved to be costly to the national economy and wasteful, as the state in Tunisia and the public agency Fond de Promotion et de Décentralisation Industrielle, (FOPRODI) had discovered belatedly and at their own expense. In Egypt, too, during the 1970s, much needed public funds extended to private businessmen on very easy terms were wasted. A viable business project does not depend on cheap credit and should survive under market-rate credit conditions.

Indeed, the claim that capital shortages in LDCs is the main handicap to development may require reconsideration. National rates of savings in Third World countries tend to be quite high in relation to GDP, and also the rate of investment. In 1984, national savings in Tunisia amounted to 31 percent of GDP.[44] The rate of investment was as high as 23 percent of GDP in the sixties and went up to near 27 percent in the early seventies.[45] Later it rose to as high a rate as 32 percent of GDP.[46] Comparatively speaking, those rates are higher than in advanced industrial countries. It is the use of capital rather than its quantity that makes the difference between success and failure. Governments in LDCs should realize that easy credit and tax exemptions are not the most productive ways of promoting business.

Governments in LDCs can contribute to economic development by first removing official disincentives and controls and then by extending services *in kind,* such as, to name a few: promotion in exports, information, and research; provision of adequate infrastructure, facilitating credit at market rates; and providing free sanitary services in poultry and animal husbandry.

Privatization, however, does not necessarily mean democratization; witness the case of Pinochet's Chile and, to a lesser extent, Syria and Iraq. It is, however, a process that cannot be considered irrelevant or insignificant for democratization. For one thing, to the extent to which public authorities disengage from direct economic activities, corresponding degrees of freedom are acquired by individuals and groups. Arguments that the poor and the labor force suffer loss of economic freedom and benefits as a result are not convincing. If labor has gained some economic benefits under the tutelage of the public sector which are not viable under a market system economy, then those privileges could not be in the national interest and should not stay. They could benefit labor only in the short run. The question of the poor is more complicated and cannot be fully discussed in this brief context. However, from a humanitarian point of view and in the national interest, the very poor segment of the population should receive subsidized basic goods and services regardless of whether a country is under state socialism or a market economy.

In other respects, privatization leads to greater economic powers for individuals and groups, who then could use these powers in such a way as to affect decision making and provide society with a countervailing force vis-à-vis the charmed circle of an exclusive political elite.

Third, in most countries of the region where there have been privatization trends, we witness relaxation of political controls and a relative tolerance of opposition. In Tunisia, a multiparty system has emerged in principle and may well lead eventually to a genuinely pluralist polity. So far, however, the official party has not suffered any losses, but in principle the opportunity is there. It should be remembered in this context that privatization is still in its beginning stage and has not gone far enough to transform the patron character of the Tunisian state. The state remains the dominant entrepreneur and still spends extensively on welfare services, while one political party continues to have hegemony over the political system. Privatization has contributed to greater freedom of expression and assembly and has given the Tunisians the right to challenge official ideology and authority.

In short, the postcolonial state tends to have ambitions far greater than its endowments permit and it accumulates political powers which breed elite self-deception. The new economic burdens assumed by the patron state tempt policy makers to extract from productive elements to spend on extensive programs of services, welfare, inefficient state business enterprises, and an overgrown bureaucracy.

The enormous role which the patron state assigns to itself leads to the development of a large and unwieldy bureaucracy. The extractive policies of the state affect both the private sector and the state business enterprises. Thus, in addition to the multitude of inadequate state management of business enterprises, official policy contributes to the poor performance of its own enterprises. The burdens of its policies catch up with it, and the patron state starts to curtail the growth of its self-assigned role and to encourage the private sector, upon which it had imposed severe constraints. Resort to the international community for assistance and for loans accelerates and so does the debt burden. Eventually, the state realizes that economic powers do not always translate into political power, and it starts to consider shedding some of its burdens by divesting itself from some of its business enterprises. In the case of Tunisia, and indeed most Arab countries, the process of denationalization remains very slow, although it is safe to say that Tunisia and Egypt have made more progress in that direction than other Arab states.

Finally, we have noted how the private sector suffers from its own inherent weaknesses, long aggravated by hostile official policies. We have also seen how it continues to suffer during the liberalization period from restrictive policies such as price controls, currency restrictions, and bureaucratic hurdles, all of which belong to the preceding *étatiste* era. It also suffers from its own inexperience in business and from adventurism. Well-intentioned government policies, such as making easy credit available, add to the problem. More would be achieved if the state lifted its restrictive policies, contributed to the development of infrastructure, and offered services in kind. Nevertheless, and despite all difficulties, the private sector in Tunisia has made progress and has shown signs of considerable ingenuity and promise.

Notes

1. The field research on which this chapter is based was made possible by grants from the Social Science Research Council, Fulbright and Fulbright-Hays, during 1987 and 1988. The Centre d'Etudes Maghrebine and particularly its director, Mrs. Jean Mrad, have provided me with invaluable assistance. During the period I spent in Tunisia, I was associated formally with the Centre d'Etudes Economiques et Sociales, of the University of Tunis. I am

also indebted to a large number of individuals who have been generous to me and to whom I am grateful. In particular, I would like to mention Mohamed Midoun, Moncef Bouchrara, Salah el Hannachi, Mohamed el Haj Mansour, and Mohamed Boudiehe. It goes without saying that none of the mentioned organizations or individuals could be held responsible for what is stated in this paper. The responsibility for contributions as for shortcomings rests with the author alone.

2. Now Minister of Foreign Affairs.

3. Interview in *Le Renouveau,* 24 May 1988. Mr. Khelil has become the Minister of Foreign Affairs in the cabinet formed in March 1990.

4. See chapter 1 for a discussion of this term.

5. *Middle East Economic Digest (MEED),* 24 August 1989.

6. Reuters dispatch, 14 November 1989.

7. Ibid.

8. Allan Findlay, in Richard Lawless and Allan Findlay, eds., *North Africa: Contemporary Politics and Economic Development* (London: Croom Helm, 1984), p. 232.

9. The public sector added, during the 1970s, 120 new enterprises. See Mohamed Midoun, "Entreprises Publiques et Développement Economique," in *Administration et Développement en Tunisie* (Tunis: Institut International des Sciences Administratives et Association Tunisienne des Sciences Administratives, 1985), p. 97.

10. According to a news release to Reuters by the governor of the Central Bank, Ismail Khelil, in March 1989.

11. Arrêté no. 134, 27 January 1982.

12. See his interview, *Le Renouveau,* 24 May 1988.

13. Ibid.

14. Ibid.

15. Source of data is *Ministère du Plan,* cited by Midoun, "Entreprises Publiques," pp. 104–105, and Leila Haouaoui, *Les Subventions de l'Etat aux Entreprise Publiques en Tunisie,* Faculté de Droit et des Sciences Politiques et Economiques de Tunis, October 1984.

16. *Ministère du Plan,* cited by Haouaoui, *Les Subventions.*

17. Midoun, "Entreprises Publiques," p. 105.

18. See *La Presse de Tunisie,* 6 May 1988, p. 7.

19. On the average, the GDP then was about 6 billion dinars.

20. Khaled El Manoubi and Abdeljelil Bedoui, *Economie Tunisienne, Etat et Capital Mondial,* (Tunis: Centre d'Etudes et de Recherches Economiques et Sociales, 1987), pp. 67–68, 88.

21. See *La Presse de Tunisie,* 31 May 1988, p. 10.

22. Such as Tunis Air, telecommunications, railways, electricity, oil and gas, and the like.

23. For a brief statement on those years, see Clement Henry Moore, "Tunisia and Bourguibisme: Twenty Years of Crisis," *Third World Quarterly* (January 1988).

24. Bechir el Younsi, "Les modalités de la privatisation et le marche des capitaux," *Finances et Développement au Maghreb,* no. 2 Tunis (December 1987), p. 57.

25. *Information Economique Africaine* (Tunis) mentions one firm, Chaffoteaux et Maury, as having been put up for sale through the Bourse in 1989. See September 1989 issue, no. 192, p. 33.

26. Figure confirmed by an official of the Ministry of Tourism and Transport.

27. *La Presse de Tunisie,* 7 September 1988. Of this some 600 thousand dinars came from proceeds of 1987.

28. Ibid., an interview.

29. Nights spent by tourists increased from 218,962 nights (January to July), 1987 to 237,869 for the same period, 1988. Room occupancy for that period rose from 52.5 percent to 54.6 percent. *La Presse de Tunisie,* 7 September 1988.

30. The governor of the Central Bank announced in March that the three Tanits were next on the government's list for privatization. News release to Reuters, March 1989. By the end of the year, he made good on his word.

31. See *Information Economique Africaine,* September 1989, no. 192, p. 33.

32. Reported in *Information Economique Africaine,* January 1990.

33. The Economist Intelligence Unit (EIU), Country Report, *Tunisia, Malta,* no. 1, 1988, p. 22.

34. World Bank, *World Development Report 1988* (New York: Oxford University Press, 1988).

35. Findlay and Lawless, *North Africa,* p. 228.

36. Ibid.

37. Figures from the Planning Ministry, quoted by Midoun, "Entreprises Publiques," pp. 98–99.

38. J. Ballion, M. Bouchrara, and D. Thery, *Une Industrie Dynamique: La Briqueterie en Tunisie* (Tunis: Ministère de l'Équipement, du Logement, de l'Aménagement du Territoire et des Transports, 1987).

39. For the first two years' record, see Findlay and Lawless, *North Africa,* pp. 230–31.

40. This represents a drop in the cost of subsidies, which had reached nearly 300 MD in 1984. Statement by the Minister of Planning, Ismail Khelil, given to *al Iqtisaad wa al A'maal,* Beirut, April 1984.

41. Ezzeddine Abaoub, "Analyze Financière de l'Appareil Productif Tunisien," *La Presse de Tunisie,* 31 August 1988.

42. *Réalités* (no. 148), Tunis, 10 June 1988.

43. See reform measures in the dailies *al Sabaah* and *La Presse de Tunisie,* 27 May 1988.

44. *The Middle East and North Africa* (Europa Publication, 1988), p. 777.

45. Mohsen Trabelsi, *L'Industrie Manufacturière Tunisienne et sa Place dans l'Economie Nationale* (Tunis: Centre d'Etudes et de Recherches Economiques et Sociales, 1985), p. 22.

46. National savings have in recent years dropped to 18 percent of GNP due to the recession and persistent droughts.

Contributors

ABDEL MONEM SAID ALY is the Deputy Director for Research and Publishing at the Al-Ahram Foundation's Center for Political and Strategic Studies in Cairo and a former Middle East Guest Fellow at the Brookings Institution. His publications include *Back to the Fold?: Egypt and the Arab World*, *The Arabs and the Future of the World System*, and *The Arabs and Their Neighbors: A Study of the Future*.

LAURIE A. BRAND is Assistant Professor of International Relations at the University of Southern California. She is the author of *Palestinians in the Arab World: Institution Building and the Search for State* and is currently completing a study of the role of economic policy in Jordan's inter-Arab relations.

KIREN AZIZ CHAUDHRY is Assistant Professor of Political Science at the University of California at Berkeley. Her articles have appeared in *International Organization* and *Middle East Report*.

ILIYA HARIK is Professor of Political Science at Indiana University and former Director of the American Research Center in Egypt. He is author of *The Political Mobilization of Peasants: A Study of the Egyptian Community* and coeditor (with Louis J. Cantori) of *Local Politics and Development in the Middle East*.

FRED H. LAWSON is Associate Professor of Government at Mills College. He is the author of *The Social Origins of Egyptian Expansionism during the Muhammad 'Ali Period* and *Bahrain: The Modernization of Autocracy*.

MARCIE J. PATTON is Assistant Professor of Political Science at Elmhurst College. She is currently completing a study of the political economy of Turkish development.

MARSHA PRIPSTEIN POSUSNEY is Assistant Professor of Political Science at Bryant College and an editor of *Middle East Report*. She is currently writing a monograph on Egyptian labor/state relations from 1952 to 1987.

KHALED FOUAD SHERIF is a public enterprise specialist at the World Bank. He is author of *Egypt's Liberalization Experience* and *Principles of Management* and is currently completing a book on privatization in Egypt.

REGINA M. SOOS is a doctoral candidate in political science at the University of Chicago. She is currently writing a dissertation on the politics of private-sector development in Egypt.

DENIS J. SULLIVAN is Assistant Professor of Political Science at Northeastern University. His articles have appeared in *International Journal of Middle East Studies*, *Journal of South Asian & Middle Eastern Studies*, and *Administration & Society*. He is completing a study of private voluntary organizations and development in Egypt.

DIRK VANDEWALLE is Assistant Professor of Government at Dartmouth College. He has written extensively on economic privatization in North Africa and is editing a book on the Libyan Jamahiriyah since 1969.

Index